Writing
Creatively

Joan D. Berbrich, Ph.D.

Author of other books published by Amsco

Fifteen Steps to Better Writing
Laugh Your Way Through Grammar
Macbeth: A Resource Book
101 Ways to Learn Vocabulary
Reading Around the World
Reading Today
Thirteen Steps to Better Writing
Wide World of Words
Writing About Amusing Things
Writing About Curious Things
Writing About Fascinating Things
Writing About People
Writing Logically
Writing Practically

Dedicated to serving

AMSCO

our nation's youth

AMSCO SCHOOL PUBLICATIONS, INC.
315 Hudson Street   New York, N.Y. 10013

When ordering this book, please specify:
either R 186 W or WRITING CREATIVELY.

ISBN 0-87720-375-X

Printed in the United States of America

TO THE STUDENT

Writing a novel or a poem or a play is a little like growing a tree—say, a paper birch.

The idea and the seed are both beyond human comprehension: the moment of creation is pure art, touched with witchcraft.

But after the seed has germinated, after the first green shoot has emerged from the earth, the skill takes over—and the careful gardener waters and loves and prunes until the paper birch grows tall and straight, by day tossing its lacy green brilliance against the blue of sky, by night shattering the darkness with its marble trunk. This perfect thing is the result of art and skill, of genius and sweat.

So it is with writing.

No one can teach you to write like Tolstoy, or Shakespeare, or Emily Dickinson. No one—in ten lessons or ten thousand—can teach you to create. But you *can* learn how to foster the creativity that is within you, and how to "water and love and prune" until you too have a proper paper birch.

Creative writing in the classroom is an anomaly, or seems to be. One does not write a sonnet to order, or a short story in forty-five minute segments. Yet the attempt is justified by the possible results.

And what are the results?

You can learn to use your imagination—to stimulate it deliberately and to channel it with purpose.

You can learn the power and magic of words.

You can learn the techniques that other writers have used, can play with them freely, and modify them to match your needs.

You can experiment.

You can explore the works of great writers, and good writers, and average writers, and examine the terrain they have already mapped.

And you can follow them across that terrain by imitating their styles.

Or you can experiment—discovering new patterns, new ways to express the human condition.

And what if genius is not yours? Is the creative writing course then a waste of time? No. Even if your stories never get past the slush pile (the editorial limbo to which all unsolicited manuscripts go), you can use what you have learned to give life a distinctive touch, to mark it with your personality.

In the "dead" hours of the night (between 3 and 5 a.m.) you can write poems meant for no eyes but your own—poems that sweep away depression and freshen hope.

You can write affectionately humorous gift tags,

and custom-made birthday greetings,
and a special story for a special child.

You can write a few verses that will tell better than prose of your love, or of a shared grief.

You can write a news story that will make people dig into their pockets to help crippled children . . .

> or a playlet for a community group or a young people's organization . . .
> or a coherent, interesting news release for your club or professional group.

You can turn a family experience into a filler,

> become a stringer (part-time representative) for a nearby newspaper,
> or write commercials for your local radio station.

You can even use your creative writing skills to change yourself: to improve your speech patterns, making your conversation sharper, more colorful, more effective; to alter your thought patterns, bringing improvisation and daring and creativity to your daily routine.

Creative writing is not—should not be—a course for the elite. For creative writing is related to creative living—and that is everyone's goal.

Besides, the strangest people end up by becoming truly creative writers. There was Jack London, oyster pirate and pin-boy in a bowling alley; there were Robert Frost, farmer, and Wallace Stevens, insurance company executive; there was Ann Petry, pharmacist and advertising agent; and there was Herman Melville, seaman, mutineer, beachcomber, and customs inspector. And you?

To help *you* serve an apprenticeship in writing, we have divided this text into three parts:

THE WORKSHOP which concentrates on the tools and techniques of writing: how to get ideas, how to angle them, and how to express them;

THE STUDIO which gives you the chance to use these newly learned techniques in writing successful essays, poems, scripts, and stories;

PUBLISHERS' ROW which explains how to find markets for your work and how to prepare and mail your own manuscripts.

This three-part approach is a map, no more. The work and the sweat, the inspiration and the dreaming—these you must provide if you are to reach your goal: to write creatively. Good luck—and good writing!

Joan D. Berbrich

Publisher's Note

When the author submitted the above introduction, she sent along a personal note describing how it was written. We feel that you will enjoy this account—and find it deeply moving, as we did. With the author's kind permission, here it is. . . .

You may enjoy knowing the origin of the Preface. I really had trouble with it—played with it for several weeks and no idea surfaced. One evening, extraordinarily restless, I decided to "pace" it out. It was raining but I walked our driveway, up and down, up and down, with Chips (a neighbor's dog) at my side. The rain trickled down the back of my neck and soaked my hair, and still all that would come sounded pedantic and heavy. Suddenly I passed for the 99th time our paper birch and it had become something different, special—the epitome of what I was trying to say. I mooned and paced and was rained on a bit longer, then—when it felt ripe—dashed inside and made some notes. What fascinates me about writing, even writing something as concrete as school texts, is that *each* beginning is out of one's control. One waits, and prepares, and reads, and lets simmer, and waits. Afterward, the hard work comes, but it's easy compared to those elusive beginnings!

CONTENTS

Part One
THE WORKSHOP

Unit I
GETTING IDEAS

Unit II
PLAYING WITH WORDS

Unit III
USING DETAILS

Unit IX
THE SHORT STORY

Part Three
PUBLISHERS' ROW

Unit X
MARKETING

Part One
THE WORKSHOP

. . . wherein you will learn

how to get good ideas and

how to angle them;

how to find the right words and

how to combine them;

how to create your own style,

how to intensify mood,

how to develop a sense of the comic.

Unit I
Getting Ideas

INTRODUCTION

Ideas are like apples, growing on trees. Or like zucchini, lurking on the ground under giant leaves. Or like potatoes, growing deep in the earth itself. All you have to do is pluck them; or search them out and twist them off; or dig them up.

Ideas are in your brain, hiding but available. They're in everything you see or hear or taste or smell or touch. They're in what other people say and do. They're in your dreams, waiting to be tapped. They're in your daydreams.

Ideas become inventions, and explored territory, and novels. Interplanetary travel began with an idea. Columbus' trek to America began with an idea. Progress is a chain made of links called ideas.

As a writer, you can exist without a typewriter. You can exist (though not well) without books. You can exist (maybe) without money or a publisher. But you *cannot* exist without ideas.

Ideas are the primal material without which no artist can work—as important as marble to the sculptor, as oil to the painter, as words to the writer.

Study a comic strip for several days. The best of them, instead of simply telling a continuing adventure tale, base each episode on an idea: a quirk in human nature, freshly perceived; a word examined in a new light; a historical fact studied from an unexpected angle. Where does the comic strip artist find a new idea every day?

He finds them exactly where you will: in yourself, and in the world around you. Ideas are distinctive: seen by *your* eyes; shaped by *your* experiences; polished by *your* purpose. So you are trespassing on no one's land when you reap ideas. If you don't garner them, no one else can—for your ideas are available to you alone.

A good writer must be

> curious
> flexible
> nonconforming
> ingenious
> imaginative

A good writer must have

> a sense of humor
> a thirst for experience
> a sharpened mind
> an enduring body
> a sensitive heart

To acquire these characteristics, leap, plod, and gambol your way through these MIND STRETCHERS!

1 *All About You.* Print your full name. _____

Imagine you have been asked to sign the first Declaration of Independence for the entire human race. Write your name as you would like it to appear in the everlasting archives.

_____

Using the two or three initials of your name, dream up a monogram that would jazz up your stationery and book covers.

Ann Devlin   Bruce Lyle Collins   (yours)

2 *A First.* Eat a vegetable or a fruit you have never eaten before—perhaps a mango or eggplant. Describe the taste.

_____
_____
_____
_____

3 *Deductive Experience.* Go into a supermarket. Pick up any box of cereal. Copy the ingredients exactly.

_____

_____

_____

Any conclusions? _____

_____

_____

4 *Wide-Angle Vision.* You can eat a leg of lamb, construct the leg for a chair, or cry "Break a leg!" to an actor for luck. List below as many "arm" phrases as you can.

_____

_____

_____

_____

_____

5 *Riddle.* What do you get if you merge a lunatic and a grown-up watch?

Answer: _____

(See answer at bottom of page.)

6 *Desert Island Dilemma.* If you could take only one book with you on a desert island (you'll be there alone for ten years), which book would you choose?

_____

Why? _____

_____

7 *Easel Time.* Draw a picture of a gadget with which you can break a walnut, join two pieces of wood, or shatter your little sister's piggy bank.

(Riddle answer: cuckoo clock)

8 *Dream-o-Rama.* Dream up an interesting and possibly delicious fruit or vegetable that you might develop by crossing two edible plants. (For example, one might cross a mint plant and an apple tree and get tiny, mint-flavored apples—called, of course, *applemints*.)

Give yours a name. _____

Describe it. _____

_____

_____

_____

9 *Wishing Well.* You just threw a penny into a wishing well. You are entitled to one wish and one wish only. What would you wish for?

_____

_____

_____

_____

10 *Nature Study.* Bears hibernate for the better part of the winter. If humans hibernated, how would your town be different than it is? (Example: Without heating systems being maintained, all the pipes in town would burst every year, making plumbing a favored occupation!) Let your imagination rove wildly!

_____

_____

_____

_____

_____

1. BRAINSTORMING

Brainstorming, a fairly new invention, is a technique for developing ideas. It is used by educators, businesspeople, and creative artists. You begin with a word—let that word suggest another word or phrase—and so on.

Here's an illustration starting with the word BRAINSTORMING.

Brainstorming . . .
   storm the brain . . .

Hurricane. Cyclone. Tornado.
   Cyclone of the cerebellum . . .
A man alone in a hurricane—brain damage—not physical, psychological.
   Huge cyclone? End of world?
      Effect on only human to survive . . .

We need people. Why?
   Independence vs. dependence—or interdependence.
      Charismatic movement. Encounter . . .

Brief Encounter—that was a movie.
   Meeting a stranger—one-minute conversation—influence on rest of life.
      One minute—what it is—what it can do.
      One minute to live. Frightening thought, yet fascinating. Why—when . . .

One minute to—

            the "I do" in a wedding
            a head-on collision
            being awarded the Nobel Prize . . .

Prizes—parties, school. Me? Sure. Why not? Wrap me in pretty paper, tie me with a ribbon. A nice prize? Or sheer horror? A Corpse for a Birthday.

If you've never brainstormed—by yourself—you've missed a challenging and exciting experience. It's bad enough if you've never visited another state, but it's a good deal worse if you've never visited your own mind!

Solitary brainstorming will help you to know yourself. More relevant for the creative writer is that it will treat your own mind as a lode, to be explored, to be mined for any possible gold nuggets. You may find plots, characters, climaxes—perhaps just a wisp of an idea that can be expanded and developed. But you can't find *nothing*! Every human brain is seething with bits and ends of conversations, happenings, fears, loves.

According to psychologists, everything we have ever seen, heard, done, smelled, is in our brain, waiting only for retrieval. Brainstorming is one method of retrieval.

Try it.

How to Brainstorm

Go back and look at the brainstorming "happening" on the preceding page. You begin with a word—any word. Then you let your mind carry you, willy-nilly, from that word to another word or phrase.

> **Sometimes your brain will use inversion of word-order . . . from brainstorming to storm the brain.**
>
> **Sometimes it will use simple association: storm to hurricane to cyclone to tornado.**
>
> **Sometimes it will work on a fear and jump an unknown abyss: from huge cyclone to end of the world; then (since we all fear being alone in terrifying storms) to being truly *alone*—the only person left on earth.**
>
> **Sometimes it will work to an opposite: from independence to dependence.**
>
> **Sometimes it will play with one phrase or idea: *one minute;* and try variations on that one phrase.**
>
> **Sometimes it will grow personal, even bitter: *me*, a prize?**
>
> **And sometimes it will toss up a title ready to use: A Corpse for a Birthday.**

WARNING—don't tell your brain which technique to use. You'll mess up the procedure and mar the spontaneity. Let your brain work in its own way, at its own pace. Write down *everything*—even things that seem silly. Later you can weed, muse, and select. Now's the time for digging.

As your first exercise in brainstorming, start with the word *headlights*. Work for five minutes, letting your brain take you where it will, starting with that one word.

_____

_____

_____

_____

_____

_____

_____

_____

_____

_____

Try it once more. This time your starting word is *tree*. Remember—don't control it. Let your subconscious do the work.

_____

_____

_____

_____

_____

_____

_____

_____

_____

_____

Using the Results of Brainstorming

Since one quest of most writers is to know *self*, use your brainstorming results first to learn something about yourself. From our brainstorming list at the beginning of this chapter, one can deduce a person who is intrigued by violence in nature, by the results of violence on humans, by human relationships, by *why* life develops as it does, by some self-doubt, even self-cynicism.

Analyzing the results of your own brainstorming session takes courage. Study the results from your first brainstorming (*headlights*) and try a little self-analysis. Being as objective as you can, list some qualities possessed by the person (*you*) who did the brainstorming.

_____

_____

_____

_____

_____

If you have quite recovered from your growing knowledge of self, you can go on to the next step. This time, before you can proceed, you must ask one question: what kind of idea am I looking for? An idea for a short story? For a poem? For a nonfiction article? For a birthday card? For an essay? For a script?

Usually you can find all kinds of ideas (though many will be worthless) in the results of any brainstorming experience. Let's try it on the original "brainstorming on brainstorming" (page 6).

FOR A SHORT STORY: A sci-fi yarn about the world ending in a huge cyclone with only one survivor.

A romantic tale of a young woman's thoughts sixty seconds before she is to say "I do."

A mystery story of someone receiving a pretty (but grim) gift.

FOR A POEM: Playing with the meaning of "one minute."

Sonnet on a chance meeting.

Love poem: self as a wrapped gift.

FOR A NONFICTION ARTICLE:	How six brides and six grooms felt at the moment they said "I do."
	The effect of storms on human beings (possibly through interviews).
	Why the charismatic movement is part of today's scene.
FOR A BIRTHDAY CARD:	Big clock—one minute to twelve—now it's *your* day.
	Gift idea: either giving self to the birthday person, or seeing the birthday person as a "gift to the world."
	Upheavals of nature—all in honor of your natal day.
FOR AN ESSAY:	How one minute changed my life.
	People need people.
	The role of the stranger.
FOR A SCRIPT:	Dialogue between a man who survived a hurricane on an island and the man who rescues him but did not experience it.
	Narrative. Mime. Sixty seconds to live. Actual filming of those 60 seconds.
	Group of people on a train going over a trestle at the moment tornado hits: action, dialogue.

You get it? The secret lies in studying the brainstorming results and in extracting from them as many angles and ideas as possible.

This time work with the results of your second brainstorming session (*trees*, page 7). Try to list three titles and/or topics suitable for each category of writing.

FOR A SHORT STORY: _____

_____

_____

FOR A POEM: _____

_____

_____

FOR A NONFICTION ARTICLE: _____

_____

_____

FOR A BIRTHDAY CARD: _____

_____

_____

FOR AN ESSAY: _____

_____

_____

FOR A SCRIPT: _____

_____

_____

_____

Now that you have mastered the technique of brainstorming, USE it. When you have a few minutes between classes, BRAINSTORM. When you're waiting for your dental appointment, BRAINSTORM. When you're trying to fall asleep at night, BRAIN-STORM. You will glean hundreds of ideas for all kinds of writing.

A fun-variation on solitary brainstorming is group brainstorming. If you have a congenial (or even uncongenial) group of friends, try a brainstorming session. No fewer than three; no more than ten. Appoint one person to take notes, or use a tape recorder. The advantage is obvious: many brains will come up with more varied and startling ideas than can one brain.

Best of all, everyone can use any or all of these ideas. Ten people can take the same starting idea for a story and end up with ten very different short stories. In fact, that might be an interesting experiment! Try it some rainy day.

2. JOURNAL JOTTING

A *journal* is a log of the past, a map of the present, and a navigation chart for the future. It is a storehouse of ideas, a silo for information. It is a vitally important tool for any writer.

A journal may be a bound volume, a looseleaf book, a steno pad, or a batch of 3 × 5 cards. The format doesn't matter; the contents do. With its help you can capture forever an image, a thought, a phrase, or a storyline. The experienced writer doesn't trust memory; the experienced writer trusts a journal.

Now, then—how does one keep a journal? What does one put into it? That very much depends on you—on the kind of person you are, on your needs and interests, on the kind of writing you wish to do. It may be helpful to examine—and imitate—some entries from the journals of famous writers. Don't worry if you have trouble imitating the style—we'll work on that later. Right now, imitate the content. This should help you to determine the kind of entries you will want to make in *your* journal.

Descriptions

A common type of entry in many journals is the descriptive. A writer's primary concern is to capture something so exactly that the reader can see it. To do this, he or she may use an exact detail, an image, or an accumulation of details. Study each of the entries that follows. Then look around the room or out the window and create descriptions of your own.

Exact Detail

Henry David Thoreau was fascinated by nature. Note his brief but careful use of detail in this entry.

> January 5, 1858. I see one of those fuzzy winter caterpillars, black at the two ends and brown-red in middle, crawling on a rock by the Hunt's Bridge Causeway.*

YOUR TURN _____

_____

_____

_____

_____

*From THE WRITINGS OF HENRY DAVID THOREAU edited by Bradford Torrey. Reprinted by permission of Houghton Mifflin Company.

An Image

Dorothy Wordsworth, sister of the poet, William Wordsworth, could occasionally turn a fine phrase with her pen. She used her knowledge of the sea and fishing in this entry.

> October 31, 1800. A very fine moonlit night—
> The moon shone like herrings in the water.[1]

YOUR TURN _____

_____

_____

Accumulation of Details

One of the most sensitive writers of the 20th century, Katherine Mansfield, used this technique to capture the essence of a lovely morning.

> August 12, 1920. More beautiful by far than a morning in spring or summer. The mist—the trees standing in it—not a leaf moves—not a breath stirs. There is a faint smell of burning. The sun comes slowly—slowly the room grows lighter. Suddenly, on the carpet, there is a square of pale, red light. The bird in the garden goes "snip—snip—snip"—a little wheezy, like the sound of a knifegrinder. The nasturtiums blaze in the garden: their leaves are pale. On the lawn, his paws tucked under him, sits the black and white cat . . .[2]

YOUR TURN _____

_____

_____

_____

_____

_____

_____

Portraits

Also common in writers' journals are portraits: sometimes abbreviated notes that will later evoke the image of an almost forgotten character; sometimes a nearly finished portrait; sometimes a sketch of a group of people. Plumb your memory and try to "match" each of the following portraits:

---

[1]From the JOURNALS OF DOROTHY WORDSWORTH edited by Helen Darbishire. Copyright 1958, Oxford University Press, Oxford, England.
[2]From the JOURNAL OF KATHERINE MANSFIELD by Katherine Mansfield. Copyright 1927, Alfred A. Knopf, Inc.

Abbreviated Notes

Arnold Bennett, the English novelist, favored this type of portrait-entry. Notice how much he captures in a few short lines.

> Friday, February 12th, 1909. Girl with voluptuous laugh, short and frequent. Half Scotch, half English. Age 24. Very energetic, obstinate, and "slow in the uptake." Red cheeks. Good-looking. Athletic. Shy—or rather coy . . .[1]

YOUR TURN _____

_____

_____

_____

"Finished" Portraits

In Sweden, in 1873, a fourteen-year-old girl kept a journal. Selma Lagerlöf would grow up to become a famous writer of fiction, but even at fourteen, she knew how to trap an interesting character on paper. Notice how she moved from details to comparison in her portrayal of Professor Satherberg, her instructor at the gymnasium and a poet.

> February 11, 1873. I know that Professor Satherberg is a poet . . . A slight little man and not at all good-looking. His eyes are always red, and he has a sallow complexion and deep lines around the mouth. His face is sad as though he were ill. I think that a poet should be handsome and proud and radiant like Goethe. When he went skating on the river Main he was the most distinguished-looking gentleman in all the world.[2]

YOUR TURN _____

_____

_____

_____

_____

_____

Group Sketch

The great romantic poet, George Gordon Byron, usually depicted his characters in verse, but in this entry, he made prose jump through hoops to make permanent him-

---

[1] From THE JOURNAL OF ARNOLD BENNETT. Reprinted by permission of A. P. Watt & Son, London, England.

[2] From THE DIARY OF SELMA LAGERLÖF, translated by Velma Swanston Howard. Copyright 1936, Doubleday & Company, Inc.

self, Lady H., and a few other people in a specific moment in time. A rhetorical question, hyperbole, similes, and metaphors are all called upon for this instant "snapshot" of a dinner party.

> November 30, 1813. Why does Lady H. always have that damned screen between the whole room and the fire? I, who bear cold no better than an antelope, and never yet found a sun quite *done* to my taste, was absolutely petrified, and could not even shiver. All the rest, too, looked as if they were just unpacked, like salmon from an ice-basket, and set down to table for that day only. When she retired, I watched their looks as I dismissed the screen, and every cheek thawed, and every nose reddened with the anticipated glow . . .[1]

YOUR TURN _____

_____

_____

_____

_____

_____

_____

_____

Dialogue

The inexperienced writer often has the football player speaking in exactly the same way as the society matron. Making one person's speech distinctive requires a good ear and an equally good memory. The right kind of journal entry will help you to develop both. You can use entries of this type simply to record an important speech or to take down, verbatim, an example of dialect.

Important Speech

After Selma Lagerlöf described Professor Satherberg in her journal, she went on to record a few moments of dialogue between herself and the Professor. He was, remember, a teacher in the gymnasium as well as a poet.

> February, 1873. [the first speaker is the writer of the journal]
> "Is it a pleasure to write verse?" . . .
> "Yes," said the Professor . . . "But it is also a pleasure to straighten crooked backs and make stiff joints flexible . . ."
> He had given me a beautiful answer, but I did not think he was right. Now, if I could write poetry I should never care to do anything else.[2]

---

[1]From THE LIFE, LETTERS AND JOURNALS OF LORD BYRON by Thomas Moore. Reprinted by permission of John Murray (Publishers) Ltd., London, England.
[2]From THE DIARY OF SELMA LAGERLÖF, translated by Velma Swanston Howard. Copyright 1936, Doubleday & Company, Inc.

YOUR TURN _____

_____

_____

_____

_____

_____

Dialect

One time when Mark Twain was on a ship, the crew and passengers spotted what seemed to be a tremendous fire. They sailed toward it, watching with fear and excitement. But it wasn't a fire at all. An old woman who had watched for hours summed up the experience in her own inimitable fashion, and Twain recorded her speech.

> December 20, 1866. For the land's sake [the old woman said] I sot here and sot here all this blessed night calculating to see a whole boatload of sorrowful roasted corpses and now it ain't nothin' after all but a lot of nasty turtles.[1]

YOUR TURN _____

_____

_____

_____

_____

Brief Observations and Reactions

Your journal should also include brief observations and reactions. You may notice an interesting sign or building or vehicle and have an instant reaction to it. Record it. Or you may see something not unusual in itself, but something that triggers an unusual reaction in you. Record it. Both types of entries may later suggest a short story or help to round out a character.

Interesting Observations

Like any good novelist, Arnold Bennett was always alert for the odd, the doubly meaningful. One fall day in 1912, while he was out riding, he noticed a strange sign. That night he wrote:

> Tuesday, October 1st, 1912. Hospital for Incurables. West Hill. What must be feelings of patient as he drives into entrance of this Hospital and sees the big sign, "Hospital for Incurables"?[2]

[1]From MARK TWAIN'S NOTEBOOK edited by Alfred Bigelow Paine, Harper & Row, Publishers, Inc.
[2]From THE JOURNAL OF ARNOLD BENNETT. Reprinted by permission of A. P. Watt & Son, London, England.

_____

_____

_____

_____

_____

Interesting Reactions

Thomas Merton, the priest-contemplative and writer, was interested in the world around him, but still more interested in the way a natural event may affect a human being. This experience, too, occurred on a fall day, but Merton's reaction is wrier, more ironic than Bennett's.

> October 12, 1947. All the hills and woods are red and brown and copper, and the sky is clear, with one or two very small clouds. A buzzard comes by and investigates me, but I am not dead yet.[1]

YOUR TURN _____

_____

_____

_____

_____

Comments on Life

From Baton Rouge to the Bay of Fundy there is no writer who does not love to introspect: to play with life, to mull over it, to extract from it a thoughtful or clever aphorism. An event may trigger it; or a cynical observation; or just a sudden internal awareness. It is this kind of awareness—and comment—that stimulates the writer's sensitivity and helps him to understand others and the world through self.

An Event

Few men in the 19th century were more thoughtful than Ralph Waldo Emerson. In 1848, when he was traveling in France, he recalled the Revolution of a few months before and noted the havoc it had caused. He commented:

> May 6, 1848. The boulevards [in Paris] have lost all their fine trees, which were all cut down for the barricades in February. At the end of a year we shall take account, and see if the Revolution was worth the trees.[2]

---

[1] Reprinted from THE SIGN OF JONAS by Thomas Merton by permission of Harcourt Brace Jovanovich, Inc.
[2] From THE HEART OF EMERSON'S JOURNALS edited by Bliss Perry. Reprinted by permission of Houghton Mifflin Company.

_____

_____

_____

_____

_____

_____

An Observation

Emerson didn't need a historic event to start his brain cells leaping and racing. We don't know exactly what caused the following comment, but it was probably a passing glance at a small child handling a knife or pruning shears. (Note how this comment makes better—and more bitter—sense today than it did in 1832.)

> January 20, 1832. Don't trust children with edge tools. Don't trust man, great God, with more power than he has, until he has learned to use that a little better. What a hell should we make of the world if we could do what we would! Put a button on the foil till the young fencers have learned not to put each other's eyes out.*

YOUR TURN _____

_____

_____

_____

_____

_____

Internal Awareness

The Swiss writer, Henri Frédéric Amiel, kept his journal for over thirty years, covering thousands of sheets of paper. His journal was . . . "the confidant of his most private and intimate thoughts; a means whereby the thinker became conscious of his own inner life . . ." How true this is can be seen in the following entry in which Amiel learns something about himself; and we, his readers, ruefully learn something about ourselves, too.

> September 24, 1857. We are never more discontented with others than when we are discontented with ourselves. The consciousness of wrongdoing makes us irritable, and our heart, in its cunning, quarrels with what is outside it, in order that it may deafen the clamor within.

---

*From THE HEART OF EMERSON'S JOURNALS edited by Bliss Perry. Reprinted by permission of Houghton Mifflin Company.

_____

_____

_____

_____

Storylines

Whether the writer pens an occasional sonnet or twelve novels a year, he or she is always seeking storylines: something that can be developed and expanded and manipulated into a finished literary work. The storyline may be a complete plot with a beginning, middle, and end; or it may be a wisp of an idea. It may eventually provide the structure for a long novel, or one phrase in one line of a short poem. Because storylines are so vital, most writers jealously record every possibility and consider them the "emeralds" of their journals.

Incident

In the following entry, Arnold Bennett records in great detail an incident that came to his notice in 1907. For ten years the incident remained just part of one entry in his journal. Then, in the novel *Riceyman Steps*, he found the perfect way to use it. Here is the entry.

> Sunday, October 20th, 1907. A curious instance of avarice from Calvocoressi. An old lady living in a 9,000 fr. apartment in the Avenue de la Grande Armée, who pays two servants 150 fr. per month each in order to induce them to stand her avaricious ways. There is a story in this. If a piece of mutton was bought that was too much for one day and not enough for two, she would say to the servant, "Supposing I don't eat any today, will there be enough for tomorrow?" "Yes, Madame!" And she would starve. If her son was reading the paper in the evening she would say, "Anything interesting in the paper?" "No, nothing special." "Then let us turn off the light and sit in the dark and talk." When alone in the evening, in order to save the electric light, she would spend her time promenading on the staircase.*

YOUR TURN _____

_____

_____

_____

_____

_____

_____

_____

*From THE JOURNAL OF ARNOLD BENNETT. Reprinted by permission of A. P. Watt & Son, London, England.

Plot

Henry James wrote some of the most carefully constructed novels and short stories in the 20th century. He considered an artist a craftsman and applied this to himself by keeping long notebooks in which he kept track of every possible storyline that he might someday be interested in using. Here are two entries[1]—each short, yet each strong enough to provide a plot for a complete story or novel.

> May 16th, 1899. The Coward—...The man who by a fluke has done a great bravery in the past; knows he can't do it again and lives in *terror* of the occasion that shall put him to the test. DIES of that terror.

> October 19th, 1901. Lamb House. Something like the man who subscribes to an agency for "clippings" ... to send him everything "that appears about him," and finds that nothing ever appears, that he never receives anything.

YOUR TURN

_____

_____

_____

_____

_____

_____

_____

Miscellaneous

All around us are "things" waiting to be recorded—deserving to be recorded; "things" that can later enlighten, enrich, sharpen our writing. Have you heard some interesting names lately? Record them. Have you watched a baseball game? Record a moment of suspense. Have you cried while walking in the rain? Record the feeling. One writer took her notebook to her mother's funeral. Another took hers regularly to church. *Everything* is important to the writer—all of life is interesting and exciting. Here are two entries: one by Henry James in which he simply lists names that he might like to use sometime; the other by Sir Walter Scott who was faced by a familiar chore and found just the right image to describe it.

> Rome, Hotel de L'Europe, May 16th, 1899. Names. Pilbeam—Kenardington—Penardington—Ardington—Lindock—Sturch—Morrison—Morgan—Mallow—Newsome—Ludovick—Bream . . .[2]

> December 7, 1825. Wrote answers to one or two letters which have been lying on my desk like snakes, hissing at me for my dilatoriness...

[1,2]From THE NOTEBOOKS OF HENRY JAMES, edited by F. O. Matthiessen and Kenneth Murdock. Copyright © 1947 by Oxford University Press, Inc.; renewed by Kenneth B. Murdock and Mrs. Peters Putnam.

_____

_____

_____

_____

_____

_____

Writing on Writing

Finally, the writer uses the journal to communicate with self. *What* do I observe? *Why* do I observe? *How* shall I use it? The writer asks the questions—and posits the answers. Virginia Woolf, a brilliant and sensitive novelist, made this entry not long before her death.

> March 8, 1941. Brighton. Like a foreign town: the first spring day. Women sitting on seats. A pretty hat in a teashop—how fashion revives the eye! And the shell encrusted old women, rouged, decked, cadaverous as the teashop. The waitress in checked cotton. No: I intend no introspection. I mark Henry James' sentence: observe perpetually. Observe the oncome of age. Observe greed. Observe my own despondency. By that means it becomes serviceable. Or so I hope. I insist upon spending this time to the best advantage. I will go down with my colours flying. This I see verges on introspection . . .*

YOUR TURN _____

_____

_____

_____

_____

_____

_____

It you have not already started a journal, start one now. Write in it every night (or every morning); or carry it with you; or make notes in spare moments. *How* you do it doesn't matter—just do it. It will make you a more aware person, and help you to become a better writer.

---

*Reprinted from A WRITER'S DIARY by Virginia Woolf by permission of Harcourt Brace Jovanovich, Inc.

3. BROWSING WITH EYE AND EAR

Need ideas? Wander through a supermarket.

Open your eyes, and see.

Notice the names of products. They have a kind of poetry of their own.

Notice the colors that are used most often in displays.

Notice the exotic products you have never seen before—shelved not too far from the more prosaic cereals and potatoes.

Notice the way pyramids of cans are formed—the cart containing day-old bread at reduced prices—the "specials" prominently displayed at the front of the store.

Notice the vegetable and fruit section: the apple reds and the tomato reds; the cucumber greens and the lettuce greens; the squash yellow and the orange orange.

Notice the people: the woman in curlers and yesterday's rumpled slacks; the middle-aged man with a paunch in jazzy Bermuda shorts; the old couple, slow but content, turning their shopping into a morning's expedition; the five-year-old snitching candy while his mother is weighing onions.

Notice the sunlight, flashing through the windows, startling the cans of green peas into sudden glory.

Open your ears, and hear.

Listen to the rumbling of voices through the store, some highpitched, some deep and low, but all merging under some invisible conductor's baton.

Listen to the *ping* of cans dropped into a cart, the *plop* of frozen foods, the ominous *crackle* of bottles.

Listen to the ever-ringing bell as embattled cashiers summon the manager.

Listen at the check-out counter to the voices: the bored voices, the enthusiastic voices, the complaining voices, the angry voices.

Listen—just outside the store—to cars braking, and other cars starting up.

All right. So you've wandered through the store. You've seen and you've heard. So what? Where are the ideas?

You already have them—they're waiting to be recognized. Examine your notes.

Need an idea for an article? How about one on why certain colors are used in displays? Or one explaining how products get their names?

Need an idea for a poem? Those exotic foods nestling near the canned potatoes—hmmm—a nice analogy, isn't it, for the way all kinds of people live "cheek by jowl" in the same world?

Need an idea for a story? That old couple—what are they shopping for? Perhaps for a solitary dinner for their 50th wedding anniversary—solitary because their five children are scattered all over the country, too successful and too busy to share in a celebration.

Or that angry voice . . . why is he angry? What happened before he even entered the store? What effect will his tirade have on the young cashier whose eyes are already glazed with tears?

Sometimes ideas come in other ways. Look at some of the phrases: CUCUMBER GREEN would make an interesting title for a poem or story; AT REDUCED PRICES, as a title, has possibilities; so does DAY-OLD BREAD.

Pair things that weren't actually paired: the woman in curlers and the man in jazzy Bermudas. Suppose they had been married thirteen years ago, divorced seven years ago. She's studying the prices of detergents. With his shopping cart, he rounds the corner, just past the ginger ale. They see each other. How do they react? Will they be embarrassed, nod briefly, and walk on? Or will they rediscover their youthful romance?

Get it? Look and listen. Then examine your observations in every kind of light—sunlight and electric light, at dawn and at dusk. Extract from them ideas, analogies, images.

Try it.

Exploring the Classroom

Look around you. *Really* look. Then jot down five things you see. Don't choose the first five that come to mind. Look for things you haven't seen before, or noticed before . . . an odd pair of earrings, a girl who never smiles, a graffiti-decorated T-shirt.

_____

_____

_____

_____

Listen . . . Can you hear a radiator or an air-conditioner? The scratching of pencils? Suppressed giggles? List five things you hear.

_____

_____

_____

_____

Now study your lists carefully. Think about them. Then jot down at least three phrases or ideas that could be used in some kind of writing. In each case explain how you might be able to use the phrase or idea.

_____

_____

_____

_____

_____

_____

_____

_____

_____

Exploring the Cafeteria

Today (or tomorrow) take this workbook to lunch. As you eat, look and listen. Explore the cafeteria as you did the classroom: list five things you see, five you hear, and three ideas you can glean from your observation.

LOOK _____

_____

_____

_____

_____

LISTEN _____

_____

_____

_____

_____

IDEAS _____

_____

_____

_____

_____

_____

Custom-Made Safari

For your final experiment, visit (with your workbook) one of the following places:

> gas station
> community park
> laundromat
> pizza parlor
> nursery, or school playground.

Look. Listen. Note. Deduce.

LOOK _____
_____
_____
_____
_____

LISTEN _____
_____
_____
_____
_____

IDEAS _____
_____
_____
_____
_____
_____

Don't stop now. Carry your journal or notebook with you wherever you go. A family dinner can be a marvelous opportunity to look and listen—and to take notes; so can a family spat.

Get into the habit of browsing with eye and ear—of thinking with a writer's mind—and you will have more ideas than you can handle in three lifetimes!

---

4. MULLING AND MUSING

One of the loveliest techniques for ferreting out ideas is the constructive daydream. You're familiar with the ordinary daydream, that will-o'-the-wisp that has you romping in the country on a sunny day when you should be paying attention to your math teacher! From time to time you have probably reprimanded yourself for daydreaming. Perhaps you've even worried about it.

Don't. Everyone daydreams, even your prosaic pal who would deny it with horror. It's part of being a human being. The trick is—learn to use your daydreams. Learn to daydream constructively. Inventors know this; so do writers.

Of course, most people (even writers!) can't just daydream on demand. Lie down on your bed, stretch happily, and let your mind wander free. Chances are you'll fall asleep. Instead—channel your mind. Provide it with a gimmick to play with, and daydreaming—and ideas—will almost surely follow.

Here's a whole bag of gimmicks to get you started.

Daydream Yourself Into a Situation

You may have read the short story, "The Secret Life of Walter Mitty" by James Thurber. (And there's a writer who must have been a master of daydreaming!) Walter Mitty, a meek, rather henpecked man, during one short shopping trip with his wife, dreamed of being the commander of a Navy hydroplane, a great surgeon, an expert with a gun, the captain of a bomber, and a lone man facing the firing squad. The story has universal appeal because it deals with something we all understand: the need to daydream when we have been belittled and hurt.

All right—it's your turn now. Become anything you like—an American spy; the commander of a nuclear submarine; the first human to step on the surface of Mars; a superb chef—anything at all!

YOUR CHOICE _____

Before you actually begin, remember—daydream concretely. See yourself in a particular situation, doing a particular thing. Are you an American spy? What has just happened? Have you just been caught? Are you being interrogated and tortured? In the next five minutes, as you daydream, enjoy having the lead role in the drama you are creating. After the five minutes are up, summarize your daydream below.

_____

_____

_____

_____

_____

_____

_____

You may not have a great story there, but you had fun and you widened your horizons a bit. *Bonus hint:* if you often become a secret agent in your daydreams, research the field. Read everything that is relevant, in fiction and especially in nonfiction. You will glean all sorts of colorful details to make your daydream more exciting—and more useful in your writing.

Daydream Yourself Into a Celebrity

Ever wonder what it feels like to be Barbra Streisand or Robert Redford? To be Henry Aaron or Chris Evert? To be Queen Elizabeth or Muhammad Ali? Here's your chance. Become one of them. Choose a celebrity—any celebrity.

YOUR CHOICE _____

For five minutes, become the person you chose. See yourself attending the premiere of your latest picture, or winning a baseball game, or leading the procession to Westminster in a horse-drawn coach. Provide as many details as you can. After your five-minute spree, summarize your daydream.

_____

_____

_____

_____

_____

_____

_____

Daydream Yourself Into Your Best Friend

Sometimes you get tired of being just Jane Doe; even being Jane Roe would be better. Try it. Become your best friend. You have an advantage here—you know your friend's family, house, general environment, even personality. So, for five minutes, swap personalities. Try to look like that friend. It's possible. (Spencer Tracy, when making the film *The Rugged Path*, refused makeup that would simulate a beard growth. But he had to look like a man who had been drifting around in the ocean for eight days. Tracy insisted he could look unshaven just by thinking himself unshaven. And he did!) Think like your friend. Act (in your mind) like your friend. After the five minutes are up, describe how it felt to be someone else.

_____

_____

_____

_____

_____

_____

The "If" Game

This is always fun; you may have played it before. Simply posit an "if"—then day-dream. Here are a few possibilities:

> If I Had a Million Dollars
> If I Were President for Six Months
> If I Won a Round-the-World Trip

YOUR CHOICE   (any of the above or your own) _____

Again, spend five minutes daydreaming. Describe your daydream below.

_____

_____

_____

_____

_____

_____

_____

_____

Variation

Play the "if" game again; but this time role-play your best friend in the same situation. If you daydreamed about "If I Had a Million Dollars," now daydream about the same topic, from your friend's point of view. Describe the daydream.

_____

_____

_____

_____

_____

_____

The special value of the Variation is that it forces you to step into someone else's shoes, to see with another pair of eyes, to think with another brain. It's marvelous exercise for a writer.

It will also help you to know your friend better and—by comparison—to know yourself better. As an additional Variation, try the same procedure sometime by stepping into the shoes of your mother or father or teacher. It could be an enlightening experience!

Title Triggers

For a totally different approach to daydreaming, trigger your mind with titles. Titles of novels and movies are meant to tantalize and they often do. For best results, choose the title of a work you are not familiar with. Then for five minutes, daydream about the title. What does it mean? How can it be used? What kind of story does it suggest? Here's a list of some provocative titles. Choose one. Daydream. Summarize the story *you* would write if you had created the title.

> *Heaven Has No Favorites* (Erich Maria Remarque)
> *The Magic Mountain* (Thomas Mann)
> *Ship of Fools* (Katherine Anne Porter)
> *The Moon Is Down* (John Steinbeck)
> *Player Piano* (Kurt Vonnegut)

YOUR CHOICE _____

YOUR STORY _____

_____

_____

_____

_____

_____

_____

_____

For an extra dividend, read the novel whose title you chose. Compare the author's thinking with your own. A hundred daydreamers can start at the same place yet end at a hundred different destinations! Such is the power of the imagination.

The Invention Game

This is a pretty difficult game. Its purpose is to invent a "brand-new" gadget or procedure. The easiest way to start is to think about your problems, large and small. Do you have trouble scrubbing the kitchen floor? Or remembering to turn off the lights when leaving a room? Or coping with the noise of your next-door neighbor? Choose one problem; then daydream your way to an invention that might solve that problem. Since this is an exercise for the imagination, you don't have to worry about whether the invention is practical or marketable. Just dream it up!

YOUR PROBLEM _____

YOUR INVENTION _____

_____

_____

_____

Worry an Idea

If you have ever watched a cat play with a ball of yarn, you know how to worry an idea. You examine it, take it apart, pounce on it from different directions; smell it; paw it; get entangled in it; taste it. That's what you're going to do—worry an idea. It's a very specialized form of daydreaming. You can start anywhere ... with MONEY, for example. MONEY suggests—Wall Street and banks and J. P. Morgan; shiny new Cadillacs and gleaming white yachts; earning it (sometimes grim) and spending it (with a grin!); million-dollar bank robberies and kidnappers and ransom notes; numismatists, often dedicated, and counterfeiters, also "dedicated"; skiing in Switzerland and/or Swiss bank accounts; a lemonade stand or IBM. The list could go on and on . . . . . .

Here are some possible ideas for you to worry:

> courage
> war
> leaf
> trade
> chocolate
> doubt

Choose one (or your own) and see if you can identify twelve distinctly different aspects of the idea or concept.

YOUR CHOICE _____

TWELVE ASPECTS _____

_____

_____

_____

_____

_____

_____

_____

_____

_____

_____

_____

There are still other gimmicks, of course, but these should get you started. Glance back over what you have written in this chapter. Aren't there at least a few ideas for stories or poems that intrigue you? If there are, start writing.

If there aren't—at least you are well on your way to becoming a daydreaming expert. Record your best results in your journal. It's an unbeatable combination:

constructive daydreaming + notation = dozens of ideas!

5. "I CRIED TO DREAM AGAIN . . ."

Everybody dreams. Even you. Even if you don't remember dreaming. According to dream-experts, if you don't dream, you can become mentally or emotionally disturbed. For dreams provide a release from tension; occasionally they even provide solutions to problems.

Dreaming is as old as humanity. The ancient Egyptians had a complex method for interpreting dreams. So did the Assyrians and the Greeks and the Romans. To the Jews of the Old Testament, dreams were often sacred messages sent by God: note Jacob's dream of a ladder with angels ascending and descending. When Jacob looked up, God looked down, and it was then He promised Jacob the land around him for him and his descendants. To the early Christians, too, dreams were usually from God. It was in a dream, remember, that Joseph was told to take Mary as his wife and that the child she bore would be the Messiah.

But all of this was long ago. What about today? In recent years dream-clairvoyants have become increasingly popular. They try to locate kidnapped children and stolen masterpieces. Occasionally one will be asked to predict the winner of the Kentucky Derby. Two decades ago the AEC (Atomic Energy Commission) actually considered using dream-clairvoyants to determine probable targets of enemy bombs.

Fascinating, you say—but useless to you? Not at all. Many writers are deliberate dreamers. They seek in their dreams ideas, procedures, even whole poems and stories.

ITEM: Voltaire, the French satirist and poet, dreamed an entire canto of *La Henriade*.

ITEM: Charlotte Brontë, the English novelist, sometimes had difficulty writing about an emotion that she herself hadn't experienced. When this happened, she thought about the problem every night as she was falling asleep. Weeks might pass, but eventually the morning would come when she awakened with her problem solved.

ITEM: Samuel Taylor Coleridge, the British romantic poet, once took a three-hour nap and woke up with the poem, "Kubla Khan," completely written (in his head, of course!).

ITEM: Robert Louis Stevenson used dreaming "on demand" when he needed money, and therefore needed to write and sell a story. He would order himself to dream and then simply "put together" the story that evolved. One of his greatest works, *Dr. Jekyll and Mr. Hyde*, started as the result of a dream.

ITEM: Edgar Allan Poe found in his dreams both the moods and themes of his stories and poems. If you have ever awakened from a bad dream with your heart pounding and thumping, you can guess the origin of "The Tell-Tale Heart."

Convinced? Learn to use *your* dreams.

Remember a Dream

Begin by searching your memory for the most vivid dream you have ever had. Describe it.

_____

_____

_____

_____

_____

_____

Borrow a Dream

Start asking people about *their* dreams. You will have no trouble getting them to talk, but you may have plenty of trouble getting them to stop. Choose the most interesting dream described to you and borrow it. Summarize it.

_____

_____

_____

_____

_____

_____

How to Recall a Dream

If you have trouble remembering your dreams, try this tonight. Tell yourself firmly that you *will* dream and that you *will* remember your dream. Place a pad and pencil within easy reach. If you awaken during the night, lie quietly for a few minutes trying to hold the dream. Then make a few notes to help you recall it later. If you do *not* awaken during the night, follow the same procedure when you wake up in the morning: lie quietly, hold the dream, make a few notes. Later in the day, write the results below.

_____

_____

_____

_____

_____

_____

Experiment With Dreams

Role-play Charlotte Brontë. If you have a writing problem, try to dream your way to a solution. Perhaps you have the kind of character you want to use in a short story, but you don't know how that person would speak or act. *Be* that character just before you fall asleep. See what happens. Perhaps you want to convey a particular mood and you just can't. Think about it as you twist and turn at night. See what happens. Describe at least one experiment of this type and the results.

_____

_____

_____

_____

_____

The Dream as Vehicle

The writer uses the dream in still another way: as the consciously constructed vehicle for a theme. The entire literary work may be a dream, or a dream may play a small but vital role in the development of the plot.

The Dream Allegory

Pilgrim's Progress by John Bunyan is a dream allegory. The novel is based on a dream and, through the action of the dream, teaches readers how to live their lives in order to be saved. Bunyan begins his novel this way:

> As I walked through the wilderness of this world,
> I lighted on a certain place where was a Den, and
> I laid me down in that place to sleep; and, as I slept,
> I dreamed a dream.

Bunyan then describes how, in the dream, he watched the pilgrim Christian make a journey through the Slough of Despond, the Valley of Humiliation, and the city of Vanity Fair.

Let your imagination wander free and try to think of a dream allegory that you would be interested in developing. (Perhaps in a dream you can outline a plan for lasting peace, or design a world in which goodness equals happiness.) Describe briefly the contents of the dream-as-vehicle and the purpose of the dream allegory.

_____

_____

_____

_____

_____

_____

The Dream Episode

For *Julius Caesar*, Shakespeare found his plot in history; but in Act II he used a dream to foreshadow Caesar's assassination. Calpurnia, Caesar's wife, has a dream in which she sees her husband's statue issuing blood. She begs him not to leave the house that day, and he agrees—but one of the conspirators reinterprets the dream and persuades the "mighty Caesar" to go to the Capitol. In this play the dream prepares the reader for the pivotal action of the plot, establishes a mood of fear and suspicion, and suggests the irony that pervades the play and, indeed, life itself.

Create a dilemma. (For example, your best friend has told you that she is planning to run away from home. Should you tell anyone? Should you do anything?) Then create a dream that will foreshadow what is to come and thus heighten the suspense.

_____

_____

_____

_____

_____

_____

_____

Use your dreams. They are probably the result of your own subconscious meandering, and they belong to you. Note them in your journal; they will yield both ideas and solutions. And enjoy them, for they can take you into strange lands and wondrous situations. It was Caliban, the warped spirit in Shakespeare's *The Tempest*, who said wistfully—

—and then in dreaming
The clouds methought would open; and show riches
Ready to drop upon me, that when I wak'd
I cried to dream again.

6. CALENDAR CALCULATIONS

The calendar, like the clock, has become a modern-day tyrant. It tells us when to change from light to heavy-weight clothing, when to be in a holiday mood, and when to pay our bills. Even the writer suffers from calendaritis—especially when deadlines approach.

But, to the writer, the calendar is slave as well as tyrant. It's an idea giver: a whisper in the ear, a nudge from an elbow.

Major Holidays

What will I write about? I check the calendar and am reminded that Thanksgiving is only a few months away. So, depending on my mood and the type of writer I am, I can

—write a short story about a reunion at a Thanksgiving Day dinner

—write an article about how the traditional Thanksgiving Day menu came into existence

—investigate and write about comparable festivities in other lands

—write appropriate verses for Thanksgiving Day cards

—write a children's story in which the Gobbler is the main character

—interview a dozen people and find out what Thanksgiving means to them

—write a nostalgic essay about Thanksgiving when I was a child (or when my grandmother was a child)

—break the word into its two main components: "giving" and "thanks" and write an article about how people have *given thanks* throughout the centuries

—write an article about the origin of Thanksgiving Day in this country

—talk to several doctors about patient complaints the day after Thanksgiving and write an article about the results of overeating

—write a sonnet about Thanksgiving—or a haiku, or free verse

—write a story about an American youth overseas on Thanksgiving Day—his feelings and his thoughts

The dozen suggestions given above form only the tip of the iceberg. Given fifteen minutes and a good imagination, any writer could come up with two dozen more. And somewhere in those three dozen will be at least one idea crying to be developed.

Choose a major holiday (other than Thanksgiving Day) and list at least twelve suggestions for related writing ideas.

HOLIDAY _____

_____
_____
_____
_____
_____
_____
_____
_____
_____
_____
_____
_____

Minor Holidays

New Year's Day, Independence Day, Labor Day, Veterans (or Armistice) Day, Thanksgiving Day, and Christmas Day are celebrated in all fifty states. In addition many lesser holidays are celebrated in one or several states. First you have to find out what holidays are celebrated. Almost any annual almanac will help you. Here are a few favorites that may well appeal to writers. (In each case, only one state is given although the holiday may be celebrated in several.)

Confederate Memorial Day (Georgia)
Mardi Gras (Louisiana)
Farmers Day (Florida)
Pioneer Day (Utah)
Seward's Day (Alaska)
Town Meeting Day (Vermont)
Kamehameka Day (Hawaii)
Arbor Day (New Mexico)
Three Kings' Day (Puerto Rico)

Do some research. What special minor holidays are celebrated in your state? List them below, with dates.

_____
_____
_____

Choose any one lesser holiday and list six writing ideas.

HOLIDAY _____

_____

_____

_____

_____

_____

Another possible source for ideas is *religious holidays*. If you're interested in this field, check them and add them here or in your journal.

_____

_____

_____

_____

Special Days

Special days, weeks, or months have been put aside for extra attention for a particular group or interest. These, too, can provide ideas for the writer. There are well-known ones, like

American Education Week
Mother's Day (2nd Sunday in May)
Father's Day (3rd Sunday in June)
Pearl Harbor Day (December 7)
Boy Scout Week
Girl Scout Week
Flag Day (June 14)
Groundhog Day (February 2)
Halloween (October 31)
National 4-H Club Week

—and lesser known ones like National Allergy Month and National School Lunch Week. Scout around. Ask questions. Check almanacs. Then make a list of five "specials" that interest you.

_____

_____

_____

_____

_____

"Special" Specials

Even more fascinating (and a richer lode for the beginning writer) are the "special" specials: the days important only to a particular area or village. These come in a variety of forms. In each category below, add a couple of examples suitable for your school and/or community.

Events   the Kentucky Derby; the Indianapolis 500 race; the Balloon Festival in Glens Falls

YOURS _____

_____

Celebrities   For Niles, Ohio: William McKinley born on January 29, 1843
For Lamar, Missouri: Harry S. Truman born on May 8, 1884
For West Hills, N.Y.: Walt Whitman born on May 31, 1819

YOURS _____

_____

Disasters   For Hanna, Wyoming: coal mine disaster, June 30, 1903, in which 169 people were killed
For scattered villages in Missouri, Indiana, and Illinois: tornado on March 18, 1925, which caused 689 deaths

YOURS _____

_____

Anniversaries. Interesting anniversaries are all around you. Any one of them might give you an idea for a local newspaper story.

Date (day, month, and year) on which your high school first opened its doors for classes _____

Date on which your town library opened _____

Date your town was settled _____

Date your church was founded _____

Date your present mayor was born _____

Add two of your own:

_____

_____

School Newspaper

While you're preparing to break into the professional market, practice in your school newspaper. How about a column called "On This Date ..." or "In This Month ..."? Include both items of recent vintage and items from history. For example:

ON THIS DATE ... April 23

In 1924 the seniors at our school held the first school dance.

In 1564 William Shakespeare was born.

In 1904 our first mayor, John C. Grant, started his term of office.

In 1973 our school held its first coed phys ed class.

In 1970 President Nixon abolished draft deferments for fathers.

In 1962 U.S. and Soviet scientists agreed to establish a world weather-watch network.

In 1964 all classes were suspended for two days because of a fire in the cafeteria.

The feature should include at least six items of different types. It's a good idea to alternate items of purely local interest and items of state or national interest. Possible sources: school newspaper file; yearbooks; annual almanacs; encyclopedia yearbooks; *Famous First Facts;* books of dates and holidays.

Try a feature column of your own. Set it up for tomorrow's date. Do some quick research. Ask people. See what you can come up with in 24 hours.

ON THIS DATE ... _____

_____

_____

_____

_____

_____

_____

_____

_____

_____

The brain is like a pump: it needs priming. Calendar calculations can prime your brain and make the ideas really flow. Set up your own calendar at the end of your journal. Give a separate page to each month. Enter the major holidays, the minor holidays, and any "special" days relevant to you and your area. A quick glance now and then will start the priming, and some creative thinking will complete it.

Suggestion: some writers keep *two* calendars on their desks: a current one, and one that is six months "fast." The second one reminds them that it's time to start working on that Christmas special or to begin researching "Groundhog Day." There's a hidden bonus: you get the chance to enjoy every holiday twice!

Unit II
Playing With Words

WORDS | ROGET | DICTIONARY | WORD POWER | SYNONYMS | SLANG | ENCYCLOPEDIA | USAGE | WORD ORIGINS | TROPES

WHISTLE

NARROW

S.W.I.Veller

PANDORA'S PIZZA

Bitter-sweet

BUZZZZ

ELONGATE

"in the sepulchre there by the sea"

A word is a word is a word . . .

You can hear it buzz or whistle.

You can see it elongate or narrow.

You can feel it pucker your lips.

You can explore the story behind the word: as in sandwich, or bloomer, or derby.

You can create fascinating names.

You can make a part stand for the whole—or a thing for a man.

You can combine likely words— or unlikely ones.

You can do anything you like with words, once you have learned to control them.

A word is a word is a word.

UNABRIDGED DICTIONARY

1 *All About You.* List the ten words you consider most beautiful.

_____   _____

_____   _____

_____   _____

_____   _____

_____   _____

Now list the ten words you consider most ugly.

_____   _____

_____   _____

_____   _____

_____   _____

_____   _____

Analyze your two lists. What do your choices reveal about you?

_____

_____

_____

_____

2 *A First.* At home, offer to do something you have never done before: wash dishes; cook an omelette; clean the windows; scrub a floor. Describe (*a*) how you felt when you made the offer; (*b*) the reaction of your parents; (*c*) how you felt doing the task.

_____

_____

_____

_____

3 *Perception Plus.* Wear two unmatched shoes on a school day. Record: how much time elapses before anyone notices the two different shoes; what people say; how some people show they are embarrassed for you.

_____

_____

_____

_____

4 *The Key Family*. Choose a new last name for yourself and your (hypothetical) husband or wife. Now assume you have three children. For the children, select first names that will form fun-phrases when linked with the new last name. (Example: the Key family; the children: Don Key; Monk Key; Syl Key.)

_____

_____

_____

5 *Novel Arithmetic*.   Try to solve these six puzzles in three minutes.

(*a*) What number becomes even by subtracting one letter? _____

(*b*) What number becomes heavy by adding one letter? _____

(*c*) What number belongs to us by subtracting one letter? _____

(*d*) What number increases ten times by adding one letter? _____

(*e*) What number is elevated by adding one letter? _____

(*f*) What number is finished by adding one letter? _____

6 *Desert Island Dilemma*.   You will be on a desert island for ten years. You may have one companion, and one only. Describe the person you would prefer. It may be someone you know, a celebrity, or a completely hypothetical "perfect" person.

_____

_____

_____

_____

7 *Dream-o-Rama*.   Old John is half-crippled with arthritis and has trouble pulling the crab grass out of his lawn. Dream up an invention that will do the job. (Remember it doesn't have to work; and the wilder, the better!)

_____

_____

_____

8 *Nature Study*.   The kinkajou has a tail twice as long as its body. Each night it curls it up to make a cozy bed. Think of three other things you could do with a tail if you had one twelve feet long.

_____

_____

_____

_____

9 *Easel Time.* Look out the window. Copy a cloud. (If there aren't any clouds, copy a tree or another object.) Now look at your drawing from all angles, turning the paper slowly. List the different objects it suggests.

_____

_____

_____

_____

10 *Improvisation.* Here is a brick—an ordinary brick—the kind used in building houses. List ten non-traditional ways the brick might be used. (Example: as a paperweight.)

_____

_____

_____

_____

_____

_____

_____

_____

_____

7. THE WORD-SHELF

You want to be a writer?

How many words do you know? 20,000? 30,000? Not enough. A ten-year-old knows as many. 100,000? 200,000? Still not enough. A college sophomore can equal that.* 500,000? Never enough.

Words are necessary to express ideas, to communicate. You need all the words in the world, and then a few more. So if you want to write, become (if you are not already) a word-watcher, a word-hoarder, a word-user.

This is a straightforward chapter, designed to introduce you to a shelf of word books. Each exercise concentrates on one word book. You will become familiar with the book, discover its riches, and evaluate its use for you. Word books are tools: handle them with skill and care.

Dictionary

Any good dictionary will give you

> —the meaning, pronunciation, and derivation of a word
> —the parts of speech of a word
> —some synonyms

In addition, most good dictionaries will give you a few notes on usage, and identifications of proper names (people and places). You will, of course, use the dictionary to check spelling and usage, but you can also use it to begin research of many kinds. First, choose a dictionary.

TITLE OF DICTIONARY CHOSEN _____

Using your dictionary, try to solve some problems a free-lance writer might encounter.

Dental Problem

For a magazine for dentists, writer Carl Zeller wants to write a filler (a short interesting feature). Since you are Zeller's assistant, it is your job to find appropriate material. Use *tooth* and *dentist* as starting entries. Move on to other related words. For example, as you look up *dentist*, you will find many words beginning with *dent-*, including *denticulate*. You discover *denticulate* can refer to a form of architecture in which teeth-like rectangles project beneath a cornice. List several other examples of information related to dentistry that you can find in the dictionary.

_____

_____

_____

_____

_____

*Figures from Norman Lewis' WORD POWER MADE EASY, published by Doubleday & Company, Inc.

After studying your notes, suggest a theme for a suitable filler.

_____

_____

Murder, Inc.

As she plans an article on homicides in her state, Maria DeLong becomes curious about the word "kill." How many definitions would she find for "kill" if she were consulting your dictionary? _____ List two unusual definitions that would give her article a fillip.

_____

_____

Key Solution

Jack Proust is writing a short story that is set in a small town on the Atlantic Coast. His main character owns a yacht. Proust is writing—

With the stars blocked out and the storm manhandling his ship, young Hawley

headed anxiously for the _____. On the mainland, he would have dinner

before setting out once more to find his abandoned guest.

Proust paused. Did he want *quay* or *cay*? Although the two words sound alike, they have very different meanings. Check both words. How is *cay* different from *quay*? Which word does Proust want?

_____

_____

_____

Guessing Won't Make It So

Here are a few words writer Janice Gray used in a recent article. You may think you know them, but you probably don't. Use your imagination to try to guess the meaning of each word before you look it up in the dictionary.

foolscap: YOUR GUESS _____

DEFINITION _____

goldbrick: YOUR GUESS _____

DEFINITION _____

running head: YOUR GUESS _____

DEFINITION _____

watch glass: YOUR GUESS _____

                 DEFINITION _____

hamlet: YOUR GUESS _____

                 DEFINITION _____

Convinced? In the future—don't guess; look it up!

Roget's Thesaurus

This reference book provides a large number of synonyms or near-synonyms for almost any word you can think of. Erica Fishman is writing a short story. She has used "he said" and "she said" so often she is boring herself. Check all entries under *say* and *said* and see if you can find twenty substitute words that might be helpful to Erica.

_____   _____

_____   _____

_____   _____

_____   _____

_____   _____

_____   _____

_____   _____

_____   _____

_____   _____

_____   _____

Apply your new knowledge. In each of the following sentences insert a sharper, more exact verb for "said."

EXAMPLE: "Be quiet so the monster doesn't hear us," she (said) _____*whispered*_____ to her little brother as they slipped underneath the bed.

1   "I *hate* girls!" three-year-old Leo (said) _____ as he set out for the party.

2   "I—I don't wa-want to j-join," Lulu (said) _____ as the initiation began.

3   "You can't join the circus," Jim (said) _____ as his eighty-year-old grandmother packed a knapsack.

4   "I *will* run, even if *no one* wants me," the veteran presidential candidate (said) _____ stoutly.

5   "My voice sounds like a frog's," (said) _____ Edwin.

Dictionary of Contemporary American Usage
(Bergen & Cornelia Evans)

This is a fine reference book for the writer who is revising an article or story. Sam Ellerman just completed an essay on organic farming. He is doubtful about three things. Help him.

1 In the essay Sam used "picture of health," "pet peeve," and "go the whole hog." Why should he probably eliminate all three terms?

_____

_____

_____

2 Should Sam use "good will" or "goodwill" in describing a well-known philanthropist? How are the two terms different?

_____

_____

3 In describing one farmer's education, Sam is uncertain whether to say "he graduated from high school" or "he graduated high school" or "he was graduated from high school." Which is correct?

_____

A Dictionary of Modern English Usage (H. W. Fowler)

This is another fine reference book for the writer who is busy with revision. Like Sam, Suzanne Perrault has some problems.

1 Is "news" singular or plural? Should she say "the news *is* bad" or "the news *are* bad"? Why?

_____

_____

2 When are the new "-ize" verbs—like *slenderize* and *finalize*—acceptable? When are they not acceptable?

_____

_____

3 To denote a red, four-year-old, female deer, should she use hart, doe, stag, hind, or buck? _____ What kind of deer exactly does each term indicate?

_____

_____

_____

There are other fine reference books on the Word-Shelf. Browse through

Funk & Wagnalls *Standard Handbook of Synonyms, Antonyms, and Prepositions* (James C. Fernald).

Partridge, Eric. *Dictionary of Slang and Unconventional English.*

> *Writers are browsers; and one of their favorite pastimes is browsing through word books.*

8. MUD-PUDDLE MAGIC

All words are magical, but some words are more magical than others.

For basic word magic, consider this: you say "apple" and anyone who hears you (and understands English) knows exactly what you are talking about. That's magic! If you don't believe it, look at birds and elephants: they can and do communicate; yet without words, they never get much beyond mating calls and danger signals.

But there are other words that are more magical than "apple"—that have magic in their very sound. Consider the word "mud." It sounds like what it is: sticky, soft wet dirt. Mud plops and thuds; it certainly doesn't flow or leap. To a mother, it's messy footprints on the kitchen floor and small grimy faces. To a child, it's dough for pies, and clay for forts; marvelous muck to slosh through; harmless but nasty missiles.

Knowing the meaning of "mud," you can guess what a mudfish is, or a mud hen, even if you've never heard those terms before. You wouldn't want your opponent to be a mudslinger, and you know why a mudguard is used on some vehicles. You may not recognize "mudlark" but you can see, can't you, why it is the word used in England to indicate a dirty but merry street urchin?

Now consider the word "puddle." *The American Heritage Dictionary* defines it as "a small pool of usually dirty, stagnant water." But it's considerably more than that. Remember coming out of school on a rainy afternoon when you were little, and wading happily through squishy puddles? Remember sailing boats in puddles along the curbs, and having races of matchsticks or bits of straw? Remember the sun glistening on a puddle, turning dirty water into rainbow? Remember building bridges over some puddles, and walls around others? Remember trudging back and forth with small pails of dirt as you fought bravely to turn an ordinary puddle into a mud puddle?

To a writer, the word or phrase that sounds right—like "mud puddle"—and that also has rich connotations is the finest of all raw materials. E. E. Cummings knew this well. In his poem, "in Just-spring," Cummings describes the world as "mud-luscious" and later as "puddle-wonderful." He used separately the two parts of a phrase locked in almost every adult memory, linked each with an unexpected adjective, and came up with two new phrases that evoke the delight of spring. Notice the adjectives he used: "luscious"—the perfect description of mud if you happen to be five years old; and "wonderful"—trite in many situations but invigorating when linked with "puddle." This is magic carried to a high degree, and even Cummings reached it only occasionally. But it is every writer's goal.

Onomatopoeia

The official term for words that *sound* like what they mean is *onomatopoeia*. Some of the more obvious examples are the following:

buzzed	shrieked
crackled	thundered
wheezed	babbled
droned	roared
whimpered	popped

Say each word aloud. Listen to the sound echo the meaning. Used in writing, these words deliver a double punch. Try it. From the above list of ten onomatopoeic words, select the one that will support the meaning of each sentence and make each effective.

1 Beneath his feet, the brittle snow _____.

2 Becoming almost a part of the hot June stillness, the teacher's voice _____ on for thirty minutes.

3 Caught up in the excitement of the day, the two-year-old _____ of dolls, goldenrod, and candied cakes.

4 The puppy, its paw torn and bleeding, _____ for its small owner.

5 "Surprise!" shouted the guests as they _____ out of their hiding places.

Sound Play I

Teach your ears to *hear*. Add three words (suitable both as to sound and meaning) to each of the following categories. (There are no right and wrong answers. Not everyone reacts emotionally to the same stimulus.)

"Cool" words: brook chill _____

"Hot" words: warmth radiant _____

"Noisy" words: loud shrill _____

"Quiet" words: soft gentle _____

"Shapeless" words: blob plop _____

Sound Play II

This will really force both your imagination and ears to work. Listen to a common sound: the slamming of a door, the clicking of typewriter keys, the revving of a motor. Then describe it, using both regular and coined onomatopoeic words. (A coined word is a word invented to fill a particular need. You shouldn't do it regularly but it's fine when it's justified: when there's no word already in existence that will do the job you want it to do.)

Shakespeare once wrote

> Then nightly sings the staring owl,
> *Tu-whit, to-who!*

YOUR TURN _____
_____

Subtle Onomatopoeia

Onomatopoeia-blunt can be effective, but far more useful is onomatopoeia-subtle.

Which suggests movement: light or flash? _____
(REASON: the initial "fl" *flickers*.)

Which suggests repetition: jabber or talk? _____
(REASON: the suffix -er (or -le) *continues*.)

Which suggests littleness: inch or yard? _____
(REASON: the short "i" *diminishes*.)

Continue.

Which suggests slipperiness: slime or mud? _____

(REASON: _____)

Which suggests lightheartedness: merry or happy? _____

(REASON: _____)

Which suggests heaviness: ounce or ton? _____

(REASON: _____)

Continue.

What sound in *skinny* suggests the angular? _____

What sound in *slim* suggests the smooth? _____

What sound in *sun* suggests light and play? _____

What sound in *moon* suggests darkness and romance? _____

Continue.

If you had to choose between feeling *zaggoted* or *meressed* (both terms just coined), which would you choose?

Why? _____
_____

If you had to choose between eating *mallotoni* or *muz*, which would you choose?

Why? _____
_____

Continue.

Coin new onomatopoeic words for the following definitions:

A new land-air-water vehicle with a soft,
purring motor _____

A new cereal that whistles when milk is
poured over it _____

A new dance step in which each partner
stamps, glides, twists, and stamps again _____

Thimble Your Thesaurus

Most of the time, though, you won't be coining words; you'll be seeking the word that already exists and that *sounds* right and *is* right. *Roget's Thesaurus* or any good dictionary of synonyms can be helpful.

For example: you want to describe someone who hates to spend money. You look up "stingy." You find, among other adjectives, parsimonious, mean, niggardly, frugal, grudging, churlish, and avaricious. All you have to do now is be sure you know the meaning of each of these, and then decide which meaning *and* sound best rounds out your description.

Use your thesaurus to find five vivid synonyms for each of the following:

chatter _____ _____ _____ _____ _____

pain _____ _____ _____ _____ _____

hard _____ _____ _____ _____ _____

walk (noun) _____ _____ _____ _____ _____

gap (noun) _____ _____ _____ _____ _____

From your lists of synonyms, choose the three words you consider most onomatopoeic. In each case, explain why the sound of the word appeals to you.

1 _____

_____

2 _____

_____

3 _____

_____

The Master of Onomatopoeia

Edgar Allan Poe knew the importance of *sound* as few other writers have. In an essay called "The Philosophy of Composition" (1846), Poe wrote: "I have often thought how interesting a magazine paper might be written by any author who would—that is to say, who could—detail, step by step, the processes by which any one of his compositions attained its ultimate point of completion."*

Having posed the problem succinctly, Poe went on to solve it; and in this essay explains exactly how he wrote his famous poem, "The Raven." One section of this essay deals with his choice of *Nevermore* as the keystone of his refrain. You probably remember the line—

Quoth the Raven, "Nevermore."

---

*From "The Philosophy of Composition" in THE WORKS OF EDGAR ALLAN POE IN ONE VOLUME by Edgar Allan Poe. Copyright 1927. Reprinted by permission of Walter J. Black, Inc.

He began his search, Poe wrote, by reminding himself that a refrain "must be sonorous and susceptible of protracted emphasis ..." The long "o" seemed to him the most sonorous vowel; the "r" seemed the most producible consonant. Since he had already determined that the poem would be melancholy, he had to find a word that included the long "o" and the "r", preferably connected, and had a melancholy connotation. He concluded:

> In such a search it would have been absolutely impossible to overlook the word "Nevermore." In fact it was the very first which presented itself.[1]

Poe admitted that the "o" in "Nevermore" is not quite long—but it is almost so, and the word was perfect for his purpose in every other respect. More than a century later, with "The Raven" one of the best-known poems to adults and children alike, we can confirm Poe's choice. The man knew the tools of his trade.

Become a master. Study each of the following selections and see if you can, unerringly, with sound and meaning as your guides, select the superior word, the word the author chose. Explain briefly your choice.

1

> The skies they were ashen and sober;
> The leaves they were crisped and sere—
> The leaves they were withering and sere;
> It was night in the lonesome October
> Of my most _____ year.

(immemorial or unforgettable)   Edgar Allan Poe. "Ulalume"[2]

YOUR CHOICE _____

REASON _____
_____

2

> Until God loosen over sea and land
> The _____ of the trumpets of the night.

(blasting or thunder)   Algernon Swinburne. "Laus Veneris"

YOUR CHOICE _____

REASON _____
_____

[1]From "The Philosophy of Composition" in THE WORKS OF EDGAR ALLAN POE IN ONE VOLUME by Edgar Allan Poe. Copyright 1927. Reprinted by permission of Walter J. Black, Inc.
[2]"Ulalume" in THE WORKS OF EDGAR ALLAN POE IN ONE VOLUME by Edgar Allan Poe. Copyright 1927. Reprinted by permission of Walter J. Black, Inc.

3

They dined on mince, and slices of quince,
    Which they ate with a _____ spoon,
And hand in hand, on the edge of the sand,
    They danced by the light of the moon.

(runcible or silver)   Edward Lear. "The Owl and the Pussy-Cat"*

YOUR CHOICE   _____

REASON   _____

_____

4

He had his nest of wishes _____ to him all the time.

(piping or singing)   George Meredith. *Diana of the Crossways*

YOUR CHOICE   _____

REASON   _____

_____

> **The magic wand of onomatopoeia is within your grasp. Touch it lightly to a muffled line and hear words sing!**

*Edward Lear's "The Owl and the Pussy-Cat" in THE BOOK OF HUMOROUS VERSE, compiled by Carolyn Wells. Copyright 1920, Doubleday & Company, Inc. Reprinted by permission of Maurice O'Connell, Jr.

9. THE WORD AND ITS STORY

> Monday's child is fair of face,
> Tuesday's child is full of grace,
> Wednesday's child is full of woe,
> Thursday's child has far to go,
> Friday's child is loving and giving,
> Saturday's child works hard for its living,
> And a child that's born on the Sabbath day
> Is fair and wise and good and gay.
>
> (as quoted by A. E. Bray,
>   *Traditions of Devonshire*, 1838)*

So children have been chanting as their parents nodded wisely for at least a couple of centuries, probably far longer. Of course the days have names; of course a child's name-day shapes its future. So said the folk tales. But where did the names come from? And what do they mean? A browse through books of mythology supplies this information.

Monday: the *moon's* day.

Tuesday: *Tiu's* day; (also Tyr); the Norse god of war and for a while the chief god.

Wednesday: *Woden's* day; (also Odin); the chief Norse god whose major duty was to postpone the day of doom when the world would be destroyed.

Thursday: *Thor's* day; the strongest Norse god; the god of thunder and lightning who sent rain and caused the earth to bear fruit.

Friday: *Frigga's* day; the mother of the Norse gods, and originally also the goddess of love and beauty.

Saturday: *Saturn's* day; the Roman god of agriculture, of sowing and reaping. Saturn presided in the Golden Age when life was simple and good. His feast, the Saturnalia, in December, lasted seven days and was celebrated with great feasting and wild merriment.

Sunday: the *sun's* day.

Take a few minutes to seek a relationship between the old rhyme and the still older name-derivations. The poet must have been aware, consciously or subconsciously, of the varied mythological origins, for they partly determined his descriptions. The story behind a word often affects our appreciation and use of the word.

---

*A. E. Bray's *Traditions of Devonshire* in THE OXFORD DICTIONARY OF QUOTATIONS, Second Edition, Oxford University Press, Oxford, England. Copyrights from 1941 to 1955.

People-Words

Many words are named for people. *Odyssey* (a long journey) comes from Odysseus who took ten years to return to Greece after the Trojan War. *Mercurial* (changeable and quick) comes from Mercury, the messenger of the Roman gods, known for his swift and mischievous errands. Here are some more people-words. Starting with the dictionary and going on to encyclopedias and word-books, find out as much as you can about the origin of each.

tantalize _____

_____

caesarian _____

_____

derby _____

_____

bloomer _____

_____

lunch _____

_____

(And a few more to play with: guy; martial; cereal; guillotine; volcano; siren; pyrrhic; cardigan; to hector)

Place-Words

Other words are named for places. You've heard of a *sardonic* grin—a bitter, scornful grin; but did you know it was named after a poisonous plant that grows in Sardinia and that twists and distorts the face of the eater? Track down the origin of these place-words.

laconic _____

_____

limousine _____

_____

vaudeville _____

_____

antimacassar _____

_____

marathon _____

_____

(And a couple more: shanghai; milliner)

Animal-Words

The names of animals, most often, come from their appearance. The *wapiti*, for example, is a large American deer that received its name, inelegantly, from the Shawnee word for its distinctive white rump! (*Kangaroo* is an exception, though. When Captain Cook visited Australia, he asked the natives what that strange animal was called. They shrugged and said "kangaroo"—meaning "I don't know" or "I don't understand"—and the kangaroo was forthwith baptized.) Investigate the origin of these animal-words.

hippopotamus _____

_____

squirrel _____

_____

jack rabbit _____

_____

secretary bird _____

_____

rhinoceros _____

_____

Writing a Filler

Knowledge of such word-origins makes a writer more sensitive in using words; but this knowledge has an immediate, practical use, too. A clever, interesting word-origin story makes a fine filler; and fillers are used by most magazines and many newspapers. (A *filler* is a short item used by a publication to fill up a column.)

To write a filler, follow these few steps:

1 Start with a word-origin that interests you.

2 Check encyclopedias and other reference books for related information.

3 Write.

4 Cut from your writing everything that isn't necessary. Be ruthless. A filler should be short and should carry only one idea.

5 Check your first and last sentences. Does the first sentence capture the reader's interest? Does the last sentence drive home the point of the anecdote? If they don't, rewrite until they do.

6 Make a clean, finished copy.

An Example . . . .

There's a possible filler in the name and appearance of the mule deer. A quick check of five reference books yielded this information. The mule deer

. . . has a large white patch on the rump

. . . has a tail tipped with black

. . . is one of more than thirty species of deer

. . . moves with a jerky gait, as if all four feet touched the ground at the same time

. . . has odd, double-branched antlers

. . . Lewis and Clark said of it: "It does not lope but jumps."

. . . is handsome

. . . has huge ears; hears tiniest sound; sudden noise makes it jump into air before fleeing

. . . bounds with great stiff-legged leaps like a "runaway pogo stick"

. . . prefers a rocky landscape, from western Mexico to British Columbia

. . . often found in the Rocky Mountains

. . . looks like a mule

. . . likes both mountains and deserts

. . . makes dust beds on slopes—called "mule deer hotels"

. . . reddish-brown coat in summer; steel-blue in winter

Here's the first draft of a possible filler.

> Rudolph may have a red nose, but the *mule deer* of the Rocky Mountains has a good deal more to contend with. His peculiar double-branched antlers, his white rump, and his black-tipped tail all set him off from the more than thirty other species of deer that roam the earth. It's a handsome creature, the mule deer, and a fascinating one. Its coat changes from reddish-brown in summer to steel-blue in winter. On the steep mountain slopes it burrows out dust beds laconically known as "mule deer hotels." But its real oddness—as well as its name—comes from two other characteristics: it has huge ears (like a mule's), is extraordinarily sensitive to sound; and when frightened, jumps into the air, then takes off with a jerky gait like a "runaway pogo stick," all four feet hitting the ground simultaneously. When Lewis and Clark first saw the mule deer in action, they noted with astonishment: "It does not lope but jumps!"

It won't do. It's too long (more than 150 words); a filler should seldom be more than a hundred. It contains too much information and too many kinds of information. The second sentence will have to go, and the third, fourth, and fifth. Then the whole paragraph needs tightening. The beginning is satisfactory, with an allusion that will have meaning for almost every reader; and the ending isn't bad but should be sharpened.

Here, after a couple of intermediate drafts, is the final revision:

Rudolph may have a red nose, but the *mule deer* of the Rocky Mountains has a good deal more to contend with. As its name suggests, it *looks* like a mule, with a mule-shaped head and huge mule-like ears. It walks like a mule, too. Instead of running like all the other deer, it jumps into the air, then bounds away stiff-legged, all four feet hitting the ground simultaneously—like an animated pogo stick. Said the astonished Lewis and Clark as they watched their first mule deer in action: "It does not lope but jumps!"

As you can see, it is a good deal tighter and more unified than the first version. It *might* sell.

It's your turn now. From the word-origins you've already investigated, choose the one that interests you the most. Explore reference books for related materials. Write. Cut and polish. Copy the final revision below.

_____

_____

_____

_____

_____

_____

_____

_____

_____

Writing a filler seems easy—but it isn't. It demands all the basic steps necessary to any writing job. It even demands skill in marketing. Ask yourself: "To what kind of people would my filler appeal?" Your answer should suggest possible markets. The "mule deer" filler might go to a children's or young people's magazine, or to a local newspaper. A filler about a child might go to a women's magazine. The filler about the mule deer has been made more marketable by the allusion to *Rudolph*, making it a possibility for almost any publication around Christmas time.

Study your filler. Consider possible markets. (And if you really want to write for a living, start studying magazines *now*.) If you're satisfied with your filler, if you think it's well-written, send it off. (Check the last unit of this book for marketing procedures.) And don't forget your school newspaper. It may not pay cash, but it often will print—and seeing something you wrote in print is marvelous payment for the beginning writer!

Writing a Longer Filler

Now that you've become market-conscious, consider writing longer fillers—ones aimed at a particular market. If you are sports-minded, for example, you might try one on the origins of game names: tennis, golf, soccer, etc. Or (still on sports) one on the origin of arena, athletics, gymnasium, and calisthenics. The trick here is to find several related words, all of which have interesting origins.

Choose sports, or one of the groups below.

RELIGION: basilica, ecclesiastic, homily, pagan, seminary, pastor, Bible, shrine, evangelist, chapel

POLITICS: candidate, census, caucus, poll, governor, gerrymander

EDUCATION: college, academy, pedagogue, precocious, symposium, dean

MILITARY: martial, stratagem, ambulance, soldier, parachute, jeep, infantry, pistol, grenade

Explore the origins of all words in the group you chose—plus any other related words you can think of. When you have enough material, try writing a longer filler—perhaps 200 words.

_____

_____

_____

_____

_____

_____

_____

_____

_____

_____

_____

_____

_____

_____

_____

_____

_____

_____

The number of word-origin fillers that you can write is limited only by your imagination and endurance. There are thousands of possible words, dozens of possible groups—and plenty of possible markets! Writing fillers is

a good way to start a writing career (it teaches discipline, conciseness, and research)

a good way to earn money by writing "on the side"

a good way to bolster your ego (it's fun to wave a magazine or newspaper in front of your friends and chortle: "See what I wrote!")

A Grab Bag of Additional Suggestions

1 For your local newspaper, investigate the origins of the names of your state, county, and city or town. Write a filler.

2 Use a word-origin to begin a longer piece of writing . . . even a term paper. A term paper on art museums would be off to a good start with the long-ago meaning of "museum."

3 Turn one of those longer fillers (a group of word-origins) into a short article for your school newspaper or other market.

4 Some additional words to explore: ostracize; ephemeral; posse; etiquette; sarcasm; sanctimonious; digital; cynic; holocaust.

5 Some good word-books for use in pursuing word-origins:

Shipley, Joseph. *Dictionary of Word Origins*

Wedeck, Harry E. *Short Dictionary of Classical Word Origins*

Barnes, Duane Clayton. *Wordlore*

Asimov, Isaac. *Words from the Myths*

and—*every* dictionary you can find!

Good hunting!

10. THE NAME IS THE GAME

What's wrong with this brief episode from a famous novel?

"A merry Christmas, uncle! God save you!" cried a cheerful voice . . .
"Bah!" said Smith. "Humbug!"

The *name* makes the difference. If Charles Dickens had named his penny-pinching, wicked old character John Smith instead of Ebenezer Scrooge, *A Christmas Carol* might never have been published. John Smith can't cause a raised eyebrow, but Ebenezer Scrooge shrivels with miserliness. In good writing, the name sets the pace for both tone and theme.

Dickens was a master at the art of choosing—or creating—names. Look at these:

Dick Swiveller	Uriah Heep
Mr. Murdstone	Peggotty
Pip	Mr. Turveydrop
Mr. Gradgrind	Abel Magwitch
Fagin	the Cheeryble brothers

Aren't they marvelous? Knowing only the names, one could write elaborate character sketches.

Other authors have also played the name-game successfully. Thackeray, in *Vanity Fair*, used Becky Sharp for his heroine, and that attractive young woman was just as hard, curt, and cruel as her name suggests. Margaret Mitchell, in *Gone With the Wind*, at first called her lead character Pansy; only later was it changed to Scarlett. Can you imagine a *Pansy* O'Hara clashing head-on with Rhett Butler, or tearing raw carrots from the earth to ward off starvation?

The name *is* the game. It makes a difference.

Storied Names

Some names are so wrapped in past story that they carry connotations instantly. As a warm-up exercise, match each name in the first column with an appropriate description from the second.

(_____) 1 Penelope   *a*   brave; crafty; skilled in strategy

(_____) 2 Cassandra   *b*   home-loving; loyal

(_____) 3 Sibyl   *c*   vulnerable; romantic

(_____) 4 Achilles   *d*   alluring; prophetic

(_____) 5 Ophelia   *e*   whining; full of woe

Establishing Names

Business owners know the monetary value of a catchy name. Here are some "establishment" names gleaned from newspaper ads. In each case explain briefly the probable reason the name was chosen (the kind of appeal intended).

6   The Colonel's Table (a restaurant) _____

_____

7   The Razor's Edge (a barber shop) _____

_____

8   Dunkin' Donuts _____

_____

9   Candy Apple Play School _____

_____

10   Mixed Media (gift shop) _____

_____

11   The Sawhorse (lumber company) _____

_____

12   Sheer Joy (candy shop) _____

(And—just for fun—what kind of establishment might be called "*Shear* Joy"?
_____)

Name Your Own

Make your imagination stretch and quiver! Search in the hidden niches of your brain and find names for the following:

13   A bowling alley _____

14   A restaurant for vegetarians _____

15   A hard rubber car that cannot be dented _____

16   A cap that can be worn while skiing, then turned into a soup bowl for supper

_____

17   A shuttle service beteen Earth and Mars _____

18   A stapler that uses invisible staples _____

Sidestep

Before we continue, work a few minutes in your telephone directory. "Let your fingers do the walking" through the Yellow Pages. Find five or six related names of stores or businesses. (Example: all may include a specific word such as *apple*, or all may have a patriotic ring.) Combine these names into a short filler that might interest your local newspaper.

THE NAMES

_____
_____
_____
_____
_____
_____

THE FILLER   (Remember—keep it short; write a catchy beginning and a forceful ending; keep it unified.)

_____
_____
_____
_____
_____
_____
_____
_____

Back to the Literary Ranch

When James Joyce wrote *A Portrait of the Artist as a Young Man*, he named his young hero Stephen Dedalus: Stephen, after Christianity's first martyr, and Dedalus, after the Greek artificer who created wax wings so that man could fly.

When Aldous Huxley wrote *Brave New World*, he gave the name Henry *Foster* to the man in charge of the Hatchery, and Mustapha Mond (Mond means world) to the Controller. But Huxley had the most fun with the pivotal point of his satire: the mechanization that started with assembly-line production. In the new robot-like culture, God gave way to Our Ford; and the sign of the cross to the sign of T (the Model-T Ford). Mustapha Mond was greeted as his "fordship" and frustrated people, as expletives, cried "Oh, Ford!"

Of course not all fictitious characters have names so complex and erudite; but most are carefully chosen for sound and connotation. Consider the difference if Twain had written not *The Adventures of Tom Sawyer* but *The Adventures of Cecil Pankhurst*. Consider the difference if Lewis Carroll had written not *Alice in Wonderland* but *Prudence in Wonderland*. What if Rudolph the Red-nosed Reindeer had been named Billy? Or if Queen Guinevere had been dubbed Queen Maisie?

Names *do* make a difference. Now that you have become name-conscious, you will want to do two things.

First, choose or create names for the following types of people that you might wish to use in a story or poem:

1   A tall, robust young man with great skill in archery who saves the heroine from death and, while doing so, saves a nation from total destruction

2   An ugly old woman who bore nine children and watched all of them die and who now takes vengeance on the world by kidnapping children whenever she can

3   A fat, middle-aged man who has concentrated solely on making money and who now is becoming aware of what he has missed

4   An attractive young woman who runs a lumber camp in Oregon, owns a paper mill in the Adirondack region, and sets the policies for 100 newspapers across the country

In addition, you will need names for settings. Name these:

5   A mansion built in 1751 that has been vacant for 46 years and that is supposed to be haunted. It is built on a high hill and surrounded by 93 acres of uncared-for grounds

6   A small town (population 342) that discourages the introduction of anything new or different. It has been unchanged for at least 37 years and really is little different from the original settlement of 200 years ago

7   A large city (population 15 million) that is built of glass and filled with unruly inhabitants. It is not quite complete, and probably never will be

8   A good-sized pond that is rumored to be bottomless. At least half a dozen people drown in it each year, and residents of the rural area that surround it whisper of a monster that can be seen at midnight on October 31

The second thing you will want to do is start collecting interesting names. When you hear a name (person or place) that intrigues you, make a note of it in your journal. The next time you need a name for a fictitious character, consult this list. If James Joyce and Charles Dickens and Aldous Huxley could spend hours of their time and generous slabs of their imagination to conjure up just the "right" names, then you—as a beginning writer—cannot afford to do otherwise.

Note: If you have trouble thinking of "right" names, hold a brainstorming session (see Chapter 1). That will start your creative juices flowing!

11. WHEN A PART IS MORE THAN THE WHOLE

The mathematician insists that the equation 2 + 2 = 4 tells the truth precisely and completely.

The scientist insists that the formula H_2O best defines water.

They're both right, in their chosen fields; but they're both wrong in their shared field: in their humanity. For $2 + $2 may equal triumph if you need three dollars for a pet project; or disaster, if you need five. And water may mean rain on your face at dusk, or the ocean pounding on the shore, or a tall cold drink after you have mowed the lawn.

The formula defines, in the narrowest sense—but it does not draw distinctions between water in a deep well and water from a city tap—or, for that matter, from water in a sewer. It doesn't realize, or care, that to one person water is joyful recreation, while to another it spells fear and death by drowning.

Denotation and Connotation

The formula *denotes;* the word *denotes* AND *connotes.* **To denote** is to serve as a name, to provide a literal meaning. **To connote** is to imply or suggest something beyond the literal meaning. For example: the word "apple" denotes a specific kind of fruit; but it connotes many things: sin (the apple in the Garden of Eden); disagreement or war (the apple of discord in Greek mythology); self-confidence (the apple William Tell placed on his son's head and then shot off); and simple pleasure (the tang of warm apple pie on an autumn afternoon, the fun of picking apples, or ducking for apples on Halloween). Some or all of these things are suggested when a writer uses the word "apple."

Just as a car's battery needs to be charged to keep operating, so writing needs to be charged to be effective. And the best way to charge your writing is to use words rich in connotation.

A Tiger in Your Tank

Train yourself to become alert to the connotation as well as the denotation of words. This exercise should help you. For each word at the left, write the dictionary definition (denotation) and one or more connotations.

TIGER   *Denotation:* _____

             Connotations: _____

             _____

HOME   *Denotation:* _____

             Connotations: _____

             _____

LOLLIPOP   *Denotation:*   _____

            Connotations: _____

                                  _____

GRAVE   *Denotation:*   _____

(noun)   *Connotations:*   _____

                                  _____

CRYSTAL   *Denotation:*   _____

             Connotations: _____

                                  _____

You Are . . . I Am . . .

Another way to sharpen your awareness of connotation is to play the "You are . . . I am . . ." game. It goes like this:

"You are gluttonous, but I have a good appetite."

Or like this:

"You are miserly, but I am thrifty."

Notice that, in each case, "you and I" share a similar quality, but the choice of words turns the quality into an insult for you and a compliment for me. If you can come up with five good "You are . . . I am . . ." sentences, you have grasped the basic meaning of word-connotation.

You are _____, but I am _____.

You are _____, but I am _____.

You are _____, but I am _____.

You are _____, but I am _____.

You are _____, but I am _____.

Synecdoche

Connotation makes a *word* more than it is; synecdoche makes a *thing* more than it is. Sounds complicated, doesn't it? If you were to explore *all* the aspects of synecdoche, you would find it complex indeed. But the average writer needs to be concerned with only one.

Synecdoche is simple to grasp: **let a part stand for the whole**. You probably use synecdoche frequently. Remember the last time you referred disdainfully to the "boob tube"? You were referring to a complete television set, not to a tube; but you chose to indicate it by naming one of its parts. That's synecdoche. When a first mate announces sternly, "All hands on deck!" he'd be shocked if he were suddenly confronted by twelve pairs of hands dancing around his feet. He meant, of course, *sailors*—but he chose to indicate them by naming one of their parts. That's synecdoche.

Smarten your sense of synecdoche by inserting a *part* of a whole in each of the following blanks:

1 A sailor, standing on a rapidly sinking ship, is anxiously scanning the horizon. He sees another ship approaching and cries with relief: "A _____, a _____!"

2 A cattle rancher who needs money plans to sell off his stock. He orders: "Send 5,000 _____ to the market tomorrow, and the other 5,000 next week."

3 Jerry, who has just bought his first car, brags to his friends: "Come out and take a look at my _____."

4 Suzy is in charge of setting up a booth for the carnival. She looks at the four husky males nearby and says: "I need four pairs of _____. Any available?"

5 Antony, speaking after the assassination of Julius Caesar, wanted his audience to listen closely to his words. He said: "Friends, Romans, countrymen; lend me your _____."

Synecdoche is easy to appreciate, but difficult to create. Challenge yourself: create a couple of examples of synecdoche. Think about things you like to do: motorcycling; biking; surfing; painting. Then ask yourself which *part* of the whole is central. Use that part, as synecdoche, in a sentence.

_____
_____
_____
_____
_____
_____

Metonymy

Not too different from synecdoche is *metonymy*. Metonymy comes from the Greek word, metonymia, meaning "substitute naming." To put it more simply—if two objects are closely associated, one may take on the attributes of the other. When you hear that the White House has delivered an ultimatum, you know perfectly well that the building hasn't suddenly burst into speech. You know that the President of the United States has spoken. The concepts, White House and President, have been associated for so long that the former has taken on, through metonymy, some of the attributes of the latter.

Metonymy also exists as a result of similarity in appearance. When your host asks you if you would like some ginger ale and you reply: "Yes, on the rocks, please," you do not expect him to go out to the garden and start digging. Both of you know that "rocks" is used, metonymically, for "ice cubes."

In the following sentences, underline the example of metonymy and explain the relationship between the metonymical word and the word for which it is a substitute.

1 "She sets a good table," Jed said with satisfaction.

_____

_____

2 The old salt tottered down the street, his legs still unused to the solid feel of pavement.

_____

_____

3 At fifty, restless and seeking new challenges, he abandoned the scalpel and began to write poetry.

_____

_____

4 Within a half hour, sixteen people had reported the sighting of a flying saucer. The Governor called up the National Guard.

_____

_____

5 After the jury brought in the verdict, the bench pronounced sentence.

_____

_____

That was a warm-up session. Now you're ready to analyze metonymy as used by professional writers. In each of the following quotations, underline the metonymical word or words; then explain two things: (1) the original word for which the metonymical term is a substitute; and (2) the probable reason why the author chose to employ metonymy.

1 "Give us this day our daily bread." (Gospel according to St. Matthew)

_____

_____

_____

2 "The pen is mightier than the sword." (Edward Bulwer-Lytton in *Richelieu*)

_____

_____

_____

3 "In the bottle, discontent seeks for comfort, cowardice for courage, and bashfulness for confidence." (Samuel Johnson)

_____

_____

_____

_____

_____

4 "No pain, no palm; no thorns, no throne; no gall, no glory; no cross, no crown." (William Penn)

_____

_____

_____

_____

_____

5

> The glories of our birth and state
> Are shadows, not substantial things;
> There is no armour against fate;
>   Death lays his icy hand on kings.
>   Sceptre and crown
>   Must tumble down,
>   And in the dust be equal made
> With the poor crooked scythe and spade.

James Shirley. *The Contention of Ajax and Ulysses**

_____

_____

_____

_____

_____

Connotation, with its assistants *synecdoche* and *metonymy*, is a powerful tool for sculpting chiseled sentences. This "tool" you will use often; keep it in sight when you are at your workbench.

_____

*James Shirley's *The Contention of Ajax and Ulysses* in THE CAMBRIDGE BOOK OF POETRY AND SONG. Copyright 1882, Thomas Y. Crowell & Company, Inc.

12. FELICITOUS PHRASING

Sometimes a word, by itself, is just a word; but when it is linked with another word, something magical occurs. "Doornail" is a nondescript kind of word; combined with "dead"—as in "dead as a doornail"—it changes. It becomes a pleasure to the ear, a tickle of the imagination. After it has been used a few thousand times, it becomes trite. But the first writer who used the phrase (possibly William Langland) created something special, something enduring; and he did it by employing alliteration.

Alliteration

Alliteration is the repetition of the initial sound in two or more words. Often it's the repetition of the initial letter, but not always. You might say "felicitous fish," repeating the initial letter; but you might also say "felicitous phrasing," repeating the initial sound. ("Celestial canaries" is *not* alliterative; the letter is repeated, but the sound is not; and it is the repeated sound that is important.)

Alliteration is the most popular of the figures of speech. To prove this to yourself, complete the following alliterative phrases, many of them terribly trite:

... in the wild and _____ west.

I'll do or _____!

He's penny-wise, _____-foolish.

The new miracle drug will _____ or cure.

... rock 'n' _____ music ...

Don't get on your _____ horse with me!

Sell more than your competitor; be a _____-getter.

Dollars to _____ he won't be back.

Sticks and _____ may break my bones ...

You can have fun with alliteration.

You can create political slogans:

VOTE FOR VALERIE
RIDE HIGH WITH RONALD

YOUR TURN _____

Or create travel ads:

Come to ... snowy Switzerland
... beautiful Bermuda

YOUR TURN _____

Or create a name for your house:

> Howell's Haven
> D'Amato's Den

YOUR TURN _____

You can even create tongue-twisters. Remember your favorite when you were little?

> Peter Piper picked a peck of pickled pepper;
> A peck of pickled pepper Peter Piper picked;
> If Peter Piper picked a peck of pickled pepper,
> Where's the peck of pickled pepper Peter Piper picked?

> (from *Peter Piper's Practical Principles of*
> *Plain and Perfect Pronunciation*, 1819)

Choose a letter: p, or s, or t, or any other letter you like. Consult both brain and dictionary and make a list of at least twenty words beginning with the letter chosen.

_____	_____	_____	_____	_____
_____	_____	_____	_____	_____
_____	_____	_____	_____	_____
_____	_____	_____	_____	_____
_____	_____	_____	_____	_____

Now roll each word around on your tongue. Select the six or eight that roll best and combine them into a sentence of small-sense. After that, just follow the Peter Piper formula and presto: your very own tongue-twister! Copy it below. Later you can swap your masterpieces and try them out. Determine which twists the tongue most tightly!

_____

_____

_____

_____

Back to the Workbench

So much for fun and games. Look, now, at the way professionals use alliteration. In each of the following quotations, choose the alliterative word in parentheses. That's easy. But after you have chosen it, read the quotation first with the wrong word, then with the right word. *Hear* the difference. Become aware of how the choice of one word can make or break a sentence.

> In her sepulchre there by the sea,

> In her tomb by the _____ sea. (pounding, sounding)

> Poe. "Annabel Lee"

Keen as are the arrows

Of that _____ sphere. (argent, silver)

Shelley. "To a Skylark"

So sweetly mawkish, and so _____ dull. (plainly, smoothly)

Pope. "The Dunciad"

On to Oxymoron

And now—make haste slowly to oxymoron. *Oxymoron* is the blending of two contradictory terms. It all comes clear when you notice the derivation of the word: "oxy" meaning sharp, and "moros" meaning stupid or foolish; hence, a sharp-stupid saying. And that's exactly what oxymoron is: a phrase that seems stupid at first, then—on further thought—turns out to be quite sharp. Consider "to make haste slowly." Sometimes you have to slow down in order to hurry. Alliteration is a union of words; oxymoron is a much more sophisticated union of words. You will not use it frequently, but it can, at times, be an effective and forceful technique.

First Step

Begin to master the oxymoron by filling in the blanks in the following sentences with words that are contradictory, yet meaningful:

1 Your mother looks at your room and shakes her head. "A _____ mess you've made of it," she chides.

2 The doctor has just finished examining you. "Do anything you like; go anywhere you like," she says. "You're _____ healthy!"

3 As Juliet said to Romeo: "Parting is such _____ sorrow."

Second Step

Continue to develop mastery of the oxymoron by defining the seven examples below. (Example: "to make haste slowly" means to slow down in order to hasten a successful completion of a task.)

4 free servitude _____

_____

5 mournful optimist _____

_____

6 cheerful pessimist _____

_____

7 cruel kindness _____

_____

8   wise fool _____

    _____

9   serious vanity _____

    _____

10 living corpse _____

    _____

Third Step

Few writers have used oxymoron so often and so well as did William Shakespeare. Shortly after Romeo and Juliet met and loved, Romeo killed Tybalt, Juliet's cousin. Juliet, distraught with loving hate and hating love, cried bitterly:

> Beautiful tyrant, fiend angelical!
> Dove-feather'd raven, wolvish-rav'ning lamb!
> Despised substance of divinest show!
> Just opposite to what thou justly seem'st,
> A damned saint, an honorable villain!

Read the above five lines several times. Then underline the examples of oxymoron. Below, explain why Shakespeare chose to use this technique so heavily in this particular passage.

_____

_____

_____

Fourth (and Final) Step

Proceed now, with plodding glee, to construct your own dull-bright examples of oxymoron. (Aim for three.)

_____

_____

_____

Tropes are simply figures of speech: techniques to charge our expression with provocative thought and vivid imagery. You have now mastered five tropes:

onomatopoeia synecdoche metonymy alliteration oxymoron

> **As the skilled carpenter carves with precision, as the skilled potter shapes with love, as the skilled weaver designs with an eye to color and texture, so the skilled writer carves and shapes and designs—using as tools the literary techniques developed over the centuries.**

Unit III
Using Details

INTRODUCTION

A detail tells a rat from a rabbit,
     defines a giraffe,
       profiles an elephant.

A detail is a fingerprint of the character, making it specific, and different, and unique.

A detail may evoke a face, or a forest, or a fragrance. It may even evoke an idea.

Details can be gleaned by the senses,
                by research, or
                by analysis.

Details are the multitudes of images of a Brueghel, or the broad, wild colors of a Kandinsky.

Details make up the macabre in Poe,
            the loving loneliness in Emily Dickinson,
            the brutal wisdom in Shakespeare.

Details crawl and leap and strut and slither and whine.

Details are red, white, blue, green, black, yellow.

Details sound hard and soft, melodic and discordant, shrill and reassuring.

Details comfort, dismay, appall, appeal, and shock.

A detail turns a home run into a pop fly, or
            a gutter ball into a strike.

A detail may turn a victory into a rout, but a different detail
            may turn a rout into a victory.

Details are as plentiful as grains of sand on a beach,
            as varied as apples picked in the same orchard,
            as colorful as tumbling leaves in October.

To the writer, details are red corpuscles providing sustenance, and strength, and life itself.

For life is made up of details.
And details re-create life.

1 *All About You.* If you could keep only one of the following—automobile, radio, refrigerator, or television—which would you keep?

_____ Why? _____

_____

Which would you find it easiest to discard?

_____ Why? _____

_____

What do your choices tell you about yourself? _____

_____

_____

_____

2 *A First.* Be creative in an unfamiliar field. If you have never painted a picture, paint one now. If you have never written a poem, write one now. If you have never strummed a guitar or pounded on a piano, use one now to compose a short song. Afterwards, describe how you felt while you were painting, or writing, or composing, and then describe the result of your endeavors.

_____

_____

_____

_____

_____

3 *Acronym Antics.* WAC, as everyone knows, is an acronym for *Women's Army Corps.* A few years ago one WAC with a hearty appetite noted idly that WAC might just as well stand for—*Where Are Calories?* A sister WAC who had lost the caloric battle retorted: *"Collecting At Waistlines!"*, turning the acronym around. Choose any well-known acronym and create a new meaning for the letters. If you feel really sharp, try the double-twist: a question (forward) and an answer (reverse). Some possibilities: NOW (National Organization for Women); ZIP (Zone Improvement Plan); CARE (Cooperative for American Relief Everywhere); NATO (North Atlantic Treaty Organization).

ACRONYM _____

QUESTION _____

_____

ANSWER _____

_____

4 *Improvisation.* You want to take a bath, but the stopper in the bathtub is broken. It's too late to go to the store. Using only objects found in most homes, how could you improvise a stopper that would work well enough to permit you to take a leisurely bath?

_____

_____

_____

5 *Dilemma.* If you *had* to sacrifice one of your five senses—sight, hearing, taste, touch, smell—which would you give up? _____ Why? _____

_____

6 *Deductive Experience.* Take a survey. Ask twenty people this question: "What is your favorite taste?" After you have completed the survey, tabulate the results and record them below.

_____

_____

_____

Any conclusions? _____

_____

7 *Daffy Definitions.* A snorer has been defined as a *sound* sleeper, and a dentist as a man who runs a *filling* station. Put your wits to work and create daffy definitions for the following:

a dog _____

an electrician _____

an umpire _____

an automobile driver _____

a sophomore _____

8 *Magic Spectacles.* You are a Martian and your spaceship is hovering over your (real) school. You have special eyeglasses that enable you to see through roofs and ceilings. Keeping in mind that you are totally unfamiliar with humans and human activities, describe what you see as you look down into the school building.

_____

_____

_____

_____

_____

_____

_____

9 *Riddle.* Why is an elephant better equipped to travel than a fox or a rooster?

Answer: _____

_____

(See answer below.)

10 *Dream-o-Rama.*   Dream up a new flavor of ice cream. It must be (*a*) truly new, one never tried before; (*b*) delicious; and (*c*) potentially popular.

_____

Because the elephant always has his trunk with him, while the fox has only a brush and the rooster a comb!

13. SENSE SENSITIVITY

You have five windows on the world—five senses that can help you to know the world and to understand it. Some lucky writers have been sense-sensitive by instinct; others have had to train themselves to deliberate and skillful use of these versatile tools.

So this is a training session: a time to see and to hear, a time to smell and to taste, a time to touch.

The Sense of Sight

Start with this short quiz:

1 You have handled many one-dollar bills.

   (a)   Whose picture is on it? _____

   (b)   Where on the bill does the Great Seal of the United States appear? _____

   (c)   Not counting the serial number or dates, how often does the numeral "1" appear?

   _____

2 What color are the walls of the school cafeteria? _____

3 Most pencils aren't quite round. Do they have four, six, or eight sides? _____

All three questions deal with things you see almost daily. You should have a perfect score. Do you? If you missed even one answer, you are not using your eyes with full effectiveness.

First Phase

Look. Look at the wall to your right. Look hard and long. Describe it as completely as possible. Note details.

_____

_____

_____

_____

_____

_____

_____

_____

Look at the top of your desk. Describe it. Note details.

_____

_____

_____

_____

_____

Study the Rorschach-type test figure below. (A Rorschach test measures a person's personality through the interpretation of an abstract design.) Let your imagination aid your eyes. What do you see?

_____

_____

_____

_____

Second Phase

The photographer and the artist use perspective almost automatically. The writer often forgets it exists. Study some object—perhaps a bowl of fruit—from a distance of at least twenty feet (a long shot); then move in to three feet or less (a close-up); finally peer at it through a magnifying lens. After each part of the experiment, describe what you see.

(*a*) A Long Shot _____

_____

_____

(*b*) A Close-Up _____

_____

_____

(*c*) Under the Magnifying Lens _____

_____

_____

Third Phase

Colors appear not only on an artist's palette, but also in a writer's mind. Often a simple *red* will not suffice; you may need a blood-red or a cherry-red, quite different hues. This time let memory aid your eyes. Find modifiers that will convey very different shades of the following colors:

RED	BLUE	GREEN	YELLOW
blood-red	midnight-blue	cucumber-green	mustard-yellow
_____	_____	_____	_____
_____	_____	_____	_____
_____	_____	_____	_____

Fourth Phase

Take a one-block walk. During your block-long trek, take five word snapshots of things you *see*. The snapshots should be one sentence in length and may record the ordinary (e.g., halfway along the block is a mustard-yellow house with filmy windows and a sagging door); or the not-so-ordinary (e.g., muddy water along the curb—in the sun, an iridescent puddle—a cigarette wrapper drifts lazily).

1 _____

_____

2 _____

_____

3 _____

_____

4 _____

_____

5 _____

_____

The Sense of Hearing

Most people hear even less than they see. You will have to work harder at training this sense.

First Phase

For about two minutes sit very quietly and listen. Listen intently to sounds within the classroom and to sounds in the hall or outside the building. List all the sounds you can hear.

_____

_____

_____

_____

_____

_____

Second Phase

Now that your ears have started to hear, force them to become more specific. Think about bells. Describe, in just a few words, the *sound* of each of the following bells:

1 The School Bell _____

_____

2 The Church Bell _____

_____

3 Your Door Bell _____

_____

4 A Telephone Bell (or Ring) _____

_____

5 A _____ Bell (you name it) _____

_____

Third Phase

This time try to describe a cluster of sounds. Listen to someone typing on either a manual or electric typewriter. Isolate each sound; determine the sequence; combine into a whole. Instead of describing the typing process, you may prefer to work with the sounds made by someone going to the chalkboard, writing a sentence, and then erasing it. Your sound perception may be enhanced by closing your eyes; this throws the burden on your ears.

_____

_____

_____

_____

_____

Fourth Phase

It's time to walk again—one block. As you walk, listen. What do you hear? Take five word snapshots: one-sentence descriptions of *sounds*. (e.g., An oil truck rumbles past, its motor turning hard and fast; the horn honks once, a long blaring, scaring note.)

1 _____

_____

2 _____

_____

3 _____

_____

4 _____

_____

5 _____

_____

The Sense of Smell

Some psychologists claim that the sense of smell—more than any other sense—is likely to evoke long-ago memories. An unexpected smell of turnips, for example, may suddenly waft you back to a dinner when you were four years old; the smell of hot tar may waltz you back to a summer when you stupidly insisted on going barefoot! The sense of smell, then, becomes an important tool in the writer's kit.

First Phase

Probe your memory. If you were writing a story or a poem about school, what common school smells would you include? Don't be satisfied with the first smells that you remember. Probe. Consider classrooms, the cafeteria, the gym, etc. Aim for half a dozen "school" smells.

_____

_____

_____

_____

_____

Second Phase

By now, your nose should be twitching just a bit. Good. Walk into three stores—specific stores. You might choose a barber shop or a beauty parlor, a butcher's, and a delicatessen. Put your nose to work. What smell predominates? What other smells exist? (Try to be inconspicuous or you may find yourself the object of curious stares.) *After* you leave each store, describe as vividly as you can the predominating (most forceful) smell and any additional smells.

STORE # 1 _____

_____
_____
_____

STORE # 2 _____

_____
_____
_____

STORE #3 _____

_____
_____
_____

Third Phase

Back to your memory. Explore your file of smells. What smells do you remember that evoke

a spring day _____

a garage _____

a dog that's been out in the rain _____

Thanksgiving Day _____

Continue with two more smells that have a special significance for you. Describe briefly the memory or emotion that each evokes.

_____
_____

Fourth Phase

Walking time again. (Tell your feet this is your last short walk.) Walk one block. Concentrate on what you smell. This may be difficult. You will have to capture subtle smells as well as blatant ones. Take five "smell" snapshots (e.g., the overpowering, acrid smell of gasoline from a passing car or bus).

1 _____

2 _____

3 _____

4 _____

5 _____

Sense of Taste

A very pleasant sense, generally, is the sense of taste. Yours may be rather primitive, or—if you have trained it—it may be quite sophisticated. Some industries (wineries, for one) employ professional tasters to assure that taste quality is high and uniform. As a writer, you do not have to become a connoisseur of taste, but you do have to become aware of tastes.

First Phase

You'll enjoy this. Eat or drink five different foods. After each tasting, describe the experience in as much detail as possible. Do *not* at this time name the food you are tasting and do not use visual description at all. Example: bland and cool to the tongue; soft and smooth; with a rich, near-cloying sweetness. (Would you recognize ice cream?)

1 _____

2 _____

3 _____

4 _____

5 _____

Now swap books with a friend or take turns reading the descriptions aloud. Try to guess what food is being described in each case. Don't be discouraged if most of the guesses are wide of the mark. It is difficult to describe a taste accurately and identifiably without resorting to help from the sense of sight or smell.

Second Phase

This time you're being asked to really probe your memory. Try to remember a taste experience that you had at least ten years ago. If possible, choose a taste experience that you have not since repeated. Duplicate this taste experience now. Compare and contrast the taste from memory and the taste today. Some possibilities: cotton candy; licorice sticks; lollipops; baby food (if you have a really terrific memory!).

_____

_____

_____

_____

_____

Third Phase

In this round, experiment with the effect of one taste on another. Eat a bit of pickle, then a teaspoonful of ice cream. Nibble on a potato chip, then on a square of dark chocolate. Choose each pair of foods, keeping in mind contrast and sharpness of flavor. Work with five different pairs and record your taste observations below. (*Taste* each food only; eating ten different foods in quantity may result in a stomachache rather than in improved taste perception.)

1 _____ and _____

_____

_____

2 _____ and _____

_____

_____

3 _____ and _____

_____

_____

4 _____ and _____

_____

_____

5 _____ and _____

_____

_____

The Sense of Touch

If you have ever tried to "read" Braille, you know how clumsy and inept most of us are with the sense of touch. Yet the potential is there. We have fingertips that are marvelous in their sensitivity and ability to "read." They simply need training.

First Phase

This is easy. Without looking, reach into your purse or your pocket for an object: any object. Leaving it where it is, explore it with your fingers. (Use your non-writing hand. Save the writing hand for notetaking.) Describe the object as fully as you can, using only your sense of touch. You should be able to handle approximate size, shape, surface (smooth, rough), projections, indentations, degree of slipperiness, etc.

_____

_____

_____

_____

_____

Read your description out loud. See if someone else can identify the object from your description.

Second Phase

This will be a bit more difficult. Let someone place in your hand (out of sight, anyway) an object that does not belong to you. Explore it with your fingers. Note below all characteristics that can be detected by the sense of touch. When you have exhausted the object, study your notes and try to identify the object.

_____

_____

_____

_____

_____

Third Phase

Finally, touch five things with distinctly different surfaces. Some possibilities: sandpaper, velvet, porcelain, unfinished wood, polished stone, plastic, blotter, carpet. Take your time with this experiment. Start with the first object you have chosen. Caress it with your fingertips, lightly and gently. Press hard on it. Rub it. Try touching it with your cheek. If it is clean, try touching it with your tongue. Make detailed notations before proceeding to the second object.

1st: _____

_____

_____

2nd: _____

_____

_____

3rd: _____

_____

_____

4th: _____

_____

_____

5th: _____

_____

_____

For the Daring Writer Only: Synesthesia

Some writers claim that reactions to the senses sometimes correspond: that it is possible to hear a color, or to see the sound of a trumpet as scarlet (as Samuel Johnson noted). This sort of crossing of the lines between the senses is known as *synesthesia*, a technique both challenging and alluring.

To help you grasp the idea of synesthesia, here are a few questions. There are no absolute answers; sense-correspondences tend to be highly personal.

What color is noisy and clamorous? _____

What color is low-pitched and quiet? _____

How does green smell? _____

What kind of bell-sound duplicates purple? _____

Is a sweet taste melodic or discordant? _____

If you touch yellow, is it hot or cold? _____

If you could hear the scent of cedar, how would it sound? _____

Do you prefer "spicy red" or "spicy blue"? _____ Why? _____

_____

_____

You may not often employ synesthesia, but you will want to be aware of it in the writing of others; and there will be times—especially when you are trying to create a mood—when you will find this technique richly satisfying.

Far more important, though, are the experiments you tried with the basic five senses. Your job as a writer is to help a reader to understand and to experience—and you can best do that by appealing to a reader's five senses.

14. OBSERVATION PLATFORM

The weather observer has to note all the changes, all the details, all the movements of the weather in his area. The observer of the heavens must be quick to recognize the slightest alteration in the smallest star. You—as a writer—must be an observer of people and their world. You must be aware of their appearance and their behavior, their speech and their gestures, their relationships and their place in the universe.

Since you are interested in writing, you probably consider yourself a pretty good observer already. Want to prove it? Here's a trivia test: trivia for everybody but the writer. For the writer, it's the most important test of all. Use it to measure your O.Q.— observation quotient.

1 Are your best friend's eyebrows thick, thin, or average? _____ Dark or light? _____ Wide or narrow? _____ Does your friend "use" them (raise, lower, etc.) often? _____ To convey what attitude? _____

2 Draw or describe in detail the shape of a maple leaf.

What country uses the maple leaf on its flag? _____

3 Is the skin of an orange thicker or thinner than the skin of a tangerine? _____

4 In the morning, do you put on your right shoe first—or your left? _____

5 Do you have any teachers who are left-handed? _____

6 Does your voice change when you talk to a small child? _____ If so, how?
_____

Do most people change their voices when they speak to a child? _____

7 In most theaters, how is the end of an intermission signaled?
_____

In most stores, how is the closing time signaled?
_____

8 Does the clock in your classroom (don't look at it!) have Roman numerals or Arabic numbers? _____

9 What fruit or vegetable is "in season" in your area in July? _____ in August? _____ in September? _____

10 How does rainy weather affect you? _____

How does it affect most people? _____

We're willing to bet that you were unable to answer at least one of those questions! Yet, as Thoreau said, "... a man must see, before he can say." Before you can write, you must observe—closely and uniquely—and from more than one point of view.

A to Z

The first game-plan will simply help you to be more observant and more conscious of the names of things. Complete (as far as possible) each of the following A to Z lists. If necessary, wander around your home or garage or school. Look. Notice. Take notes.

	OBJECTS FOUND IN THE HOME	OBJECTS FOUND IN A GARAGE	OBJECTS FOUND IN A SCHOOL
Samples:	album	tire	chalk
A			
B			
C			
D			
E			
F			
G			
H			
I			
J			
K			
L			
M			
N			
O			
P			
Q			
R			
S			

T   _____   _____   _____

U   _____   _____   _____

V   _____   _____   _____

W   _____   _____   _____

X   _____   _____   _____

Y   _____   _____   _____

Z   _____   _____   _____

Develop your own categories and play the game whenever you have a few minutes. Try it with birds, flowers, cars. Each list you complete will make you more word-conscious and more observant.

Item Inventory

On the following page is a picture of a dozen common items. Look at the drawing for about one minute. Turn back to this page and list as many items as you can.

_____

_____

_____

_____

_____

_____

Did you get all of them?

This time study the picture for three minutes. Note details. Then turn back to this page and answer the following questions:

1 Whose picture is on the ten-cent stamp? _____

2 How many pieces of luggage are there? _____

3 How big is the fish in proportion to the man? _____

4 According to the wristwatch, what time is it? _____

5 What name is on the tote bag? _____

6 Is the top of the garbage can on the can, on the ground, or neither? _____

7 How many pieces of silverware are pictured? _____

8 To whom does the Social Security card belong? _____

Are you as observant as you thought you were? Remember—the use of detail is of major importance to any writer.

Training by Television

If you are an average American, you spend more time than you will admit in watching television. Put that time to work. Try the following experiment:

First, turn on the TV set and tune in to a soap opera, drama, or variety show. Then turn off the sound. Watch for at least five minutes. Notice the setting. What does it tell you? Notice the way people are dressed, the things they are doing, the gestures they make. Notice facial expressions. As you watch, make a few notes below.

_____

_____

_____

_____

_____

Now turn on the sound. Watch and listen for at least five minutes. Notice the voices: loud or soft, shrill or deep. Notice the speech patterns, accents, even pauses. Notice sound effects. As you watch and listen, take notes.

_____

_____

_____

_____

_____

Give yourself a session with the television set at least twice a week. Your observation will become sharper, and the notes you make will be invaluable when you write.

Group Analysis

This exercise works best on a bus, train, or subway. If you *never* find yourself in such a vehicle, then try it in the cafeteria or even in a classroom. The important thing is that plenty of people be present.

Get comfortable; take a notebook and pencil in your hand. And look. Look at faces: Do they all bear the same expression, or are they varied? Are many people smiling? Frowning? Are they doing anything—reading a paper or book? Knitting? Just staring? Do they notice each other, or has each insulated herself or himself within a kind of invisible booth? Is there any conversation? What is the noise level? Do body movements or gestures reveal uneasiness, fear, annoyance? How about the color of clothing? Who's carrying what? Are some straining for the nearest exit? Is anybody sleeping? Notice as much as you can; make copious notes.

_____

_____

_____

_____

_____

_____

_____

_____

_____

Process-Server

You probably, at one time or another, have listed the steps in a particular process; but you probably have *not* spent much thought on the important tiny details in that process. For example, in describing the making of jam, one would outline the cutting and mashing of fruit, the mixing of it with sugar and possibly some spices, the boiling of it, the skimming, and finally the ladling into jars. The outline describes the technical process. But what about the small human details that are so important to a writer? What about the moment when the crabapple jelly boils into a rich pink foam looking like a churned sunrise? Or the searing short pain when a drop or two of the hot mixture leaps from the pot and assaults the wrist? Or that delectable moment when, spotting a bit of jam that has spilled on the outside of the jar, you surreptitiously scoop it up with a finger and tuck it inside your mouth?

Choose any process with which you are familiar: nailing two pieces of wood together; mowing a lawn; making a peanut-butter sandwich—and reconstruct the process. You may do this from memory, or you may choose to actually repeat the process. Watch for the small *human* details. Then describe the process, including the technical steps but dwelling on the small details.

_____

_____

_____

_____

_____

_____

Dinner Table Data

When you describe a character, you will constantly be referring to people you know. And the people you know best are the people you live with. You will wonder—how does someone indicate he is angry? What gesture would a woman use at that moment? What particular facial expressions suggest pouting or sulking? Because the people you know best are the people you live with, you should study them frequently.

At the dinner table, become a detached observer. Normally you are involved; and therefore you do not notice or remember details. But if you detach yourself, if you remove yourself emotionally from the discussion, you will be able to note and to remember. Try it—tonight, if possible. Be quiet; watch; listen. Notice how people react to each other. As soon as dinner is over, make a few notes. Later, at your leisure, you can develop them.

_____

_____

_____

_____

_____

_____

_____

Pantomime Play

Anyone who has ever seen Presidential candidates making a speech will have noticed different kinds of hand action: the right hand jabbing at the air to accent a point; the left arm flung to the left as if to embrace the whole country; both hands—half-raised, palms upward—in a grand though mute appeal. Gestures betray us; they give us away. Fortunately for us, most people are almost unaware of the gestures they and other people make. The writer *must* become aware of these gestures. Mentioned in your writing, they contribute immensely to a reader's understanding of a character.

Investigate the sign language used by some of the deaf. It is beautiful and revealing. To indicate sadness, one uses the hands to "draw" a long face. To indicate love, one clasps the two hands closely to the chest in a provocative manner. To indicate hate, one pushes the two hands away from the body, palms out, as though repelling something disliked.

Then investigate the gestures of people around you. Think about your own. (This is difficult; you may become self-conscious.) After you have investigated, noticed, and pondered, describe the gesture (*not* the facial expression) you think would best accompany and symbolize each of the following:

touching something hot _____

feeling cold _____

crying _____

anger _____

conveying a sense of distance _____

frustration _____

withdrawal _____

protest _____

worship _____

puzzlement _____

Pad and Pencil Tour

Every place has an aura of its own: a smell; a sound pattern; a grouping; a design of reactions. Choose a place you would like to investigate. It may be a service station, a restaurant, a store, or a bowling alley. Plan to spend at least a half hour there, preferably an hour. Take your pad and pencil. Be as unobtrusive as possible; but take notes about everything you see, hear, and smell. You will discover, for instance, that there is one attitude in a "coed" department store, a different one in a shop that caters to women; and still a third one in a hardware store where most customers and saleshelp are men.

Later, after you have completed your tour and your notetaking, study your notes, think about them, and write a description that includes both significant detail and any conclusions you may have arrived at.

_____

_____

_____

_____

_____

_____

_____

_____

_____

The Town Dump

For the final and most sophisticated step in training your observation powers, you really should have available a town dump. If you don't, you may have to follow a garbage truck for a block or two; but the town dump is infinitely superior.

Again, take your pad and pencil. You may receive some curious glances, but persist. Study the contents of the dump. Really look at the trash. Identify. Make notes. List *everything* you can identify, and toss in a few descriptive words. (For example: an iron frame for a bed, rusty, broken, with one side missing.)

_____

_____

_____

_____

_____

_____

_____

_____

Now you have your list of junked objects. Look at them from different points of view. *You*, as a person, have one point of view; *you*, as a writer, must have many points of view. You must, in short, be able to empathize with others—to see things as others see them.

First, role-play an ecologist. You are concerned about the environment. Look at the list of items found at the dump. What do you see? How do you feel?

_____

_____

_____

Next, role-play a sociologist. You are interested in people and their problems. What do you see? How do you feel?

_____

_____

_____

Now role-play a junk artist—an artist who creates sculptured works, collages, etc., out of junk. What do you see? How do you feel?

_____

_____

_____

Role-play an aesthete. (Look it up if you don't know the word.) What do you see? How do you feel?

_____

_____

_____

Role-play a bored ten-year-old. What do you see? How do you feel?

_____

_____

_____

The series of experiments is complete. You should be more observant now, and more sophisticated in your observation. But work at it—constantly. And make notes of your observations.

> **Your journal is a good place for notes: if you serve *it* well, it will serve you well through many stories, poems, and articles.**

15. RESEARCH: FOUR VARIETIES

After you have trained your five senses and sharpened your observation powers until Thoreau himself would nod approval, there may still be details you need and do not have. That is the moment when you become a researcher.

Let us suppose you are writing a short story with a historical background. The story is to take place in Boise, Idaho, in the early 1920's. (If you live in Boise, set the story in Tallahassee, Florida, instead.) You cannot possibly write this story until you steep yourself in the history and geography of Idaho, specifically of Boise, Idaho. Now how do you go about finding what you want? (Before you begin, though, decide what kind of story you might like to write: a mystery, a western, a character study, etc.)

First Variety: Library Research

"A library is a wondrous thing, God wot." Shakespeare didn't say that, but he might have. Where else but in some friend's library did he learn of Bermuda (*The Tempest*), of the procedures of law courts (*The Merchant of Venice*), of Scotland's medieval kings (*Macbeth*)? Your task is easier; all you have to learn about is Boise, Idaho.

Start with an *atlas*. In it, find a map of Idaho. Explain exactly where Idaho is in the United States, and where Boise is in Idaho.

IDAHO _____

_____

_____

BOISE _____

_____

_____

Continue with the atlas. Any large mountain ranges near Boise? _____

Where exactly? _____

Any large rivers? _____ Where? _____

_____

Now turn to a good *encyclopedia*. Look up IDAHO. You will find several pages of information, and you will have to decide what kinds of details you are looking for. Below are some questions to help you get started. After you have answered them, add any other details that may be helpful in writing *your* story.

What does "Idaho" mean? _____

When did Idaho enter the Union? _____

When was Boise founded, and what stimulated its being established as a major city?

_____

Which political party prevailed in Idaho in the 1920's? _____

Other details: _____

_____

_____

Now look up BOISE. You will find another entry, shorter but more specific. Follow the same procedure.

What was the population of Boise in 1920? _____

How far above sea level is Boise? _____

Other details: _____

_____

_____

Go on to a good *almanac*. In the index, look up IDAHO.

What is the state flag? _____

What is the state flower? _____

What is the state song? _____

Other details: _____

_____

_____

_____

Other library resources worth considering:

Statistical Abstract of the United States, an annual published by the U.S. Bureau of the Census; outstanding for statistics about everything.

Dictionary of American Biography: useful if you come across a name or two that you would like to explore.

Card Catalog: for books on Idaho, or—less helpful—books on the United States. A check of indexes will indicate whether Idaho is discussed in detail.

Check at least one of the above and add relevant details to your notes.

Source: _____

Details: _____

_____

_____

By now, you have a pretty good idea of the history and general profile of Boise, Idaho. If you were writing a novel, you would want to go much further. For a short story, you probably have enough detail to go on to the second step.

Second Variety: Newspaper Research

Old newspapers are invaluable for general information and anecdotes. The best starting point is the New York *Times* Index for the year you are interested in: 1922, 1924, or whatever. Look up IDAHO and BOISE. This will give you an idea as to what relevant stories were of national interest in the time span in which you are interested.

If you come across something that looks really promising, ask the librarian for the microfilm of the New York *Times* for the appropriate month and year. Find your articles and read them. Take notes.

The next step, ideally, would be to go to Boise and check the newspaper files of local newspapers. If you live near enough, do just that. But if you live at a distance, there is something else you can try. Go to your local library and ask if any of your own local newspapers are on file. If they are, check the volume or microfilm for the year in which you are interested. You may not find stories about Boise, Idaho; but you will find a wealth of information that can be very useful. For example, study the advertisements. They will give you an idea of what people were interested in and how prices were. Study the news stories. They will provide a background of timely national news. Study the weather reports: they will often indicate weather trends all over the nation. Study the crime reports: they will reflect the kinds of crimes then prevalent and popular attitudes toward different types of criminals.

Note below other interesting (and useful) details that you have gleaned from newspaper sources. In each case, indicate the source. (By the way, any writer must keep careful track of the sources of all information. It is not unusual, a year or two after publication, for some doubtful reader to question a historical fact or a statistic. If you have a record, you can answer questions easily and quickly and will suffer less from acute humiliation!)

_____

_____

_____

_____

_____

_____

_____

_____

_____

_____

Third Variety: People Research

People are a very valuable source of information.

● Begin in a general way. Ask your friends, your parents, and your teachers if they know anyone from Idaho. Ask the school librarian and the town librarian. Ask business people. You may find nothing; then again you may find someone who lived in Boise in the 1920's and is a rich and exciting source of details.

Focus now on specific people. Find out the names of the U.S. senators from Idaho and the representatives from the Boise area. Write to them. Tell them you are writing a story about Boise and would like to learn more about the city. They will surely answer. If they can't give you material, they will suggest other people whom you can contact.

● Find out the name of the leading newspaper in Boise. Write to the editor.

● Write to the Chamber of Commerce of Boise. Ask for help.

● Write to the mayor, or to the public relations office, or to the post office.

From these collective sources, you will certainly obtain interesting and usable material. List below additional Boise-1920's material acquired through any of the above procedures.

_____

_____

_____

_____

_____

_____

Fourth Variety: Places Research

If you are writing fiction, you will also want to research places. Ideally, of course, if you were writing a story about Boise, you would visit Boise, spend a few weeks there, wander around the city, explore the Snake River, climb the Salmon River Mountains, investigate the state penitentiary, wander through the sandstone quarries, look amazed at the Arrowrock Dam, and spend some time in the municipal airport. You would want to check out stores and government buildings; drive down main highways and along narrow back roads; stand on corners and watch people go by, noting their clothing, their attitudes, their expressions.

If you are a professional writer, with an assignment and an expense account, you can do just that. But you are not. You can't afford to travel to Boise, Idaho, but you want to know it, physically and emotionally, as well as intellectually.

Well, there are several possibilities. Check out a few tour guidebooks. Many of them give maps of major cities. Study the street map of Boise. Notice where historical buildings are, and read the descriptions. Learn the streets and intersections just as you would if you had moved to Boise.

- Check a nearby travel agency. Ask for material about Boise.

- Thumb through travel magazines. Study the ads. If any of them relate to Boise, or Idaho, and offer free information, write.

- Check railroad schedules to see which trains go to Boise.

- Check airline schedules to see which planes go to Boise.

- Check bus schedules to see which buses go to Boise.

Then move in closer.

You have a great deal of information; you know much about Boise. But you have never seen the Salmon River Mountains, and your main character is going to spend some time climbing them. First read everything you can find in the library about these mountains. Then try to experience the mountains *vicariously*. Here's how you do it.

Look around you for the nearest mountains. The Rockies will do, or the Adirondacks, or the Catskills, or the Appalachians. Try climbing just a little. Notice how your feet feel—how your body reacts to climbing up and climbing down—what the hazards are—what the pleasures are. (If you have never climbed before, don't try anything dangerous. And don't go far. Getting lost in the mountains is a high price to pay for a possible story!) If there are no mountains in your area, you can try the same experiment with hills—but be aware that there is a world of difference.

After your experiment, combine what you read about the Salmon River Mountains with what you felt during your short hike. You should come close to an accurate description.

Try this vicarious research now. Explore one of the following (vicariously):

> the Salmon River Mountains
> the Snake River
> Craters of the Moon National Monument
> Arrowrock Dam
> the Snake River plains (agricultural region)
> the city itself (Boise)

Remember—first read everything you can about your choice. Then find a comparable site in your own area. Explore it. Combine your book knowledge with your foot-knowledge. When you have finished with the experiment, write a description of the site you chose and copy it below.

_____

_____

_____

_____

_____

_____

_____

_____

_____

_____

_____

_____

_____

_____

_____

> *Details are the red corpuscles of writing. No amount of effort is too great to get the details you need to make your writing vivid, alive, and accurate. Keep in mind the four varieties of research: library, newspapers, people, and places. They will give flesh to your characters and substance to your setting. Use them often and well, and they will contribute a professionalism and polish to your stories.*

16. PARSING A POTATO

Parsing is to break down, to analyze, to describe. Good writers parse everything—even potatoes. For this exercise, *we* will take a potato, and *you* take an orange or onion or apple. Ready?

Sense of Sight

First we'll parse by visual study. We'll look at the potato; you look at the fruit or vegetable of your choice.

Color:

Our potato is brown—somewhere between tan and dark-brown; closer to tan, though.

(YOURS) _____
_____

Size:

Our potato is about three inches long and about two and a half inches wide. (You can measure by using the first joint of your thumb; it's about one inch long.)

(YOURS) _____
_____

Shape:

Our potato is approximately oval in shape, although it tapers slightly at one end.

(YOURS) _____
_____

Surface:

Our potato has one knob-like projection at the wider end, as well as two quarter-inch cavities. At the narrower end, it has two small shallow dents.

(YOURS) _____
_____

Irregularities:

Our potato has a scaling skin in four places. It has three large brown spots (each about one-quarter inch in diameter) and dozens of tiny brown spots. The wider end, however, has no spots at all.

(YOURS) _____

_____

_____

_____

Sense of Touch

Now we'll parse by touching. Let your fingers caress the object, then press harder on it.

Smoothness:

Our potato is quite smooth, although the fingers detect small bumps and dents not apparent to the eye. Where the skin is scaling, it feels slightly rough, like fine sandpaper. The surface of the indentations is rougher than the other skin.

(YOURS) _____

_____

_____

_____

Temperature:

Our potato is cool to the touch, almost cold. It is uncomfortable to hold tightly.

(YOURS) _____

_____

_____

Solidity:

Our potato is basically solid, but—unlike metal—it gives slightly when pressed. It almost has a "pulse." A fingernail can cut through the skin, leaving a noticeable scar.

(YOURS) _____

_____

_____

Weight:

Tossed from one hand to another, our potato suggests definite weight (unlike a feather). But the weight is light, rather like a rubber ball.

(YOURS) _____

_____

_____

_____

Sense of Hearing

Our potato is totally silent. Dropped a couple of inches onto a desk top, it makes a dull, thudding noise.

(YOURS) _____

_____

Sense of Taste

Our potato, touched by the tongue, tastes earthy and a bit gritty.

(YOURS) _____

_____

Sense of Smell

Our potato gives off a faint, mouldy smell made up probably of earth and starch. It is barely discernible.

(YOURS) _____

_____

_____

_____

By now, you should be able to pick out your orange (or onion or apple) even if it is mixed in with a dozen others. You are beginning to *know* it. But you're not finished yet. Before you can really know your object, you must envision it in different relationships. For example, our potato might be

—one of dozens in a burlap bag
—baked, cut open, and garnished with sour cream on a dinner plate
—placed with a squash, an eggplant, and a dried ear of corn in a bowl on Thanksgiving Day
—used as a ball by a small child
—used as a weight to hold down one corner of a plastic sheet
—boiled and placed with other boiled potatoes in a serving dish
—a still-life study for an artist

Envision your onion (or orange or apple) in at least five different situations. Really see it in your mind's eye.

_____

_____

_____

_____

_____

Play Ball!

Sometime during your life, you have handled at least one kind of ball. On the facing page are sketches of many kinds of balls. Choose one with which you are familiar and *parse* it. Use the sketch and your memory; remember the five senses and the way a ball is used. Write as complete a description as possible, in paragraph form. Don't mention the name of the ball.

_____

_____

_____

_____

_____

_____

_____

When you have finished, exchange papers with a friend and see if each of you can guess the kind of ball the other described.

More Parsing

Parse one more object. Some possibilities: a garden hose, a screwdriver, a button, a shopping bag, a book. Follow the same procedure we did with the potato, and that you did with the ball. Again, write a paragraph describing (but not naming) the object you chose.

_____

_____

_____

_____

_____

_____

_____

This time read your description aloud to others in a small group. If they can identify the object with ease, you have done a fair job. If they can't, don't identify it for them. Go back to the workbench and add more details; then try again.

You will seldom describe anything in as much detail as you have in this chapter. But you must be able to. In one story you may want to describe the feel of a porcelain vase; in another you may need the smell of lemons or the taste of crabapples. The habit of "parsing a potato" will serve you well. One word more: if you parse an edible (like the potato) really well, it may develop a personality of its own, and *that* may make you reluctant to eat it. For who wishes to dine on a friend?

17. PARSING A PERSON

Since a person is a bit more complex than a potato, parsing a person is a bit more complex than parsing a potato. But it can be done, and the procedure is similar.

Choose a person: preferably someone you see frequently, even several times a day. Give that person an alias. Use the alias only; never the correct name.

Age: Gladys (our person) is 24.

(YOURS) _____

Sense of Sight

Color:

Gladys has shoulder-length ash-blonde hair; blue-green eyes; and a light, almost pale complexion.

(YOURS) _____
_____
_____
_____

Size:

Gladys is 5'4" in height and weighs about 108 pounds. She is small-boned, indicated by small, slender hands and feet.

(YOURS) _____
_____
_____
_____

Head:

Her face is an almost perfect oval. The chin is a bit weak, the lips full and wide for the face, the teeth sparkling white and obviously in good condition. The nose is Roman, but in proportion to the size of the face. The eyes are large, shuttered by long curly lashes and crowned by thin, plucked, light-colored eyebrows.

(YOURS) _____
_____
_____
_____

Body:

Her neck is a touch longer than average, and slender. Her shoulders are thin, suggesting frailness, but the rest of her body is well-proportioned.

(YOURS) _____

_____

_____

_____

Limbs:

Gladys' legs are thin, with almost no calves. Her ankles, though, are well-formed and her feet small. Her arms are also thin, her hands small but with unexpectedly long and slender fingers.

(YOURS) _____

_____

_____

_____

Other identifying marks:

Gladys has a small mole on the right side of the jawline and a tiny scar, barely visible, over the left eyebrow. Her arms are lightly freckled, and there is a brown spot two inches below the left elbow.

(YOURS) _____

_____

_____

_____

Sense of Hearing

Voice:

Gladys has a high-pitched voice that grows shrill when she becomes excited. She seldom speaks softly, and always seems to be aiming her voice as far as possible. She frequently hums, her favorite song being "Onward Christian Soldiers." She hums not when she is happy, but when she is cross and irritable and trying not to lose her temper. Her singing voice is superb and, if trained, would possess professional virtuosity.

(YOURS) _____

_____

_____

_____

Sense of Smell

Gladys emits a constant scent of jasmine. It is apparent that she uses perfume daily and is faithful to her favorite scent. She is meticulously clean, and the smell of soap lies just below the scent of jasmine. Her hair has a clean, lemon-y fragrance, and it is clear that she washes it about three times a week.

(YOURS) _____

_____

_____

_____

_____

_____

*   *   *   *

You have a pretty good physical description now, but that's the easy part. The next section combines the physical attributes with personality. Continue.

Laugh:

Gladys laughs seldom; when she does, her laugh has an artificial ha-ha sound that is unpleasant. Her smile, though, is charming, erupting quickly, showing her teeth, and ending quickly.

(YOURS) _____

_____

_____

_____

_____

Other facial expressions:

Gladys frowns often, pressing her lips together and scowling so that the eyebrows seem to merge and the skin between them wrinkles. When she is sad, her lips open slightly, her chin drops, and her eyes narrow. She can cry real tears, on demand, and often does. When she is confused or uncertain, she throws her thick, wavy ash-blonde hair over her eyes in an unconscious effort to hide.

(YOURS) _____

_____

_____

_____

_____

_____

_____

Gestures:

Gladys' hands give her away. When she is angry, she lets her arms fall straight but the fingers half clench into fists. If the anger continues or is mixed with frustration, the fingers straighten and stiffen, like small fans. If she wants something, she uses a similar gesture, but her arms become limp and the open hands face outward in a kind of appeal. When she feels threatened, she folds her arms before her. When she is relaxed, she holds the tips of the four fingers of her left hand in the whole of the right hand.

(YOURS) _____

_____

_____

_____

_____

_____

_____

Stance:

Gladys likes to lean against things: doorways, walls, etc. If nothing is available to lean against, she will perch on the nearest desk or table. It is apparently important to her that her body be in contact with a physical object. When she sits, she most often crosses the right leg over the left, just above the knee. She also likes to lounge, stretching out on sofas on impulse. At such times she relaxes completely, lying on her left side and letting her body go limp.

(YOURS) _____

_____

_____

_____

_____

_____

_____

*   *   *   *

The third section deals with the type of person Gladys is rather than with appearance.

Education and job status:

Gladys graduated from high school, 186th in a class of 305. She attended a secretarial school for one year and is currently working as a typist-clerk in Mattedorn's Insurance Company. She is of average intelligence and has ambition, but her ambition is not career-oriented.

(YOURS) _____

_____

_____

_____

_____

_____

_____

Family background:

Gladys' father is a milkman, her mother a housewife. To them, Gladys has "made it" because she has a desk job. Gladys is the oldest of three children; she has a brother just 21, and a sister of 16. The family has never been poor, but it never has had surplus money for luxuries. Gladys lives at home, but she is rebellious because she is still sharing a room with her sixteen-year-old sister. Lately she has been talking about getting her own apartment, but she realizes that her present salary is inadequate.

(YOURS) _____

_____

_____

_____

_____

_____

_____

Ambition:

Gladys' only ambition is to get married, but not to just anyone. When she was fifteen, resenting her lack of expensive clothes and her limited spending money, Gladys decided to marry a rich man. She has not changed her mind in the intervening nine years. She is currently attracted to Rick Brummel, a thirty-year-old executive at Mattedorn's. He earns about $25,000 a year and is backed by a wealthy family.

(YOURS) _____

_____

_____

_____

_____

_____

_____

Friends:

Gladys likes people, but she rarely encourages a friendship to last beyond one year. She goes to the movies and on shopping expeditions with other young women from Mattedorn's, but she carefully avoids close or confidential relationships. She likes men better than women and flirts mildly with most of them. Real flirtations, though, are reserved for someone "worth knowing"—like Rick Brummel.

(YOURS) _____

_____

_____

_____

_____

_____

_____

_____

* * * * *

Obviously this kind of investigation could go on forever; but Gladys is rather well parsed. Here are some questions. If we can answer them about Gladys, and you can answer them about _____, then the parsing was effective. Notice that the questions require reasoning from facts known to probable conclusions.

1 If you were collecting money for the Red Cross, what approach would be most successful with the subject?

GLADYS   Mention a few names of wealthy people in the community who have donated. Mention that Rick Brummel donated $25.

YOURS   _____

_____

_____

_____

_____

_____

2 While driving on a rainy night, the subject inadvertently struck an old man. No one witnessed the crime. How would the subject act?

GLADYS   Although basically law-abiding, Gladys would probably leave the scene of the accident and not report it. She already feels some self-pity: the bad breaks she had in her adolescence in a "poor" family; and this would strike her as just another unmerited "bad break." She would also be fearful of losing Rick Brummel if her name and picture appeared in the newspapers in connection with hitting a pedestrian.

YOURS _____

_____

_____

_____

_____

_____

_____

_____

_____

3   The subject is at a buffet supper. By accident, a guest tips a plate, spilling spaghetti and meatballs all over the subject's clothing. How would the subject react?

GLADYS   If the careless guest were a woman, Gladys—after an initial exclamation—would probably clench her fists and be coldly polite. If the guest were a man, Gladys would undoubtedly smile and say it didn't matter. If it were Rick, she would insist that it was an old dress anyway and that she rather liked being spattered by meatballs!

YOURS _____

_____

_____

_____

_____

_____

The advantage of parsing Gladys before using her as a character in a short story is that you will then *know* her: know how she will act and react; how she thinks; how she feels; what things will influence her; etc. If you want to describe her in a scene in which she is thwarted, you will "see" her clenching her fists, wrinkling her eyebrows, pressing her lips; you will "hear" her voice grow more shrill; you will "smell" the scent of jasmine and contrast its sweetness with her sour mood. You will have, at the tip of your pen, a wealth of details from which you can select exactly the right one for the scene.

A second advantage of parsing Gladys is that it ensures accuracy. Nothing kills a story faster than having Gladys shoot sparks from blue eyes in paragraph one and flirt shyly with dark brown eyes in paragraph eighteen! This is true even of less obvious characteristics. If Gladys loves money (and she does), you can't have her marry a poor young man just to provide a romantic ending. If you want that particular ending, then you must somehow shock Gladys out of one behavior pattern into another.

> *Parsing a person takes time, but most writers find that it pays high dividends. Gladys is Mary is Alice disturbs the readers. Gladys must be Gladys all the way.*

18. A CATERPILLAR IS AN UPHOLSTERED WORM

The genius (anonymous) who called a caterpillar an upholstered worm displayed brilliant powers of both observation and description. To wit: the slithery bonelessness of a caterpillar *is* very like a worm; and the stuffed, rounded, ridged body *does* look upholstered. The result: a phrase, "an upholstered worm," that magnificently describes and commemorates the humble crawler.

> "Anonymous" did it with a *metaphor*.

"My love's like a red, red rose/ That's newly sprung in June" sang Robert Burns, capturing young blushing love in two short lines.

> Burns did it with a *simile*.

"Bright April shakes out her rain-drenched hair" said Sara Teasdale thoughtfully, limning the dual nature of April with unforgettable precision.

> Teasdale did it with *personification*.

"'Tis with our judgments as with our watches; none go just alike, yet each believes his own," pontificated Alexander Pope, clarifying both the universality and the individuality of a judgment.

> Pope did it with *analogy*.

Metaphor, simile, personification, and analogy—four techniques, all different, yet each describes and clarifies, and does it through skillful use of detail.

The Simile

Since the simile is the easiest, we'll start with that. Compare A and B, using *like* or *as*, and you have a simile. She is as red *as* a rose. He slept *like* a log. Notice that the two objects being compared are not similar except in one respect. The girl and the rose are very different, but they share a blushing quality. The sleeping boy and the log are very different, but they share inertia.

You use (probably all too often) similes as trite as remarks about the weather. Almost everyone would use the same words to complete the following sentences. Try it.

Max swims like a _____.

Jennifer eats like a _____ (not much), but her older sister Ellen eats like a _____ (much).

Ten-year-old Jimmy crept like a _____ to school on Monday morning.

Her dress was as white as _____.

Mary Lou was as strong as an _____.

These similes you will, in the future, eschew (take pains to avoid). You will seek, instead, the original simile—the startling simile—the simile as unexpected as the flamingo in a cage of canaries.

Gore Vidal once wrote: "Like ancient trees, we die from the top." Think about that. To create this simile, Vidal had to observe how old trees die and then to discern a similarity between the way they die and the way humans die. The simile not only describes our dying; it also is provocative, making us consider our brains with a new tenderness.

The good simile will do more than describe and clarify; it will add a new dimension—something to flick the imagination and set it running. Below are ten words or phrases that have served in similes. Read them. Then read the quotations that follow them. Decide which word or phrase best completes each simile.

a cloud   an obelisk
a dress   sentries
a flat blade of ice   a shaft of light
a grenadier   a sick oyster at low tide
knives   a stone-wall

1 Alcott, Louisa May: "Now I am beginning to live a little, and feel less like _____."

2 Bee, Bernard Elliott: "See, there is Jackson, standing like _____."

3-4 Conrad, Joseph: "She strode like _____, was strong and upright like _____."

5 Dahl, Roald: ". . . the wind was like _____ on his cheeks."

6 Dole, Nathan H. "Where pillared cliffs like _____ stand . . ."

7 Herschberger, Ruth: ". . . the clouds brushed like _____ over the spacious sun . . ."

8 Lowell, James Russell: "Mishaps are like _____, that either serve us or cut us, as we grasp them by the blade or the handle."

9   Tennyson, Alfred: "When shall . . . universal peace/ Lie like _____

across the land?"

10   Wordsworth, William: "I wandered lonely as _____."

Choose the two similes you found most effective and explain *why* they worked for you. Be as explicit as possible.

_____: _____

_____

_____

_____: _____

_____

_____

By this time you are (naturally) as eager and hopeful as a Little Leaguer on the first day of the baseball season. You want to bat a few of your own, to toss a simile into the air and watch it spin in the sun! Fine. Here's your chance.

Start with an ordinary substance: a scouring pad, or powder, or relish. Choose a universal: love, or grief, or avarice. Ponder *one* characteristic shared by the universal and by the ordinary substance. Combine with skill.

TO WIT   the universal: *love*
            the ordinary substance: *a scouring pad*
THE COMBINATION   Love, like a brand-new scouring pad, makes our lives shine.

That may not be brilliant, but it is an original simile and it does say something: it emphasizes the ability of love to purify and transform our lives. The procedure is fairly simple. Go to it. Your goal: three original similes.

_____

_____

_____

_____

_____

_____

The Metaphor

The metaphor is first cousin to the simile. Like the simile, it compares two objects; unlike the simile, it does not use *like* or *as*.

SIMILE: Her teeth are *like* pearls.
METAPHOR: Her teeth are pearls.
              (*or*) Her hearty laugh displayed her magnificent pearly teeth.

Just as there are trite similes, so there are trite metaphors. "He is a pig!" or "She is a cat!" are too trite to be effective; but *good* metaphors say a great deal in few words. Herman Melville once wrote: "A whale ship was my Yale College and my Harvard." Reading that, one suddenly realizes that real education can be gained anywhere—that the lessons learned on a whaling ship can be more valuable than an advanced degree from an Ivy League college. The metaphor says it all.

Here are a few metaphors for you to ponder. In each case underline the two objects being compared and then explain briefly why the metaphor is effective.

1 "My heart is a lonely hunter . . ." (William Sharp)

_____

_____

_____

2 "Mosquito critics with a poisonous sting . . ." (William Wetmore Story)

_____

_____

_____

3 "Time is but the stream I go a-fishing in." (Henry David Thoreau)

_____

_____

_____

4 "My love she is a kitten,
    And my heart's a ball of string." (Henry S. Leigh)

_____

_____

_____

5 "And merry larks are ploughmen's clocks . . ." (William Shakespeare)

_____

_____

_____

_____

Worktime, now. Create some metaphors for parts of your body. For example: "When I do my math homework, my *brain* is a *computer*!" Proceed.

1 My legs were _____ as I raced for the tape.

2 Faced with failure, my heart was a(an) _____.

3 As the audience watched aghast, my fingers became _____,
stumbling over the ivory keys.

4 As I licked the spoon, my tongue was a(an) _____,
seeking out the last drop of whipped cream.

5 My feet were _____ as I set out to investigate
the strange noises coming from the cellar.

Personification

Personification creates a different kind of imagery. It is simply the transference of the characteristics of a person to a nonperson: to an object, an animal, an idea. In the example given at the beginning of this chapter ("Bright April shakes out her rain-drenched hair"), April (the month) could hardly shake her (nonexistent) hair; but the personification combines the brightness and raininess of April with the kicking youthfulness of early spring. And so it is effective.

Some more examples: Thomas Campbell writes that the hallowed ground *gives birth* to sacred thoughts, and Felicia Hemans that the bright waters *hear* the call of spring and *awaken*; E. A. Robinson talks of Time so *vicious* in his reaping; and Edna St. Vincent Millay of the woods, on an autumn day, that "*ache* and *sag* and all but *cry* with color!"

Stephen Crane in *The Red Badge of Courage* used personification heavily and with lasting effect. In battle, young Fleming saw the approaching shells as having "rows of cruel teeth that grinned at him"; the cannon "grunted and grumbled"; and the disturbed trees "waved their arms." After the battle was over, "the trees began softly to sing a hymn of twilight." In the hands of a lesser writer, the recurring personification might have become sentimental and grotesque; but Crane knew what he was doing. With deliberate care, he drew subtle relationships between humanity and the world of nature until war becomes a monster that gnaws not only on mortal flesh but on the earth itself.

Write a paragraph of about 50 to 75 words in which personification helps to create the prevailing mood. Here's a situation to start you off. You are alone in your living room. No one else is in the house. It is 1:30 a.m. and there is no moon. It is a dark night, with a wind of near-gale intensity. Rain is falling hard. Apart from the other noises, you hear a rustling at the front door and, as you watch, the doorknob begins to turn. Describe that moment, using personification as skillfully as you can.

_____

_____

_____

_____

_____

_____

_____

_____

Analogy

An analogy is an expanded simile. The simile needs no explanation to be understood; the analogy requires supporting detail.

When Coleridge (in "The Rime of the Ancient Mariner") wrote:

> "And every soul, it passed me by
> Like the whizz of my cross-bow!"

—the image is immediately clear.

But when Henrik Ibsen (in *An Enemy of the People*) wrote:

> "A community is like a ship . . ."

it made little sense until detail was added. Here is the complete analogy:

> "A community is like a ship; everyone
> ought to be prepared to take the helm."

That small detail: that "everyone ought to be prepared to take the helm" is necessary if the reader is to understand *how* the community is like a ship.

Analogy, as you have seen, is not so crisp and self-contained as the simile, but it is a most useful tool for the writer. The simile points out something the reader already knows; the analogy may actually suggest something new. Consider the difference between these two sentences.

> International threats must escalate in intensity if they are to continue to be effective.

> An international threat is like some drugs: to be effective, it must be given in constantly increasing doses.

Do you see the difference? The first statement is accurate and precise, but the second statement—the analogy—is clearer, gives a sharper grasp of the truth, and will linger far longer in memory.

Have you ever heard someone say: "I know what I mean, but I can't put it into words"? Here, too, the analogy can help. Ibsen (in *The League of Youth*) was trying to explain how financial leaders are not so independent as they like to think—that their fates and fortunes are actually interdependent and a change in one can trigger changes in all. He hit on a short but happy analogy: "These heroes of finance are like beads on a string—when one slips off, all the rest follow." (And how well that explains the vacillating Dow Jones industrial average given each night on the television news!)

Sharpen your critical teeth by analyzing the following analogies. In each case explain briefly the point made by the analogy, then evaluate the effectiveness of the analogy.

1 "Error is a hardy plant: it flourisheth in every soil." (Martin Tupper)

_____

_____

_____

_____

_____

_____

2   "Individuality is the salt of common life. You may have to live in a crowd, but you do not have to live like it, nor subsist on its food." (Henry Van Dyke)

_____

_____

_____

_____

_____

3   "Ideals are like stars; you will not succeed in touching them with your hands. But like the seafaring man on the desert of waters, you choose them as your guides and following them you will reach your destiny." (Carl Schurz)

_____

_____

_____

_____

_____

Continue sharpening those critical skills by developing analogies of your own. Start with a problem that's been bothering you but that you find difficult to explain. Some examples: lack of school spirit at a pep rally; the *non*-intellectual interests of some students; the dogmatism of a particular teacher; the apparent inability of parents to hear some requests. Next, ask yourself to *what* your problem can be compared. Set up a simile or metaphor, and add one or two details that elaborate and elucidate. Prune carefully (that is, eliminate all unnecessary words) and you will have an analogy. Create two.

_____

_____

_____

_____

_____

_____

_____

_____

> *Details in writing are like the stars and the moon. They are light-giving planets, emissaries from the Almighty. They dazzle the intelligence and whisper alluringly to the imagination. They are like the sun itself, creating complex minuets of shadows and light, and—through these dancing opposites—forcing eyes to see and minds to understand.*

In the above paragraph, if you didn't spot the simile in the first sentence, the metaphor in the second, the personification in the third, and the analogy in the fourth, you had better rework this chapter, my friend!

Unit IV
Putting It All Together

INTRODUCTION

Barbara Tuchman, the well-known historian, once wrote:

> . . . nothing is more satisfying than to write a good sentence. It is no fun to write lumpishly, dully, in prose the reader must plod through like wet sand. But it is a pleasure to achieve, if one can, a clear running prose that is simple yet full of surprises.

Fine, Ms. Tuchman . . . but how does one write like that?

Here is a recipe composed by fifteen professional writers:

WORK	*The art of writing is the art of applying the seat of the pants to the seat of the chair.* M. H. Vorse
OBSERVE	*The author who succeeds in his work is he who describes the interesting and significant things which it has been given him to observe and experience in his own life.* Leo Tolstoy
WORK	*Who casts to write a living line, must sweat.* Ben Jonson
ARRANGE WORDS	*Take a piece of good English writing . . . and ask why the meaning is so clear and the pleasure in reading so great. The answer lies wholly in the color and arrangement of the words.* Frank Swinnerton
WORK	*You write with ease to show your breeding But easy writing's curst hard reading.* Richard B. Sheridan
AIM FOR HARMONY	*The instructed writer is like the musician to whom the laws of harmony are so familiar that it has become instinctive in him to observe them.* Joseph Warren Beach

WORK	*You that intend to write what is worthy to be read more than once, blot frequently . . .*
	Horace
INVOLVE THE READER	*Writing or printing is like shooting with a rifle; you may hit your reader's mind or miss it.*
	Oliver Wendell Holmes
	I always write only half-sentences, and the reader himself must supply the other half.
	Johannes Brahms

WORK	*Let's face it, writing is hell.*
	William Styron
SHOW, DON'T TELL	*. . . don't narrate—paint! draw! build! Create!*
	Jack London

WORK	*True ease in writing comes from art, not chance,* *As those move easiest who have learned to dance.*
	Alexander Pope
REVISE	*As to the Adjective: when in doubt, strike it out.*
	Mark Twain
	Then, rising with Aurora's light, *The Muse invoked, sit down to write;* *Blot out, correct, insert, refine,* *Enlarge, diminish, interline.*
	Jonathan Swift

AND THIS ABOVE ALL	*Look in thy heart, and write.*
	Philip Sidney

---

1 *All About You.* List below six adjectives that you can honestly apply to yourself. (Examples: fat, ambitious, moody, intelligent.)

————————————   ————————————

————————————   ————————————

————————————   ————————————

Now, using each adjective only once, complete the following:

I am ————————————,

But I am also ————————————.

Some people consider me too ————————————,

While others praise me for being ————————————.

My friends like me because I am ————————————,

And my enemies dislike me because I am ————————————.

I am ————————————. (Repeat here the adjective used in the first line.)

Read it. Interesting, isn't it?

Bonus: How many of the six adjectives were favorable? ————————

How many unfavorable? ———————— Now think about *that!*

2 *Letter Lending.* One letter can make a world of difference.

TO WIT Why is "r" a criminal letter?
Because it turns a cook into a c*r*ook!

TO WIT Why is "b" such a hot letter?
Because it makes oil *b*oil!

Can you dream up three more?

——————————————————————————————

——————————————————————————————

——————————————————————————————

——————————————————————————————

——————————————————————————————

——————————————————————————————

3 *Under the Microscope.* Examine closely your left shoe. Describe it so exactly that anyone could identify it even if it were mixed in with thirty other shoes.

_____

_____

_____

_____

_____

(If your class is not too large and your teacher is willing, perhaps you can test your description. Put all left shoes of all class members in a pile. While one person reads a description, someone else should try to isolate the shoe described. Continue until all shoes have been returned to their rightful owners.)

4 *Graffiti Time.* Thoroughly clean one large chalkboard. Collect chalk of varying colors. For ten minutes, everyone in class should think of a drawing, a quotation, or an original statement that he or she would like to make. During the next ten minutes, everyone should have a turn at decorating the chalkboard, graffiti-style. In the last ten minutes of class, answer this question: "What does the *combination* of drawings and words suggest about the interests and attitudes of this class?"

_____

_____

_____

_____

_____

5 *Sentence Anagrams.* Take this twelve-word sentence: "The panther, a fierce hunter, savagely attacked the timid and gentle deer." Change the word order *without* adding or subtracting even one word—and build a new sentence. Example: "The panther and a gentle, timid deer attacked the savagely fierce hunter." Create at least six more sentences from the same twelve words.

_____

_____

_____

_____

_____

_____

(Helpful hint: Cut out twelve small squares from a sheet of paper. Write each word on one square. Try different arrangements.)

6   *Joke Jamboree.*   Start with this stale old joke:

> Who's that lady?
> That's no lady. That's my wife!

Keep the formula, but change the ingredients:

> Who's that scholar?
> That's no scholar. That's one of my students!

Use the formula to develop three new jokes.

_____

_____

_____

_____

_____

_____

7   *Ballooning.*   Here's a drawing. Study it.

Obviously one man has just slipped on a banana peel. The other man is looking at him. What does each say? Fill in the balloons.

8   *Simplify.*   You are sitting down to dinner: roast beef, baked potato, green peas, strawberry ice cream, and milk. Your equipment: 1 dinner plate, 1 glass, 1 knife, 1 fork, 1 spoon.

Before you may eat anything, you are forced to give up one piece of equipment. Which one will you yield? _____

Why this one? _____

Now you are forced to give up a second piece of equipment. Which one will you yield? _____

Why? _____

Finally you are forced to give up a third piece of equipment. Which one will you yield? _____

Why? _____

Any conclusion? _____

_____

9 *Improvisation.*   Here is a fly swatter.

List ten ways it can be used (excluding its purpose: to swat flies).

_____   _____

_____   _____

_____   _____

_____   _____

_____   _____

10 *Invention Interval.*   Invent an umbrella that would protect you from the rain even though your arms and hands are filled with packages and you cannot hold the umbrella. You may describe the umbrella in words and/or draw a picture of it.

_____

_____

_____

_____

_____

19. JUGGLERY AND JUXTAPOSITION

A computer can write a poem. It won't be very good and it may not make sense; but it will look like and sound like a poem. The key is juxtaposition: placing side by side certain kinds of words.

Juxtaposition

Role-Play a Computer

Start your experiment by adding five appropriate words to each of the first five categories below. Use singular nouns (without an "s") and singular verbs (with an "s").

Nouns (names of persons, places, and things)	Verbs (action words)	Prepositions (words that show relationship)	Place Names	Adjectives (words that describe)	Articles
1 elephant	wails	about	Los Angeles	roaring	the
2 _____	_____	_____	_____	_____	a
3 _____	_____	_____	_____	_____	an
4 _____	_____	_____	_____	_____	
5 _____	_____	_____	_____	_____	
6 _____	_____	_____	_____	_____	

Now that you have the *input* for the computer, it is time to set up the desired structure. Here's a structure-formula for a short poem.

> Article—Noun—Verb
> Preposition—Adjective—Place Name.
>
> Article—Noun—Verb
> Preposition—Adjective—Place Name.
>
> Article—Noun—Verb . . .

You are ready now to computer-write a poem. Poise your pencil above the column of *Articles*, close your eyes, let the point descend, and write the word so chosen in the blank space below, above (article). Follow this procedure until all blanks are filled. (If your pencil point descends between words, obviously you must try again.)

_____ (article)	_____ (noun)	_____ (verb)
_____ (preposition)	_____ (adjective)	_____ (place name).
_____ (article)	_____ (noun)	_____ (verb)
_____ (preposition)	_____ (adjective)	_____ (place name).
_____ (article)	_____ (noun)	_____ (verb) . . .

Read your "poem" aloud. Shakespeare's not trembling, but if you give it a classy title—something short and ambiguous—and read it again slowly and with dramatic pauses, you will have something that truly resembles a poem!

More About that Classy Title

Juxtaposition refers to words "side by side," but it can also refer to the relationship between title and poem. Here's one poem, "computer-written," following the formula given above.

> A house whistles
> At yellow Paris.
> A soldier trembles
> In sweet Mississippi.
> A pig roams . . .

Let's call it "Holocaust."

Read it again, keeping the title in mind. What is the poem about? Obviously, it's about a total disaster, probably a nuclear war. Paris is yellow with flame and radioactive smoke; the houses in Paris, like whistling teakettles, are boiling and teetering on the edge of ruin; Mississippi has been bombed back into primitive innocence, as the last soldier, his gun forever silenced, trembles into death. The world, too much for human intelligence, is once again the empire of dumb animals as "a pig roams."

Now call it "April."

What is the poem about? It's clear, isn't it, that it's really a lyric of springtime? Paris, clad in yellow crocuses, is a beautiful Lorelei, eliciting whistles from inanimate buildings. Mississippi, freshly sweet in magnolia blossoms, disarms even the belligerent soldier. And animals, released from winter pens and human surveillance, wander freely down rural paths.

You try it. Call it "Revolution." What is the poem about?

_____

_____

_____

_____

Once more. This time call it "Memory." What is the poem about?

_____

_____

_____

_____

_____

_____

Do you see what has been happening? Almost any two words—like "yellow" and "Paris," when combined, have several possible meanings. The title focuses and directs; like a searchlight, it disperses shadows, illuminates details, and imposes a relationship. It is the juxtaposition—the planned, deliberate arrangement—that makes sense of nonsense.

Go back to your own "poem" now. Think about it. Then select a title that will give the poem unity and meaning. Write your interpretation, based on the juxtaposition of title and poem.

TITLE _____

INTERPRETATION _____

_____

_____

_____

_____

_____

_____

Jugglery

The preceding exercise can be fun as it forces a little sense out of much nonsense. But the skilled writer doesn't rely on *accidental* juxtaposition. Like certain clowns, the writer performs miracles of jugglery every hour. Words are tossed into the air to spin and twist and somersault, until, at last, one word—the right word—descends into its proper niche.

Perfect phrases do not occur by chance. They are created with loving care. Remember the examples of oxymoron (page 73)—"cruel kindness" and "living corpse"? It is the combination that is effective—and effective combinations are found only by using one's intelligence, hearing, and intuition.

One Golden Ball

Begin sharpening your juggling skill by completing the quotations below. After each quotation, there are four words in parentheses. In each case, underline the *right* word—the word that heightens and illuminates the rest of the sentence.

1 When I behold upon the night's _____ face,
Huge cloudy symbols of a high romance. (John Keats)

(bright, dark, grim, starr'd)

2 Let us therefore brace ourselves to our duties, and so bear ourselves that, if the British Empire and its Commonwealth last for a thousand years, men will still say: "This was their _____ hour." (Winston Churchill)

(best, bravest, finest, noblest)

3 The world is a bundle of hay,
  Mankind are the _____ who pull;
Each tugs it a different way,
  And the greatest of all is John Bull. (George Gordon Byron)*

(asses, horses, mules, oxen)

4 The _____ neutrality of an impartial judge. (Edmund Burke)

(calm, clear, cold, true)

5 These are the times that _____ men's souls. (Thomas Paine)

(purify, temper, test, try)

Two Silver Orbs

Definitions are often clumsy things—accurate, but somehow superficial. Occasionally a writer with a deft touch combines a few unexpected words in an unexpected way and comes up with a satisfying definition.

In the first column below are ten words to be defined; in the second are ten deft definitions. Match them; and as you match them, note well how, in the hands of the finest artists, words and ideas merge.

(____) 1 eloquence   a "frozen music" (Goethe)
(____) 2 architecture   b "the trade of kings" (Dryden)
(____) 3 prayer   c "the unbearable repartee" (Chesterton)
(____) 4 rivers   d "the painting of thought" (Pascal)
(____) 5 self-defense   e "the ease of woe" (Crashaw)
(____) 6 silence   f "the conduct of other people" (Wilde)
(____) 7 truth   g "conversation with God" (Clement of Alexandria)
(____) 8 vulgarity   h "roads that move" (Pascal)
(____) 9 war   i "the equation of thought and thing" (Aquinas)
(____) 10 weeping   j "nature's eldest law" (Dryden)

If you managed to get seven right, you did very well indeed!

---

*From THE LIFE, LETTERS AND JOURNALS OF LORD BYRON by Thomas Moore. Reprinted by permission of John Murray (Publishers) Ltd., London, England.

Three Bronze Spheres

A third way to practice word-jugglery is to play the column game. Here, for example, are three columns, each containing five words:

ADJECTIVES	NOUNS	VERBS
golden	nation	rustled
slinky	ashtray	shrieked
melancholy	pen	wobbled
whirling	plane	raced
sterile	physician	pursued

By combining three words, one from each of the three columns, we can come up with some intriguing combinations. Some of these combinations will trigger ideas that can then be developed into rather interesting sentences.

PHRASE:	"golden pen pursued"
IDEA:	truth is difficult to grasp
SENTENCE:	Her golden pen pursued eluding truth.

PHRASE:	"melancholy physician pursues"
IDEA:	death cures all ills
SENTENCE:	Death, a melancholy physician, pursues all who live.

Now it's your turn. Make up your own columns of ten words each. Then—three times—combine, think, and develop. You will be surprised at some of the sentences you will create!

ADJECTIVES	NOUNS	VERBS
_____	_____	_____
_____	_____	_____
_____	_____	_____
_____	_____	_____
_____	_____	_____
_____	_____	_____
_____	_____	_____
_____	_____	_____
_____	_____	_____
_____	_____	_____

PHRASE: _____

IDEA: _____

SENTENCE: _____

PHRASE: _____

IDEA: _____

SENTENCE: _____

_____

PHRASE: _____

IDEA: _____

SENTENCE: _____

_____

Word-jugglery will not make you a writer; you must first have something to say. But knowing how to combine words effectively will help you translate your thoughts into crystal-like sentences: each clear, beautiful, and rich with meaning.

20. TO THE POINT

"Paul Revere rides a rocking horse."   (anonymous—20th c.)
"Absence makes the heart grow fonder." (anonymous—17th c.)

Although written three centuries apart, these two statements share one important characteristic: both are memorable. A person hearing either one is likely to remember it. Why?

That's the writer's question ... *why*? Why do certain combinations of words linger in the mind, capture the heart, and titillate the imagination? If there were one sure, clear answer, every would-be writer in the world could immediately become another Shakespeare. But there isn't. There are half answers, and "maybe" answers, and controversial answers. There are pompous answers and silly answers, answers that will amuse and answers that will anger. But there is no one answer. We simply don't know.

And that's what this chapter is all about: what we don't know.

Knowing a little, though, is better than knowing nothing. So let's analyze and ponder and beat our heads against the rock of ignorance and learn the little that we can.

Word Choice

The inventor of proverbs (often the graffitist in our time) is usually an ordinary person, not a writer. Look at those two examples again.

Paul Revere rides a rocking horse.
Absence makes the heart grow fonder.

Every word is simple and in common usage. No word needs to be defined, even for a child. In the 20th century statement, only two words are multisyllabled and one of those is a proper name. In the 17th century statement, again only two words are multisyllabled—and even those are content with two syllables each.

Conclusion: That short words only should be used. (But what about "Procrastination is the thief of time"—Edward Young, 18th century?)

Length of Sentence

"Paul Revere rides a rocking horse" is composed of six words, one of them one-letter long. "Absence makes the heart grow fonder" also has six words. Short sentences are *always* easier to remember than long sentences, aren't they?

Conclusion: That short sentences only should be used. (But what about the Shakespearean quote everyone knows—"This above all: to thine own self be true, and it must follow as the night the day, Thou canst not then be false to any man"?)

Use of Allusion

Allusions are useful jogs to memory, and the first statement contains an allusion to Paul Revere who made his famous ride on April 18, 1775. But the second contains no allusion.

Conclusion: None.

Universality of Idea

Universality of idea appeals by its nature to everyone. Maybe this is the key. Certainly the second statement expresses a belief held by many people in all times. But the first? Millions of people have probably never heard of Paul Revere. Yet the statement is memorable.

Conclusion: None.

Obviously this approach isn't working. Let's try another. This time we'll analyze one statement at a time, and do it carefully and completely.

Paul Revere . . .

"Paul Revere rides a rocking horse."

We have a six-word sentence, all simple words. We have a nice touch of alliteration: Revere . . . rides . . . rocking; and an allusion: Paul Revere.

What is a rocking horse? A toy that amuses a child, that allows the child to *pretend* to be riding a horse.

Who is Paul Revere? Revere was a patriot who worked for the independence of this country throughout the American Revolutionary War. On April 18, 1775, he learned that the British troops intended to march on Concord. Revere rode from Boston to Lexington, alerting the militia along the way, until he was captured at Lexington. Fortunately a companion got through to Concord.

What is really said in the graffito? Isn't it a "put-down" of Paul Revere, a major figure in both history and legend? Notice how easily the legendary man is reduced to a comic figure simply by substituting "rocking horse" for the real horse. (Although a sharper wit might point out that Revere's ride that night really did *rock* the British Empire!)

Nevertheless, the magic—the memorable quality of the statement—lies in the incredible gulf between the daring rider and the child in the nursery. The comparison is incongruous, and therefore snares our attention.

Try using incongruity to write a simple but memorable sentence. Insert a well-known name in the first blank of each statement. As the verb, use "needs" or "uses" or insert a verb of your own. Then in the second blank write the name of an object that we would not normally associate with that person.

1 _____ needs
                             uses   _____

2 _____ needs
                             uses   _____

3 _____ needs
                             uses   _____

Absence Makes ...

"Absence makes the heart grow fonder."

Here we have a six-word sentence, again all simple words. There is just the suggestion of personification: the heart *grows* fonder, as a power is attributed to that organ that it does not possess. Apart from that, there is nothing unusual. Why then is the sentence memorable?

Examine the content. We all know the loneliness that comes when someone we love is absent. Perhaps he will forget us; perhaps she will find someone else. We're fearful, as well as lonely. Then Anonymous put those six short words together—Absence makes the heart grow fonder—and we had a new magic formula. Those six words gave fresh hope—they seemed to promise that present pain (during absence) results in future joy (upon reunion). Like Linus' blanket, the saying became an emotional crutch to support us in difficult times.

Writing this type of sentence is not easy. There is no gimmick, no short-cut. You have to think about the problem, then think your way to a possible and probable comforting thought. Try it—in the two case histories given below:

A friend, a 17-year-old football player, has had a leg injury and cannot play in the big Thanksgiving Day game. Compose a short sentence that might reassure him and make him feel better. (Ask yourself—what is troubling him most? Use this as a starting point.)

_____

Another friend, a 16-year-old, has just been told by her parents that she cannot drive for three months. Compose a short sentence that might make her feel better.

_____

> **These are just two keys to memorable writing: the use of *incongruous detail*, and the handling of a *universal emotion*. Neither guarantees that you will compose remarkable sentences; they merely help to make it possible.**

Edward Lueders in one of his poems suggests that the writer "try untried circuitry." If you know anything about electricity, you know that's a hazardous undertaking. You may blow up—but (if you're lucky) you may also light up. And "to light up" is a writer's sole purpose.

Here's your chance to live dangerously—to "try untried circuitry." Study the following drawings. All were first published in *The Cosmopolitan* magazine in 1902. Remember universal fears and desires; remember the power of incongruous detail. Then juggle words and ideas and drawings until something clicks. After a little polishing, you should have a short but telling caption, a caption that will transform the almost-century-old drawing into a reflection on modern life. The first example should help you get started. Notice that after the drawing there are four possible captions, any one of which says more than it seems to say.

1

There is no housing problem.
or *A penny saved?*
or *The security of Social Security.*
or *A home is where the purse is.*

2

3

YOUR TURN _____

_____

YOUR TURN _____

_____

Before we close this chapter and leave behind our 1902 drawings, perform this brief experiment. Choose any one of the three drawings and, after studying it, answer the two following questions:

Drawing selected _____

Are there any incongruous details? _____ If so, describe.

_____

_____

_____

Is the idea behind the drawing universal or near-universal? _____

If so, explain. _____

The truth is that these two characteristics—via pictures or words—contribute depth and power to what we say. Together they speak to the humor and heart of humans.

21. THE SOUND OF A DIFFERENT DRUMMER

Thoreau once wrote:

> If a man does not keep pace with his companions, perhaps it is because
> he hears a different drummer. Let him step to the music which he hears,
> however measured or far away.[1]

Thoreau was referring to thinking and acting—to our willingness to walk untraveled
paths or espouse unpopular causes. And these are important to the writer. But Thoreau
might just as pointedly have been referring to writing—for the good writer must find
his own rhythm and be faithful to it.

The way word is linked to word, and phrase to phrase, and sentence to sentence—
these vary with the writer and depend on that "different drummer" that lurks in the
farthest recesses of the writer's brain. Hemingway's drummer beat out a short, almost
staccato tempo that demanded short words, short phrases, short sentences, all rich in
understatement and implication. Henry James' drummer rolled and rumbled, merging
sound with sound, into a rich complexity of melodic blends—demanding long involved
sentences that forever round on themselves and flow with incredible smoothness, each
into each.

Here is Hemingway in *A Farewell to Arms*. The narrator, Frederick Henry, has just
been seriously injured in war. Notice the short sentences, the quick sense impressions,
the curt catalog of injuries.

> They lifted me onto the table. It was hard and slippery. There were many
> strong smells, chemical smells, and the sweet smell of blood. They took off
> my trousers and the medical captain commenced dictating to the sergeant-
> adjutant while he worked, "Multiple superficial wounds of the left and
> right thigh and left and right knee and right foot. Lacerations of the
> scalp . . . with possible fracture of the skull. Incurred in the line of duty.
> That's what keeps you from being court-martialled for self-inflicted
> wounds," he said.[2]

The cold, hard rhythm of the writing reflects the cold, hard attitude of the military toward injuries; and that last sentence—unexpected, and bitter, and hurting—throws
the whole paragraph into a mixture of comic and tragic relief.

Now here's Henry James, a very different kind of writer. In *Daisy Miller* Winterbourne and Daisy, both young Americans, meet in Europe. They decide to visit Chillon.
Notice the long sentences and leisurely pace that seem to suggest that nothing is happening; yet at the end of the paragraph we have a clear picture of the two young people
and the problems that lie ahead of them.

---

[1]From "Walden" in WALDEN AND OTHER WRITINGS OF HENRY DAVID THOREAU edited by
Brooks Atkinson. Copyright 1937, The Modern Library.
[2]From A FAREWELL TO ARMS by Ernest Hemingway. Copyright 1929 by Charles Scribner's Sons and
reprinted with their permission.

The sail was not long, but Winterbourne's companion found time to say a great many things. To the young man himself their little excursion was so much of an escapade—an adventure—that, even allowing for her habitual sense of freedom, he had some expectation of seeing her regard it in the same way. But it must be confessed that, in this particular, he was disappointed. Daisy Miller was extremely animated; she was in charming spirits; but she was apparently not at all excited; she was not fluttered; she avoided neither his eyes nor those of anyone else; she blushed neither when she looked at him nor when she felt that people were looking at her. People continued to look at her a great deal, and Winterbourne took much satisfaction in his pretty companion's distinguished air. He had been a little afraid that she would talk loud, laugh overmuch, and even, perhaps, desire to move about the boat a good deal. But he quite forgot his fears; he sat, smiling, with his eyes upon her face, while, without moving from her place, she delivered herself of a great number of original reflections. It was the most charming garrulity he had ever heard. He had assented to the idea that she was "common"; but was she so, after all, or was he simply getting used to her commonness?

Two different styles—two totally different rhythms—but each is good, each is right because each is true to the writer's "different drummer."

Your hardest job as a beginning writer is to develop your own style, your own rhythm—to hear *your* drummer and to translate the beat, whatever it may be, into words that reach across to the reader.

Your Turn: A Mini-Essay

No one can teach you *your* rhythm. You must find it deep within yourself. For the next few minutes, that is your job—to find your natural rhythm in writing. This experiment might help you.

Think back to a time when you had a painful experience. Perhaps you fractured a rib or had a high fever or had a bitter quarrel with someone you loved. Remember all you can: how you felt; pain, if any; people's faces; noises; smells . . . everything. When you have brought to the surface as much of the memory as you can, describe it below, writing rapidly and with a minimum of pauses.

_____

_____

_____

_____

_____

_____

_____

_____

_____

_____

_____
_____
_____
_____

This paragraph or two will be the basis of all the work that follows. Hopefully—because you wrote rapidly and because it deals with pain (something that breaks through most inhibitions)—it will contain at least the kernel of your own rhythm. So we begin here, and go on to two techniques that will help you to improve and refine your rhythm, without basically changing it.

Parallelism

These are parallel lines:

_____
_____
_____

If one line slips out of place, this occurs:

Slippage of this kind destroys your rhythm. It turns free flowing thought into clumsy confusion. It lacerates your meaning.

Begin with the short and easy. After each example given, write one of your own, using the same type of parallelism.

FIRST, a series of **infinitives** (to + a verb)

> I like   to bowl,
>   to read mysteries, and
>   to play tennis.

> I like   to _____,
>   to _____, and
>   to _____.

SECOND, a series of **gerunds** (a verbal form with the *-ing* ending, used as a noun)

> Swimming
>   and
> skating are my favorite weekend activities.

> _____
>   and
> _____ are my favorite activities in math class.

THIRD, a series of **phrases**

His latest short story was praised for its terror,
suspense, and
surprise.

His latest test paper was praised for its _____,
_____, and
_____.

Now complete the following "short stories" by using your imagination *and* beautifully balanced parallel structure:

1 After he was introduced, Bob rose, his speech clutched in his left hand. Why had he ever agreed to speak? Speaking was not his forte; _____ing was.

2 Only one day remained until the mortgage payment was due. But she'd be all right. She had boxes of tomatoes, _____ of _____, and _____ of _____. If she sold everything, she'd have more than enough to thwart old Grimes.

3 As she stepped into the time machine to travel into the far past, she remembered the three essential directions: to dial her destination, to _____ _____, and to _____.

Continue.

FOURTH, a series of **verbs**, or **verbs plus objects**

Clyde *dashed* down Main Street, *entered* the jewelry store, and *slapped* a thousand dollar bill on the counter. "I need an engagement ring," he said breathlessly.

As she prepared for the most important date of her life, Lucia _____ _____, _____, and _____.

FIFTH, a series of **clauses**

Jason had become a citizen of the gourmet world: in France, he ate frogs' legs; in Italy, he devoured pizza; and in Japan, he dined on sukiyaki.

Phyllis was determined to become the century's greatest professional athlete:

she would _____;

she would _____;

and she would _____.

END

End this section by using parallelism to describe quickly a group of people. Here, from *Northwest Passage*, is such a description by Kenneth Roberts. Notice that in his parallel description, Roberts concentrates on the heads and faces of the women.

> As the whaleboats came slowly toward the sickle-shaped beach on which the Rangers' tents were pitched, I made out Mrs. Coit's white hair; the tight knot at the back of Sarah Hadden's head; the fat face of the German woman; the dishevelled locks of Mrs. Wick; the yellow braids and flat back of Jennie Coit; the shining black heads of the three Indian girls. They were all there. They had all come safely through.*

For your descriptive paragraph, you may want to describe five basketball players, or half a dozen musicians in the orchestra, or a few strikers on a picket line. Whatever your subject, use parallelism as Roberts did.

_____

_____

_____

_____

_____

Before you go on to the next section, go back to your mini-essay about a painful experience (page 143). Read it slowly. Note:

(*a*) whether you used parallelism at all;

(*b*) if you did, whether you used it correctly;

(*c*) if you didn't, whether use of it would improve the flow and clarify the meaning.

Revise as needed; then proceed to . . . . . .

Transitions

Here are three sentences without transitions:

_____. _____. _____.

Here are the same three sentences *with* transitions:

_____·.·_____.·¨·._____.

Notice that, in the first example, each sentence stands alone. The reader must jump from the first to the second to the third—and with each jump, face a possible break in thought. But in the second example, transitions turn the three sentences into a unified, flowing unit. Here there is little chance that the reader will lose interest or understanding.

---

*From NORTHWEST PASSAGE by Kenneth Roberts. Copyright 1936, Doubleday & Company, Inc.

In writing, a *transition* may be a word or a phrase.

- It may indicate   TIME: *immediately, at once, then.*
    . . . or CONTRAST: *but, yet, however.*
    . . . or   RESULT: *therefore, consequently.*
    . . . or ADDITION: *and, also, besides.*

- It may indicate a PURPOSE: *for this reason, to this end.*
    . . . or a CONCLUSION: *in brief, in any event, to sum up.*

- It may be simply a key word repeated, in whole or in part:

  It had been *rain*ing for three days. *Rain* made her unhappy and restless.

- It may be a pronoun that relates to a noun in the preceding sentence:

  Jim wanted to write to her. *He* knew he should, but . . .

- or a pronoun used as an adjective:

  When Adelaide was miserable, she went on a shopping spree. It was *this* habit that saved her now from drowning in self-pity.

Read the following paragraph, noting all italicized transitions. Then read carefully the notes below it. Be sure you understand how each transition operates.

> Four thousand spaceships hurtled to Earth at 1 p.m. [1]*Here* [2]*they* spewed forth flame, pestilence, and noxious gas in enormous quantities. [3]*Quickly* the news spread—"We are being invaded by eerie creatures from Outer Space!" [4]*Almost at once* newspapers printed extras with screaming headlines, and radios squawked ominous bulletins. Millions saw and heard and smelled [5]*these* beetle-like creatures. [6]*Yet* a few skeptics remained. [7]*A few* still asserted stoutly that [8]*these* three-foot-high purple beetles were from Russia or China or Africa, not from another planet.

1 *Here* (transition through place): relates to Earth.

2 *they* (transition through pronoun): relates to "spaceships" in preceding sentence.

3 *Quickly* (transition through time): relates to 1 p.m. in the first sentence and the need for urgent action implied in the second sentence.

4 *Almost at once* (transition through time): relates to "quickly" in the preceding sentence and reemphasizes need for action.

5 *these* (transition through pronoun used as an adjective): relates to panic in preceding sentence and "eerie creatures" in the sentence before that.

6 *Yet* (transition through contrast): contrasts the few who did not believe to the millions who saw, heard, and smelled.

7 *A few* (transition through repetition of a word): repeats "a few" used in preceding sentence and strengthens the idea of "a few" holdouts.

8 *these* (transition through pronoun used as an adjective): relates to the third sentence and the fifth, and rounds back to the first sentence, verifying that the ships were, indeed, spaceships.

The best way to recognize the importance of transitional words and phrases is to see how professional writers use them. Read each of the following excerpts carefully. Then, after each excerpt, explain how the transition(s) operates, using the eight notes above as guides.

1   At nine-fifteen Susan stood on the balcony of their room, gazing down at the plaza. Mr. Simms was seated *there*, his neat legs crossed, on a delicate bronze bench. (Ray Bradbury)[1]

_____

_____

_____

2   The next day was a fair one, but the peasants who had come down from the mountains, with their milk tins strapped to their backs, were saying that the weather would not hold. *It* would break tomorrow or the next day, *they* said ... (Kay Boyle)[2]

_____

_____

_____

3   Evans possessed that British rhinoceros equipment of mingled ignorance, self-confidence, and complacency which is triple-armed against all the shafts of the mind. *And yet* Winterbourne could not help liking the man. (Richard Aldington)[3]

_____

_____

_____

4   The way the land had looked this morning, still, waiting—you knew now what it was *for. For* covering up, release. *In a little while* the shoulders of stone, the dead leaves, the naked roads would be gone, drifted under a quietude as yielding as sleep. (Ruth Moore)[4]

_____

_____

_____

---

[1]From THE FOX AND THE FOREST by Ray Bradbury. © 1965. Reprinted by permission of Harold Matson Company, Inc.

[2]From AVALANCHE by Kay Boyle. Copyright 1944, Simon & Schuster, Inc. Reprinted by permission of A. Watkins, Inc.

[3]From DEATH OF A HERO by Richard Aldington. Copyright 1929, Chatto and Windus. Reprinted by permission of Rosica Colin Limited, London, England.

[4]From SPOONHANDLE by Ruth Moore. Copyright 1946, William Morrow and Company, Inc.

5   She joined parties of students during the summer and tramped the Bavarian Alps, and she danced all night at student balls. *Nevertheless*, she managed to hold herself somewhat aloof . . . (Gertrude Atherton)

_____

_____

_____

6   Along the front of the big building of which our school was a part ran a huge slope of stone steps, higher, I think, than those that lead up to St. Paul's Cathedral. On a black wintry evening he and I were wandering on *these* cold heights, which seemed as dreary as a pyramid under the stars. (G. K. Chesterton)*

_____

_____

_____

7   We were sitting at dinner in our little room, when we heard the cry of "Sail ho!" *This*, we had learned, did not always signify a vessel, but was raised whenever a woman was seen coming down from the town . . . (Richard H. Dana)

_____

_____

_____

*   *   *   *

Return now to your mini-essay (page 143) about a painful experience. This time, note whether you included enough transitional words or phrases to give your writing a flowing, easy coherence. If you did not, revise—using any of the transitional techniques considered in the section beginning on page 146.

*   *   *   *

Listen to that different drummer. Listen closely. Use parallelism and transitions to smooth and refine your rhythm, *not* to change it. The result—eventually—will be a rhythm and style recognizably yours. At that moment—when someone says, "Ah, yes. That is Jackson's writing. I can tell," you will have begun to be a writer.

_____

*From CHESTERTON'S ESSAYS by G. K. Chesterton. Reprinted by permission of Miss D. E. Collins and A. P. Watt & Son, London, England.

22. THE SEDULOUS APE

Tacitus, the Roman historian, learned from Cicero.

Edward Gibbon, who wrote *The Decline and Fall of the Roman Empire*, learned from Tacitus.

Winston Churchill, Prime Minister of England, learned from Gibbon.

And thousands of school children, as well as dozens of professional writers, still learn from Churchill.

What each one learned is, of course, "how to write." Writing cannot be taught, but it can be learned. And one of the best ways of learning to write is to imitate skilled writers.

You say you already know how to write a sentence—perhaps even two or three kinds of sentences? Fine. But no carpenter would set out to construct a fine cabinet with two or three tools. And no surgeon would begin an open-heart operation with two or three instruments. The good carpenter and the good surgeon insist that all possible equipment be available. They may use only two or three, but if they do—those two or three will be the result of *choice*. So, too, with the good writer.

To imitate is not to copy; certainly it is not to plagiarize. Rather it is depending, for a while, on someone else's structure until we find our own. When we were little, we learned to walk by holding onto chairs and coffee tables. We learned to speak by repeating sounds made by our parents. Later, we learned to drive by imitating experienced drivers; or to play football by studying a Heisman Trophy winner in action. To reinvent driving or to reinvent football would be a waste of time. We begin with the knowledge and experience of others—and then add to it. So, too, with the good writer.

So—imitate.

Imitate Sinclair Lewis

When Lewis wanted to describe the rise of the businessman in the 1920's, he wrote:

> The Romantic Hero was no longer the knight, the wandering poet, the cowpuncher, the aviator, nor the brave young district attorney, but the great sales-manager whose title of nobility was "go-getter."*

Lewis might more easily have said: The Romantic Hero was the great sales-manager, whose title of nobility was "go-getter." But it wouldn't have been as effective. Instead, he used a series of carefully chosen negatives. The knight, the poet, the cowpuncher, the aviator, and the district attorney all suggest courage, integrity, the need to be true to one's self. And this imposing series culminates in—what? In the sales-manager with only one goal: to be a "go-getter." We shudder—and that is just what Lewis meant us to do. Through contrast, he has stripped the sales-manager of the independence of the

---

*Reprinted from BABBITT by Sinclair Lewis, by permission of Harcourt Brace Jovanovich, Inc.

cowpuncher and the inspiration of the poet. He leaves him a mean little biped who thinks nobility is money. Quite a powerful sentence, isn't it?

In our first attempt at imitation, we'll define Community Leader instead of Romantic Hero. Then we'll keep the structure of the sentence but change the details.

Like this:

The _____ *Community Leader* _____ is no longer the _____ *patriot* _____, the _____ *organiz* _____ing _____ *genius* _____, the _____ *reformer* _____, the _____ *diplomat* _____, nor the _____ *gallant* _____ *daring* _____ *dreamer* _____, but the great _____ *power-lover* _____ whose _____ *token* _____ *of* _____ *success* _____ is _____ *his well-oiled political machine* _____.

Now you try it. Use as your term to be defined one of the following:

Student Most Likely to Succeed
President of the Student Organization
Star Athlete

_____ (your own term)

Then add details as needed.

The _____ is no longer the _____, the _____ing _____, the _____, the _____, nor the _____ _____ _____, but the great _____ whose _____ _____ is _____.

When you have finished, read the sentence aloud. Doesn't it have a fine rolling rhythm? And—as an added reward—note smugly that you have just used parallelism (in the series following "no longer") and contrast (following "but"). A good beginning!

Imitate Francis Bacon

Bacon was a superb constructor of sentences. Some of his sentences are so packed with meaning that they are little essays. Consider, for example, "Envy never makes holiday." One might spend a morning pondering that. Or "A wise man will make more opportunities than he finds."

We'll make this a three-round exercise: first a sentence by Francis Bacon, then an imitation of it, and finally a line on which you can write your imitation.

1 BACON: "Hope is a good breakfast, but a bad supper."
  OURS: Money is a good servant, but a bad master.

  YOURS: _____

2 BACON: "Some books are to be tasted, others to be swallowed, and some few to be chewed and digested."

OURS: Some men are to be dated, others to be courted, and some few to be loved and married.

YOURS: _____

_____

3 BACON: "Men in great place are thrice servants,—servants of the sovereign or state, servants of fame, and servants of business."

OURS: Soldiers in wartime are thrice servants,—servants of the military code, servants of the government, and servants of death.

YOURS: _____

_____

_____

Imitate Pearl S. Buck

Pearl Buck lived in China for many years and knew it well. She started one paragraph of description like this:

"The other day I stood on a mountain top in Kiangsi."

As you continue with your attempts at imitation, keep in mind that you do not have to follow word order slavishly. Keep it generally—but change when it seems right to change.

That first sentence can be imitated in dozens of ways:

Last night I stared at the stars in the Northern Hemisphere.
Today at dawn I ran across a meadow in Lisbon.
This morning I paced along the ocean's coast in Maine.

You should be ready now to imitate the complete paragraph. Choose a place you know well and that you can describe in detail. Imitate closely or loosely, as you wish.

The other day I stood on a mountain top in Kiangsi. I looked over a hundred miles of lovely Chinese country. Streams glittered in the sunshine; the Yangtse wound its leisurely way along, a huge yellow roadway to the sea; clusters of trees cuddled cosily about little thatched villages; the rice fields were clear jade green and laid as neatly as patterns in a puzzle. It seemed a scene of peace and beauty.*

_____

_____

_____

_____

---

*From MY SEVERAL WORLDS by Pearl S. Buck. Copyright 1954. Reprinted by permission of Thomas Y. Crowell Company, Inc.

_____

_____

_____

_____

_____

_____

_____

Notice that the last sentence in Buck's paragraph uses the word "seemed." The next paragraph explains that usage, since Buck goes on to show that the description is misleading—but that's another story.

Imitate Edgar Allan Poe

It's time now to imitate everybody's favorite: Edgar Allan Poe. As we have already seen, Poe loved words and used them well. Read his description of a room from the short story, "The Fall of the House of Usher." Read it several times until you *feel* the mood he is carefully constructing. Then choose a room you know well: your own room, a living room, even a classroom ... and write a description in Poe's style.

> The room in which I found myself was very large and lofty. The windows were long, narrow, and pointed, and at so vast a distance from the black oaken floor as to be altogether inaccessible from within. Feeble gleams of encrimsoned light made their way through the trellised panes, and served to render sufficiently distinct the more prominent objects around; the eye, however, struggled in vain to reach the remoter angles of the chamber, or the recesses of the vaulted and fretted ceiling. Dark draperies hung upon the walls. The general furniture was profuse, comfortless, antique, and tattered. Many books and musical instruments lay scattered about, but failed to give any vitality to the scene. I felt that I breathed an atmosphere of sorrow. An air of stern, deep, and irredeemable gloom hung over and pervaded all.*

_____

_____

_____

_____

_____

_____

_____

_____

_____

*From "The Fall of the House of Usher," by Edgar Allan Poe, in THE WORKS OF EDGAR ALLAN POE IN ONE VOLUME. Copyright 1927. Reprinted by permission of Walter J. Black, Inc.

_____

_____

_____

_____

_____

_____

_____

_____

Imitate Christopher Morley

One good way to use imitation is to choose deliberately an author whose style will counteract one of your writing faults. (You must first, of course, know your writing well enough to know your faults!) Many students find their sentences are long and heavy; they lack the light, casual touch. For such a writer, Christopher Morley is the perfect antidote.

Here is the first paragraph from one of Morley's essays. Read it several times before you begin imitating. Notice how Morley uses capital letters and parentheses to add a little humor. Both techniques are useful, but should be used sparingly.

> This was an expedition to study Geography. There were no plans and no preparations other than to pack five small suitcases (one apiece) and Scally's plaid overcoat. (Scally is a cocker spaniel.) After a long winter in town the Family had a desire to see how mountains, rivers, and roads fit together in the great jigsaw puzzle of New England.*

_____

_____

_____

_____

_____

_____

_____

_____

Imitate Ray Bradbury

Another good antidote for long, ponderous sentences is the crisp writing of Ray Bradbury. In this selection, note how strong verbs are used, and how very short sentences alternate with slightly longer ones to build intensity.

_____

*From INTERNAL REVENUE by Christopher Morley. Copyright 1933 by Christopher Morley. Copyright © renewed 1961 by Mrs. Helen F. Morley. Reprinted by permission of J. B. Lippincott Company.

The monster stopped and froze. Its great lantern eyes blinked. Its mouth gaped. It gave a sort of rumble, like a volcano. It twitched its head this way and that, as if to seek the sounds now dwindled off into the fog. It peered at the lighthouse. It rumbled again. Then its eyes caught fire. It reared up, threshed the water, and rushed at the tower, its eyes filled with angry torment.[1]

_____

_____

_____

_____

_____

_____

_____

_____

Imitate O. Henry

But perhaps your problem is different. Perhaps you already write short sentences. Each begins with a subject. Each goes on with a verb. Each ends with an object. Even you grow bored. If this is your problem, you can learn much from O. Henry. This master of the short story knew how to vary sentences and how to combine words in an infinite number of combinations. In this excerpt from "The Romance of a Busy Broker," O. Henry is describing the world of finance. Notice the simile in sentence 3, in which orders to buy and sell are compared to flights of swallows. Notice the analogy in lines 5 through 7. Be fully aware of O. Henry's word choice and word combination techniques as you start to imitate this paragraph.

The rush and pace of business grew fiercer and faster. On the floor* they were pounding† half a dozen stocks in which Maxwell's customers were heavy investors. Orders to buy and sell were coming and going as swift as the flight of swallows. Some of his own holdings were imperilled, and the man was working like some high-geared, delicate, strong machine—strung to full tension, going at full speed, accurate, never hesitating, with the proper word and decision and act ready and prompt as clockwork. Stocks and bonds, loans and mortgages, margins and securities—here was a world of finance, and there was no room in it for the human world or the world of nature.[2]

_____

*stock exchange
†depressing the value of

_____

[1]From THE FOG HORN by Ray Bradbury. © 1965. Reprinted by permission of Harold Matson Company, Inc.
[2]From "The Romance of a Busy Broker," by O. Henry, from THE COMPLETE WORKS OF O. HENRY, Vol. I. Copyright 1953, Doubleday & Company, Inc.

_____

_____

_____

_____

_____

_____

_____

_____

_____

_____

_____

_____

_____

_____

*   *   *   *   *

Don't stop now. Whenever you come across a writer whose style you admire, spend a few half-hours imitating it. Slowly you will find you are absorbing and developing certain techniques and totally rejecting others. That's fine . . . for that proves you are constructing a style of your own.

Don't feel you should apologize for finding your style through other writers. The title of this chapter, "The Sedulous Ape," comes from Robert Louis Stevenson—the Stevenson who wrote _Treasure Island_ and _Dr. Jekyll and Mr. Hyde_. Stevenson was quick to admit that he learned his trade from others. He wrote: "I have thus played the sedulous ape to Hazlitt, to Lamb, to Wordsworth, to Sir Thomas Browne, to Defoe, to Hawthorne, to Montaigne, to Beaudelaire, and to Obermann."

If the author of _Treasure Island_ could afford to admit his debt to other writers, you can too. Imitate . . . learn . . . write. Play the sedulous ape.

---

23. SUGGEST. IMPLY. CONNOTE. *SHOW.*

Mark Twain once declared: "Don't say the old lady screamed—bring her on and let her scream."

And *that* is what writing is all about. Do not *tell* your reader about something; suggest it, imply it, connote it; above all, *show* it.

Television demonstrates the value of a gesture: a farmer's wife raises her left hand, pushes some hair off her forehead, and lowers her head. We don't need words to realize that she is tired, frustrated, a little bitter.

Some movie producers have gone further. They have equipped their theaters with smell-emitters. If they want to suggest the coming of spring, the scent of lilacs and calla lilies fills the theater. If they want to suggest a battlefield, the odor of blood and gunpowder suffocates the viewers.

The writer possesses neither picture nor perfume; but words will do the job if they are used properly. And words *can* do the job more effectively and permanently than any other medium.

TV Teacher

Prepare yourself by turning on the television set. Tune in a movie, a drama, a serial—anything but a talk show or a news broadcast. Turn off the sound. Concentrate on what you see. Is a fight going on? How do you know? Is the old grandfather despondent? How do you know? Is the family's poodle in disgrace? How do you know?

Here's an example. Near the fireplace, the old grandfather sits on an orange crate. His hands hang limply between his legs. His shoulders, slumped forward, transform his frail body into a tumbling arch. His head lolls, without control; his chin is inert on his chest. His shirt is only half-buttoned, his pants baggy, his shoes scuffed and torn. (He is without hope.)

Another example: A man of about 35 is talking to a young woman. His eyebrows are drawn together, and his jaw thrusts forward. As he speaks, his lips move rapidly, as though he were biting off each word. His hands are clenched and his body leans slightly toward the woman. His shoulders hunch a little, as if he were considering physical attack. (He is angry.)

Now you try. Choose any three short scenes. Each time focus on one character. Note quickly facial expressions, gestures, body stance, clothing—anything and everything that contribute to the overall effect. At the end of your notes, state briefly, in parentheses, the emotion conveyed.

_____

_____

_____

_____

_____

_____

_____

_____

_____

_____

_____

_____

_____

Before you continue, read your notes. Contrast the simple statement of emotion (e.g., He is angry) with the many details that *imply* the emotion. The inexperienced writer states; the skilled writer forces the reader to share the work—to absorb the details and, from them, to draw a conclusion.

Vigor Through Verbs

Verbs are the power tools on a writer's workbench. Give them a chance and they will provide more action than a television camera.

Consider this incomplete sentence about Henry:

Henry _____ out of his house, _____ his dog, and _____ to the bank of the river.

Insert three weak verbs and you get this:

Henry *walked* out of his house, *called* to his dog, and *walked* to the bank of the river.

But three strong verbs can turn Henry into a happy boy:

Henry *dashed* out of his house, *whistled* to his dog, and *scampered* to the bank of the river.

Or, into an angry boy:

Henry *slammed* out of his house, *lashed* at his dog, and *strode* off to the bank of the river.

Or, into a sad boy:

Henry *moped* out of his house, *whined* at his dog, and *shuffled* to the bank of the river.

Notice that the structure of the sentence remains the same, the nouns are the same, but the verbs make the difference.

Here's a sentence for you to play with. This sentence includes three weak verbs. Replace them with three strong verbs to indicate a particular mood. (You may also change the prepositions, *down* and *to*.)

Geraldine *walked down* the street, *entered* the store, and *talked to* the butcher.

Geraldine _____ the street, _____ the store, and _____ the butcher.

Now indicate a different mood by using three different strong verbs.

Geraldine _____ the street, _____ the store, and _____ the butcher.

Once more—again different verbs for a different mood.

Geraldine _____ the street, _____ the store, and _____ the butcher.

As One Writer Put It . . .

In the following sentence from *Northwest Passage*, Kenneth Roberts could have used the verb "fell" three times. He chose not to use it at all and instead used three exact verbs to describe the action. Which verbs would you insert?

1 "I _____ after him, put my foot through a tangle of dead branches, _____ headlong and _____ against a tree with a thump that made me grunt."

After you have chosen your three verbs, compare them with the three Roberts actually used (see footnote #1).

Here are three more sentences from *Northwest Passage*. After each sentence, a weak verb is given as a clue. Insert the strong verb you would suggest.

2 "It was mid-afternoon when Ogden and I, standing on the high bank, _____ the three whaleboats heading in for Crown Point."

(Obvious choice: saw)

3 "He _____ upon me, _____ me sonorously, _____ down a full glass of flip to my health."

(Obvious choices: smiled; praised; drank)

4 "Water _____ from their beards and musket barrels."

(Obvious choice: fell)

Compare your choices with those of Kenneth Roberts. See footnotes #2, 3, and 4 below.

_____

#1. slid; pitched; rolled
#2. sighted
#3. beamed; toasted; tossed
#4. trickled

A Deluge of Details

Roger Marisot has just discovered that his last razor blade is too blunt to use.

WRITER A NOTES: Even though it was snowing and he really didn't want to go out, Roger went to the store for fresh blades. A promotion might depend on it.

WRITER B NOTES: Reluctantly, Roger laced up his boots and zipped his snorkel jacket. As he trudged through two feet of snow to Bick-Back's Five-and-Dime, he touched his chin tentatively. A fresh blade and a close shave, or—he winced bitterly—no promotion!

Which writer, A or B, makes you *see* Roger? Which makes you want to continue reading? B, of course! And B worked that magic by using details.

Here's another example:

WRITER A NOTES: Louis Mentone is a very wealthy man.

WRITER B NOTES: Louis Mentone has twelve homes, one for each month of the year. His "February home" is a thousand-acre spread in Arizona where even the cattle have their own carefully constructed swimming pool. There are two other pools for "ordinary" guests and one pool for the servants. The family pool is, of course, lined with gold. It has to be, claimed Mentone—for the comfort of the presidents and prime ministers and kings who frequently visit to consult him about international finance.

Notice that Writer B never mentioned that Louis Mentone is wealthy, but the carefully selected details impress you with his wealth as mere statement cannot.

Now you try it. We'll play Writer A; you play Writer B.

WRITER A NOTES: Steven Rawlins is a very poor man.

WRITER B NOTES: _____
_____
_____
_____
_____

Once more . . .

WRITER A NOTES: It was hot and humid, but Jennifer decided to go to the pool anyway. Maybe she would see Steve, the lifeguard, and be able to sell him the house in which he was interested.

WRITER B NOTES: _____
_____
_____
_____

Describing Action

Details can, in a sense, *create* action. In the short story, "Old Mortality," Katherine Anne Porter described the horses coming back after a race. She might have written: "The horses were coming in, looking hot and tired and sweaty." But she didn't. This is what she actually wrote:

> The horses were coming in, looking as if their hides had been drenched and rubbed with soap, their ribs heaving, their nostrils flaring and closing.

She makes you *see* the horses—in action. She does it by using details about their hides, their ribs, and their nostrils. She does it by using powerful verbs and present participles (the *-ing* form of verbs) to show that the action is *still* in progress.

Choose a bit of action with which you are familiar: perhaps your dog coming home after chasing a car; a football player making a tackle; a sophomore running down the hall trying to elude a band of roving juniors. Use Porter's sentence as a guide. Imitate her structure, but use your own details to describe an action.

_____

_____

_____

_____

Here's another example of details creating action. In *The Bolinvars*, Marguerite Bayliss described a fight between a horse and a wolf. The horse, at the moment, is the aggressor.

> She seized the red wolf. She shook it. She gave her head and her long muscular neck a twisting flip—and hurled the wolf some ten feet into the air, straight up.*

Like Porter, Bayliss used strong verbs: seized; shook; hurled. She used one participle: twisting. She used details: the *red* wolf; the horse's *long muscular neck*; the *twisting flip*; *ten feet* into the air. But she also used one other technique: two short sentences followed by a third sentence that is long but broken into three parts. By doing this, she gained intensity and urgency.

This time imitate Bayliss. Choose your own conflict: a fight between two animals, between two humans, or between a human and an animal. Again, imitate the structure but provide your own details.

_____

_____

_____

_____

_____

_____

Describing a Setting

Details can also *create* a setting.

The inexperienced writer might comment: "It was dawn, and all nature seemed alive."

But John Steinbeck knew better. In *The Pearl*, Steinbeck doesn't *tell* you that nature is alive; he *shows* you nature living. Like this:

> Kino awakened in the near dark. The stars still shone and the day had drawn only a pale wash of light in the lower sky to the east. The roosters had been crowing for some time, and the early pigs were already beginning their ceaseless turning of twigs and bits of wood to see whether anything to eat had been overlooked. Outside the brush house in the cactus clump, a covey of little birds chittered and flurried with their wings.*

Steinbeck used strong verbs and several participles. Above all, he used details.

You can do the same thing. You have learned to observe; use your observation. You have learned to see and to hear; use your senses. Use your memory and your journal. Select a different time of day: noon or dusk; or a different setting: a city street or a housing development near an industrial plant. Think! Which details would make your setting come alive? After you have decided, write a paragraph imitating Steinbeck's structure.

_____

_____

_____

_____

_____

_____

_____

_____

Before you continue with this chapter, read over the last three paragraphs you have written. Aren't they smoother, more vivid, more professional than your writing generally is? They should be, and if they are—you are progressing nicely to your goal.

Drama Through Dialogue

Another technique that will help you to show rather than to tell your story is dialogue. We will be looking closely at dialogue in a later chapter; now we will consider it only as an illustrative technique.

Here's a paragraph from a story that might have been printed in any school or town newspaper:

_____

Bob DeLuca dropped the basketball through the hoop just in time to rack up the winning points for his team against the Brambles. As the boys headed for the locker room, Bob was shouting with joy. They had won—against all the odds.

There's nothing wrong with that story, but if we add a touch of dialogue (for example, a verbatim quotation) we also add zest and action. Like this:

Bob DeLuca dropped the basketball through the hoop just in time to rack up the winning points for his team against the Brambles. As the boys headed for the locker room, Bob shouted: "We won! We really won!" Then, as his teammates pounded him happily on the back, he continued, almost in a whisper: "They said we couldn't do it, but we did!"

Much more effective, isn't it? Those few words in quotation marks put the reader on the scene, hearing, caring, sharing.

Your chance now. Choose one tiny incident that you witnessed in the last few days. Perhaps you were with your friend when he opened an envelope and discovered he had passed his driving test. Perhaps you overheard a classmate crow with delight when she received her very first "A" in science. Describe the incident briefly, ending with a verbatim quotation that acts as the punch line.

_____

_____

_____

_____

_____

_____

_____

Drama Through Illustrative Examples

One more technique that will help you place your reader in the middle of the action is the *illustrative example*. Suppose you are describing a mob scene. You note that 2,000 people were involved and that more than 100 were injured. Your reader says "Isn't that awful?" and yawns.

The numbers by themselves carry some impact but not enough.

But suppose, instead, after mentioning that 2,000 people were involved and more than 100 injured, you added:

Among the injured were three children. Susie Chilton, age 5, had one leg broken. As she waited for the ambulance, Susie cried quietly, her small, pain-twisted face pressed against the stuffed panda that she clutched. Timmy Billings, also 5, had a four-inch cut across his forehead. "I'm a big boy," Timmy said, fighting hard against his tears. "Big boys don't cry." And Carol Doyle, not yet 2. Carol lay in her mother's arms, too frightened and too confused to cry, her right arm crushed beyond repair. "She was just learning to feed herself," her mother said tearfully.

You see the difference? Giving concrete, well-chosen examples will take more thinking, more investigating, more time; but it is well worth it if it helps your readers become directly involved.

Make each of the following statements effective by providing two or three examples:

As the army retreated, thousands of people were left homeless. Among them

_____

_____

_____

_____

_____

_____

_____

Twelve Americans returned from the Olympics last night, all bearing gold medals. Before the ship had even docked, reporters surrounded them.

_____

_____

_____

_____

_____

_____

_____

_____

These are among the most important techniques to master—if you really want to write well:

> *image-making*
> *strong verbs*
> *present participles (-ing verbs)*
> *details*
> *dialogue*
> *illustrative examples*

Remember them. Use them deliberately until you begin to use them automatically. And, in time, you will know how to follow Mark Twain's advice: "Bring the old lady on and let her scream."

24. MARASCHINOS AND MARSHMALLOWS

A maraschino cherry is red, shiny, and firm to the touch. Press it lightly, and it will yield a few drops of juice. Press it hard and it will squash.

A marshmallow is white, not shiny, and floppy to the touch. Press it lightly or hard and it will flatten, then spring part-way back.

Two sweets, both different in every way.

As you start to write—a story, a poem, an article, even a filler—you will have to decide what mood or tone you want: the maraschino or the marshmallow.

If you are going to write a light, cheerful story (maraschino style), you will, of course, want to maintain a light, cheerful tone. If you are going to write a solemn or sentimental story (marshmallow style), you will want to maintain a solemn or sentimental tone.

In either case the tone must be unified, integrated, and related. A *white* maraschino cherry would be disturbing; so would a *juicy* marshmallow. The tone must be consistent, and any exceptions must be deliberate and for a specific purpose.

How exactly does one go about creating a tone or mood? Edgar Allan Poe insisted (and most writers agree) that you must first determine which effect you desire: the melancholy, the cynical, the amusing. The rest of the recipe follows.

1 Select a setting appropriate to the tone.
2 Select characters and/or incidents that will contribute to the tone.
3 Use an abundance of suitable details.
4 Choose words carefully, almost one by one.
5 Modify your own basic writing rhythm with the desired tone in mind.
6 Lace with small, occasional doses of suggestiveness.

Now that you have the recipe (and it probably seems intolerably complicated!), let's proceed to a visual "for instance."

Here are a house and a garbage can.

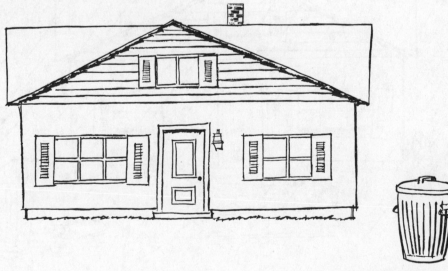

Notice that the two objects appear almost in a vacuum. We know we are dealing with a one-story house and an ordinary garbage can. That's all we know.

To provide a *setting*, we'll add some rain, one small dying tree stripped of leaves, and a muddy, broken front walk.

It's more promising now, isn't it? But not clear enough. It needs *details*, carefully chosen to build to one effect. We'll throw the cover off the garbage can and dent it a bit. The can is overflowing, showing above its top rim a bag bursting with garbage, a carton, an empty bottle. On the ground around the can is more garbage: orange peels,

egg shells, coffee grounds, dirty wet pieces of paper. In the front yard, to the left of the walk, is a child's tricycle, lying on its side, one wheel missing. The frame is rusted, the rubber holders on the handlebars worn and ripped. The grass is patchy—sparse; and the weeds have clearly taken over. In all the windows, the shades are drawn down almost to the sill.

Much more promising! It's developing a tone, a mood. Let's open the door (make it sag as it opens) and find ourselves a *character*. A man appears. (*Add details.*) He's fat, about 48; his broken suspenders are knotted and his pants sagging. He's unshaven; his eyes are bleary with sleep and drink, the lids low and heavy—like the drawn shades on the window. (Ah, there's a possibility—to draw a comparison between the man and the house: the sagging door and the sagging pants; the low-shaded windows and the heavy-lidded eyes, etc.) His hair is sparse and in tufts (like the grass).

You try it. On the following pages are three houses and three garbage cans. Add the ingredients requested in pictures 1, 2, and 3. On the lines below each picture, note briefly what you have added. (Don't fret if you have no drawing ability. Just do your best. Imagination will often compensate for lack of ability!)

1 Provide a setting for a happy, pleasant story.

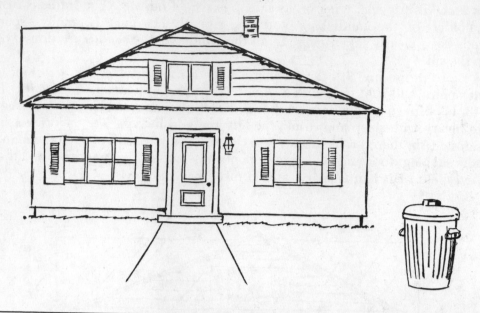

_____

_____

_____

_____

2 Add details to strengthen the cheerful tone.

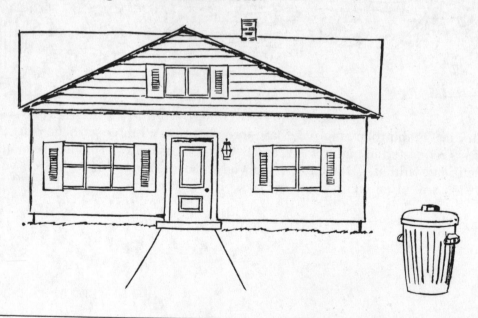

_____

_____

_____

_____

3 Add one or more characters that complement and emphasize the cheerful tone.

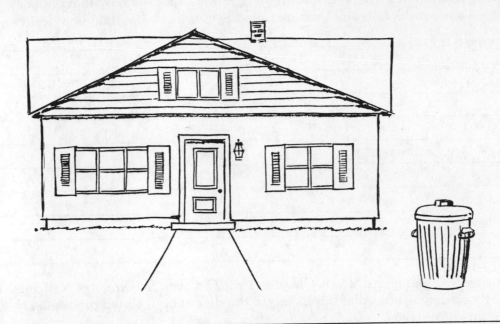

_____

_____

_____

_____

And that's about as far as we can go *visually*. We'll switch now to the verbal—for, whereas the artist has a limited canvas, the writer has an unlimited one. Here are several sketches of buildings intended to set a tone.

First, a paragraph from "The Fall of the House of Usher" by Edgar Allan Poe. This one sentence sets the tone for the entire story.

> I looked upon the scene before me—upon the mere house, and the simple landscape features of the domain—upon the bleak walls—upon the vacant eye-like windows—upon a few rank sedges—and upon a few white trunks of decayed trees—with an utter depression of soul . . .*

- Notice how Poe used details: the walls, the windows, the sedges, the trees.

- Notice how he used words: bleak, vacant, rank, decayed.

- Notice the rhythmical structure: parallel structure in which detail builds on detail until a totality of tone is reached: "an utter depression of soul."

---

*From "The Fall of the House of Usher," by Edgar Allan Poe, in THE WORKS OF EDGAR ALLAN POE IN ONE VOLUME. Copyright 1927. Reprinted by permission of Walter J. Black, Inc.

Imitate Poe's structure, using *your* house (figure #3, preceding page) or any other house seen with your mind's eye. Poe's desired effect was a melancholy tone. Specify yours. Then use your own details and your own words to achieve the tone you desire.

YOUR DESIRED EFFECT _____

YOUR DESCRIPTION _____

_____

_____

_____

_____

_____

_____

_____

Next, here's a paragraph from Chapter 1 of *The Scarlet Letter* by Nathaniel Hawthorne. By adding a little philosophizing to the description, Hawthorne quickly set the tone for an entire novel.

> ... the wooden jail was already marked with weather-stains and other indications of age, which gave a yet darker aspect to its beetle-browed and gloomy front. The rust on the ponderous iron-work of its oaken door looked more antique than anything else in the new world. Like all that pertains to crime, it seemed never to have known a youthful era. Before this ugly edifice, and between it and the wheel-track of the street, was a grass-plot, much overgrown with burdock, pig-weed, apple-peru, and such unsightly vegetation, which evidently found something congenial in the soil that had so early borne the black flower of civilized society, a prison. But, on one side of the portal, and rooted almost at the threshold, was a wild rose-bush, covered, in this month of June, with its delicate gems, which might be imagined to offer their fragrance and fragile beauty to the prisoner as he went in, and to the condemned criminal as he came forth to his doom, in token that the deep heart of Nature could pity and be kind to him.*

- Notice how Hawthorne used details: the burdock and pig-weed; the wheel-track of the street; the rust.

- Notice how he used words: beetle-browed, gloomy, rust, ponderous, black flower, fragile beauty.

- Notice the rhythmical structure: long, rich sentences, heavy with clauses and phrases that flow, but with little movement.

---

*From Norton Critical Edition of *The Scarlet Letter*, An Annotated Text, Backgrounds and Sources, Essays in Criticism, edited by Professors Bradley, Beatty, and Long. Copyright © 1961, 1962 by W. W. Norton & Company, Inc. It is reprinted here by permission of W. W. Norton & Company, Inc.

- Notice the contrast: after the description of the jail, the rose-bush; after the ponderous iron-work, delicate gems.
- Notice the philosophizing: the jail is the "black flower of civilized society"; Nature pities the criminal (though humans may judge and condemn).

In *The Scarlet Letter*, Hawthorne's desired effect was to portray good and evil in all their complexity, for good sometimes looks like evil, and evil like good. On the very first page of Chapter 1, with this vivid description, Hawthorne prepares us for what is coming.

Imitate Hawthorne's description *loosely*, using any interesting building you have seen or can imagine. Aim for contrast: the beautiful and the ugly, the exotic and the ordinary.

YOUR DESIRED EFFECT _____

YOUR DESCRIPTION _____

_____

_____

_____

_____

_____

_____

_____

_____

_____

Finally, here's a third building—but a very different kind of one. Shirley Jackson in her short story, "The Possibility of Evil," wants her tale to begin in a quiet, friendly atmosphere.

> The perfume of roses meant home, and home meant the Strangeworth House on Pleasant Street. Miss Strangeworth stopped at her own front gate, as she always did, and looked with deep pleasure at her house, with the red and pink and white roses massed along the narrow lawn, and the rambler going up along the porch; and the neat, the unbelievably trim lines of the house itself, with its slimness and its washed white look. Every window sparkled, every curtain hung stiff and straight, and even the stones of the front walk were swept and clear. People around town wondered how old Miss Strangeworth managed to keep the house looking the way it did, and there was a legend about a tourist once mistaking it for the local museum and going all through the place without finding out about his mistake.*

---

*THE POSSIBILITY OF EVIL by Shirley Jackson. Copyright © 1965 by Stanley Edgar Hyman. Reprinted by permission of Brandt & Brandt.

Read that paragraph twice more. It is a friendly and quiet house, isn't it? Earlier, we mentioned the use of suggestiveness in setting tone. The details, the words, even the rhythm indicate order and pleasure, and yet—and yet something wrong is *suggested*. We *know* it as we read. Analysis shows us that Jackson's desired effect is goodness undershot by a suspicion of evil. The lines of the house are *unbelievably* trim; *every* window sparkles; *every* curtain hangs *stiff* and *straight*. There's something inhuman about this lovely house—a willingness to sacrifice all that is merely human in order to adhere to the pattern. The last sentence of the paragraph emphasizes the same thought, but it may be too obvious. The house is not a home but a museum—not a shelter for the living, but an exhibit case for the dying and the dead. All of this is suggested, not said.

Shirley Jackson knows how to write ... she is worth imitating. Choose a building that is not what it seems to be. Describe it as it *seems* to be, letting what it *is* be suggested by key words and perhaps an occasional detail. This is not an easy assignment. (Some possibilities: a school building is a place where young people grow into free and rational adults; a hospital is a place where the ill become healthy.)

YOUR DESIRED EFFECT _____

YOUR DESCRIPTION _____

_____

_____

_____

_____

_____

_____

_____

_____

_____

_____

_____

We repeat—the tone of any piece of writing must be unified and integrated; it must be consistent. Tone or mood is not so simple and clear-cut as the maraschino cherry or the marshmallow with which we began this chapter. Sometimes you will *need* a white cherry or a juicy marshmallow. Fine ... as long as you know what you are doing, as long as the strange-looking sweet is not the result of ignorance.

Later, quite a bit later, you will want deliberately to violate tone in order to create several layers of suspense. But for now—keep your tone consistent and true; savor the maraschino and the marshmallow!

25. CUTTING TO THE BONE

Ms. Shakespeare, your English teacher, assigned a composition. "Write 250 words about . . ."

Now, thirty minutes later, you sit at your desk, counting . . . 247 - 248 - 249. Gloom overwhelms you; thunderclouds loom. You sit, staring at the wall. Then inspiration hits! You grab your pen, stick an *and* into one sentence and a *but* into another! Hallelujah! You've made it—251 words!

You've made it! Right?

Wrong.

Now that you have succeeded in putting words together effectively, your next step is to learn when to take words out. And the first two words to cut would be those late additions inserted for padding, *and* and *but*. So, you see, you are back to 249!

Revision is an art; in this chapter we will concentrate primarily on one aspect of revision: cutting. Almost any piece of writing can be improved by merciless (but judicious) cutting. Look at it this way. You can draw a line between two posts

like this   or   like this.

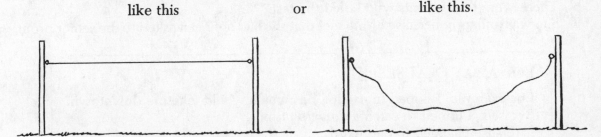

If you draw it *taut* (left figure), the line has snap, resiliency, and sharpness of profile. If you don't draw it taut (right figure), the line is limp, saggy, and blurred.

Your writing, too, should be taut, and that requires that you cut all non-essentials.

Surplus Surgery

Role-play a tree surgeon.

LOP AWAY REDUNDANCIES: UNNECESSARY REPETITION.

    For example: He repeated ~~again~~ . . .

Repeat means to state again. Therefore "to repeat again" means to state *again again*. Is *again* necessary after *repeat*? Excise it. (Cut it out.)

    For example: the cucumber was green ~~in color~~.

Green *is* a color. Why add "in color"? Excise it.

In the following sentences, excise redundancies:

1 During the exam she referred back to her notes.
2 At the five-and-dime he purchased five round balls.
3 If we cooperate together, we can win!
4 His final conclusion was that he should resign immediately.
5 In my opinion, I think everyone should graduate at the end of four years.
6 The box that arrived in the mail was square in shape.

LOP AWAY EXCESS WORDS. Sometimes we simply use too many words for the job.

> For example: The reason why he didn't go to the Broadway opening was because he had no money.

Excise "The reason why"—they add nothing to the sentence. Then excise "was." Your revised sentence: He didn't go to the Broadway opening because he had no money. Isn't it clearer, simpler, and more effective?

In the following sentences, excise unnecessary words:

7 It was in 1960 that John Fitzgerald Kennedy was elected President.
8 There were ten students who failed the test.
9 Sue was unhappy because of the fact that she had not been asked to the senior prom.

LOP AWAY CLAUSES.

For example: I hoped to catch a bus which would take me downtown.
Revised: I hoped to catch a *downtown* bus.
    (clause changed to one word)

Another example: When the sun rises, the birds begin to sing.
Revised: *At sunrise*, the birds begin to sing.
    (clause changed to prepositional phrase)

In the following sentences, reduce the clauses to single words or prepositional phrases:

10 The boys who had run away were returned to their parents.

_____

11 When autumn comes, the leaves turn red and gold.

_____

12 Joe won the election by a majority that was very small.

_____

13 When he was almost at the finish line, the miler collapsed from heat exhaustion.

_____

More Sophisticated Surgery

If this were a course in grammar, we would continue with more examples. But it is a course in creative writing, and that is quite different. You may want to use a clause instead of a phrase, you may want to use a few words that are not essential to the sense of a sentence, but are to the rhythm. (Of course, even a creative writer will *never* be guilty of using redundancies!)

As a creative writer, you must keep in mind the rhythm of the writing, the style, the content, and the intent. You must act not as a tree surgeon but as a neurosurgeon. You may eliminate an adjective because it is weak, a second adjective because it is overwhelming, or an entire phrase simply because it is intrusive or ineffective.

Take a look at this paragraph from a D. H. Lawrence manuscript. This is exactly as he wrote it in his first draft.*

> There the daffodils were lifting their glorious heads and throwing — S. 1
> back their wanton yellow curls to sport with the sun. At the foot of each — S. 2
> sloping, grey old tree a family of these healthy, happy flowers stood,
> some bursten with overfulness of splendour, some raising their heads
> slightly, modestly showing a sweet countenance, others still hiding their
> faces, leaning forward from the jaunty cluster of grey-green spears;
> many were just venturing timidly out of their sheaths, peeping about. I — S. 3
> felt inclined to hug them, I wanted desperately to know their language
> perfectly so that I might talk out my heart to them . . . They had a rich — S. 4
> perfume as of oranges; they laughed to me, and tried to reassure me . . .

Even at a first reading, one knows the description is too lush, too burdened with adjectives and personification. Let's see what D. H. Lawrence did with it as he revised. (As you study the notes below, you may find it helpful to make excisions, etc., in the original paragraph above. For example, draw a line through the adjective *glorious*.)

	REVISIONS	PROBABLE REASONS
		(although only the author knows *why* he changed something)
Sentence #1:	The adjectives, *glorious* and *wanton*, eliminated.	They slow down the pace and are unnecessary.
	The five words, *to sport with the sun*, eliminated.	Unnecessary. This is already implied.

---

*From THE FRIEDA LAWRENCE COLLECTION OF D. H. LAWRENCE MANUSCRIPTS: *A Descriptive Bibliography* by E. W. Tedlock, Jr. Copyright 1948 by the University of New Mexico Press and reprinted by their permission.

Sentence #2:	Three modifiers of "flowers"—*these, healthy, happy*—eliminated.	Weak adjectives; added nothing to the impact of the sentence.
	Reversed order of subject and verb to *stood a family of flowers*.	Places *flowers* where it should be: immediately preceding a description of them.
	overfulness of splendour changed to *golden fullness*.	Simpler; less overwhelming.
	raising changed to *lifting*.	A lighter verb.
	Participial phrase, *modestly showing a sweet countenance* changed to infinitive phrase: *to show a modest, sweet countenance*.	Smoother; wording less intrusive; more compact.
	Adverb *pensively* added after *leaning forward*.	Better for sentence rhythm; contributes a new feeling to the description.
	cluster of eliminated.	*jaunty grey-green spears* is sharper, more effective.
	many were just venturing timidly out of their sheaths, peeping about eliminated.	Personification too obvious, almost cloying.
Sentence #3:	*I felt inclined to hug them* eliminated.	Clause is childish—over-emotional.
	I wanted desperately moderated to *I wished*.	The wanting isn't lessened by the change, but a wistful quality is added.
	so that I might talk out my heart to them changed to *to talk to them distinctly*.	This further tempers the tone. The understatement has greater impact than the gushing of the first version.
Sentence #4:	Entire sentence eliminated.	Personification overdone; cloying; emotionalism rampant. The sentence detracts rather than enhances the tone.

Here is the revised paragraph from the novel, *The White Peacock*.

There the daffodils were lifting their heads and throwing back their yellow curls. At the foot of each sloping, grey old tree stood a family of flowers, some bursten with golden fullness, some lifting their heads slightly, to show a modest, sweet countenance; others still hiding their faces, leaning forward pensively from the jaunty grey-green spears; I wished I had their language, to talk to them distinctly.*

*From THE FRIEDA LAWRENCE COLLECTION OF D. H. LAWRENCE MANUSCRIPTS: *A Descriptive Bibliography* by E. W. Tedlock, Jr. Copyright 1948 by the University of New Mexico Press and reprinted by their permission.

Obviously Lawrence wanted to show not only the closeness of nature but also its separateness from humans. His first attempt made nature overwhelming; we lose sight of his purpose. His revision, as you have seen, was primarily an exercise in cutting. How hard it must have been to that still young writer to throw away so many emotionally packed words! But, by doing so, he achieved a tighter, more intense emotion.

What Lawrence did with this paragraph from *The White Peacock* is what every writer must learn to do: to cut mercilessly so that the fine, clean bone structure appears.

Now let's see how well you have learned your lesson. Here is a passage from Hemingway's story, "The Snows of Kilimanjaro." The passage describes a man's thoughts as he faces almost certain death. Hemingway would probably not recognize the paragraph as it appears here. Words, phrases, even clauses have been added. Your task is to strip away the additions, leaving the bare, stark writing for which Hemingway is noted.

So now it was all over, he thought grimly. So now he would never have

a chance to finish it—the life he had enjoyed in huge, never-satisfied gulps.

So this was the way it ended in a stupid bickering over a final drink. Since

the gangrene—a disgusting, eroding, corroding decay—started in his right

leg he had no pain at all and with the scathing pain gone the horror had

also gone and all he felt now was a great weary tiredness and a bitter rag-

ing anger that this was the end of it all. For this, that now was coming, he

had very little curiosity of any kind. For years it had obsessed him, day

and night; he had been able to think of little else; but now it meant nothing

in itself. When you thought about it, it was strange how easy being tired

enough made it.

Printed below is the paragraph *as Hemingway wrote it*. Compare your revised edition with the original. How close did you come? Before you consider this experiment closed, read aloud the padded paragraph and the original. Can you hear the difference? Can you discern the slower, more uneven rhythm of the first, the sharper rhythm of the second? Can you *feel* the value of understatement in the original, so that the description of the coming of death parallels the character's attitude toward death?

So now it was all over, he thought. So now he would never have a chance to finish it. So this was the way it ended in a bickering over a drink. Since the gangrene started in his right leg he had no pain and with the pain the horror had gone and all he felt now was a great tiredness and anger that this was the end of it. For this, that now was coming, he had very little curiosity. For years it had obsessed him; but now it meant nothing in itself. It was strange how easy being tired enough made it.*

*From "The Snows of Kilimanjaro," by Ernest Hemingway, from THE SHORT STORIES OF ERNEST HEMINGWAY, copyright 1936. Reprinted by permission of Charles Scribner's Sons.

Play the Critic

When you revise your own writing, you have to play critic to your own creation. And this is exceedingly difficult. It is easier to play the critic with others. Keeping in mind all you have learned about words and the combining of words as well as about cutting, try to solve the following problems:

1 F. Scott Fitzgerald wrote a sentence and then revised it for his story, "Crazy Sunday." Below are the two versions, not necessarily in the order written.*

   a Joel knew that this probably wasn't gibberish and yet it sounded like gibberish.

   b Joel knew that this probably wasn't gibberish and yet it didn't sound right.

   Which version is better? _____ Why? _____
   _____
   _____

2 Here are three excerpts (with revisions noted) from a recently written short story. In each case suggest a logical reason for the change.

   a She had to do the thinking for both of them. It was unusual—usually he did the thinking.

   (Revision: *unusual* changed to *uncomfortable*.)

   _____
   _____
   _____

   b For a long five minutes she stared at the cruel-edged rocks below.

   (Revision: *cruel-edged* changed to *shark-like*.)

   _____
   _____
   _____

   c She liked the crisp white apron and the yellow uniform she wore at Sheryl's; and the way the customers laughed and were happy.

   (Revision: the phrase, *and were happy*, was replaced by the clause, *when they ordered BLT's with a dash of TLC*.)

   _____
   _____
   _____

_____

*Fitzgerald sentences: as noted in WRITING, REVISING, AND EDITING, produced by Gordon Carroll with the cooperation of the Famous Writers School. Copyright 1969, Doubleday & Company, Inc.

3   Henry David Thoreau regularly kept a journal; later bits of this journal would turn up, revised, in a finished piece of work. Of the two excerpts below, the first is a journal entry from March 3, 1841; the second is a sentence from *A Week on the Concord and Merrimack Rivers*, published in 1849.

> And now I see the beauty and full meaning of that word sound. Nature always possesses a certain sonorousness, as in the hum of insects— the booming of ice—the crowing of cocks in the morning and the barking of dogs in the night—which indicates her sound state.[1]

> All these sounds, the crowing of cocks, the baying of dogs, and the hum of insects at noon, are the evidence of nature's health or *sound* state.[2]

Why did Thoreau add "at noon" after "the hum of insects"?

_____

_____

_____

Why did he change "the barking of dogs" to the "baying of dogs"?

_____

_____

_____

Why did he eliminate "in the morning" after "the crowing of cocks"?

_____

_____

_____

Why did he italicize *sound* in the finished work, but not in the journal entry?

_____

_____

_____

4   In Chapter 21, page 143, you wrote a miniature essay about a painful experience. Later in the same chapter you checked it for use of parallelism (page 144) and transitions (page 146). Now turn to it again. Study it closely. Then revise, cutting unnecessary words or redundant expressions; eliminating or adding details; substituting a strong word for a weak one. Remember: we warned you—playing critic to your own writing is painful, but it is also essential. If you cannot turn a sharp, ruthless eye on your own work, you have little chance of becoming a really fine writer.

[1,2]From Carl F. Hovde, "Nature into Art: Thoreau's Use of His Journals in *A Week*," *American Literature* 30:168 and 30:169, respectively. Copyright 1958, Duke University Press.

Copy your final revision below.

_____

_____

_____

_____

_____

_____

_____

_____

_____

_____

_____

_____

_____

_____

_____

_____

_____

_____

Finished? Good. Tired of it? Bored with it? Take heart. Lafcadio Hearn once revised a paragraph *seventeen* times; and the great Tolstoy kept rewriting until he caught himself replacing the vivid with the dull! Often, as a writer, you must bore yourself—in order to keep your reader from becoming bored.

Unit V
Developing a Sense of the Comic

LAUGHTER IS CONTAGIOUS.

182

1 *The Joke's on You.*   Do you have a sense of humor? (Yes or no) _____

   Answer these questions:

   a   Do you enjoy professional comics? _____

   b   Do you enjoy telling jokes? _____

   c   Do you try to remember jokes? _____

   d   Do you like slapstick comedy (e.g., pie in the face)? _____

   e   Do you indulge in exaggeration, just for fun? _____

   f   Do you relish wordplay (puns, etc.)? _____

   g   Do you laugh silently or aloud, or not at all? _____

   Now answer the question again. Do you have a sense of humor? _____
   Warning: it's hard to admit that you don't. But it's good (and useful) to know the
   truth about yourself.

2 *Joke Laboratory.*   On a cassette tape, record the laughter of a group of people.
   The tape should be about one minute in length. Play this tape to at least ten people.
   Summarize their reactions. Examples: one person might roar with delight,
   another might chuckle, still another might stare into space, obviously not amused,
   etc.

   _____

   _____

   _____

   Is laughter contagious? _____ Why? (No one knows for sure, but suggest a possible reason.)

   _____

   _____

3 *Joke Survey.*   Write down your favorite joke.

   _____

   _____

   _____

   Now tell the joke to at least ten people of varying ages and types (e.g., a small boy,
   a teen-age girl, your mother, a teacher, etc.). Describe briefly the various reactions.

   _____

   _____

   _____

Any conclusion? _____

_____

4 *Joke Probe*.   Check the card catalog in your school or community library. List all books cataloged under comedy, humor, joke, or wit. Follow up cross-references.

How many titles were you able to find? _____ Does the number surprise you? _____ Why, or why not? _____

_____

5 *The Joke Practical*.   List two practical jokes, or dirty tricks, you have heard of.

_____

_____

_____

_____

Examine them carefully. What common characteristic do they possess? _____

_____

Explain briefly. _____

_____

Keeping your own explanation in mind, devise two original practical jokes.

_____

_____

_____

_____

6 *The Joke Riddle*.   Accumulate (through library research or from people you know) at least a dozen riddles. Try them on your friends and family. Copy below the riddle that was most successful: i.e., enjoyed by most.

_____

_____

Explain *why* it was the most successful.

_____

Now copy the riddle that was least successful.

_____

_____

Explain *why* it was the least successful.

_____

7 *The Joke Juvenile*. Children see (or mis-see) things with a freshness that is often humorous. One child defined an elevator as a little house in which the upstairs comes down. Another child, asked to list the kinds of beans he had heard of, wrote: "Lima beans, string beans, and human beans."

Compose a couple of Jokes Juvenile, using either the zany definition or the misunderstood-word approach.

_____

_____

_____

_____

8 *Joke Ancestry*. No one really knows how the joke first came into existence, but anthropologists suspect that it was born at about the same time humans were. "Dream" yourself back to the cave and prehistoric times. Create an incident which "explains" the origin of the joke. In other words, create the very *first* joke and its background.

_____

_____

_____

_____

9 *Joke Evolution: Part I*. Read any humorous short story; then condense it into a joke. Write the title and author of the story and "your" joke below.

_____

_____

_____

_____

10 *Joke Evolution: Part II*. Write down your favorite joke.

_____

_____

_____

Now expand your joke into a 50- to 100-word anecdote, using the punch line of the joke as the punch line of your story.

_____

_____

_____

_____

_____

26. THE ABSURDITY OF IT

Life is absurd. Even everyday life is full of contradictions, odd coincidences, and unexpected events.

You reach for a phone to call Diane. The phone rings. It's Diane. You tell her you were about to call her. You both laugh.

You need a new wallet. You know you had an extra one. You search through closets. You grope through drawers. You ask people. You can't find it. You go to the store and hand over cash for a new wallet. You go home, fill in the cards, and transfer your money. You open your desk drawer—there's the "extra" wallet. You laugh (ruefully).

You are watching a basketball game. The players run out on the floor. All of the team members are six feet tall—except one, the mascot. He's two feet tall. You laugh.

A visitor to your school walks across the stage to the podium. He is beautifully dressed and his stride is proud and sure. He steps on a bit of waxed paper and slides six feet before landing on his posterior. You laugh.

You are introduced to a lovely, frail-looking woman, about five feet tall. The person who introduces you mentions that she is the finest jackhammer operator in the city, and that she's currently engaged in digging a ditch for a cable conduit. You laugh.

Why do humans laugh? And what do we laugh at? If you look closely at the five anecdotes above, you will see they share one characteristic: the unexpected, the incongruous. In each case something happened that we did not expect to happen, something violated the pattern of life.

The Comedy Angle

You can't become a comic unless you learn to think like a comic—and that means developing your own angle of comedy, your own way of perceiving the humorous in the world around you. You have already sharpened your senses; now continue, this time, noticing and recording the incongruous.

A Practice Session

For example, two men enter a room. One is beautifully dressed, well-mannered, and careful in his speech. The other is wearing dirty rags, has the juice from chewing tobacco dribbling down his chin, and grunts a lot. On a platter on the table are two turkey legs. Each man grabs a leg and starts tearing the meat off with his teeth. If you wanted to write a humorous anecdote about this, which man would you write about: the gentleman or the tramp? Why?

_____

_____

For example, you are writing a humorous sci-fi story. You are planning to have a spaceship from Saturn land on Earth. Would it be funnier to have it land (*a*) in a lonely field in Iowa or (*b*) in the middle of a lawn party on Long Island's swank North Shore? Why?

_____

_____

This World of Men and Women

A man will use a sledgehammer, and a woman will use a frying pan in this best of all possible worlds. Even as the battle continues for equal rights for women, social conventions lock us into specific roles. Anyone who breaks from the role suggests the incongruous—and becomes a target for humorists. As a writer, you can use your awareness of this to create comedy.

Your character is a male, 6'2", broad and muscular. You want to poke fun at him. You can do this by providing incongruous details. The following questions should help:

What is his occupation? (Sample answer: waiting on tables in a tiny tea shop that caters

to women) _____

What does he most enjoy eating? _____

What is his favorite hobby? _____

How does he walk? _____

This time your character is a female, 5'4", petite, pretty, and apparently frail. Answer the same questions about her, each time providing incongruous details:

What is her occupation? _____

What does she most enjoy eating? _____

What is her favorite hobby? _____

How does she walk? _____

Do you get the idea? If a professor is pedantic, it is not very funny; but if a five-year-old speaks in a pedantic manner, *that* is funny.

Candid Camera

Just about everyone has seen or heard about the television show, Candid Camera. It takes a good deal of comic ingenuity to come up with the situations they use. One segment showed a woman insisting that the gas tank of her compact car would take up to fifty gallons of gas. The gas station attendant, of course, was skeptical, and the resulting comedy lay in the bewildered expression on his face as gallons of gas continued to flow into the apparently bottomless tank. (Actually, of course, an auxiliary tank had been attached to the standard tank.) Another segment showed babies wailing, as a tape in the background played arias from well-known operas.

Practice your mastery of the incongruous by suggesting three situations that could be developed into humorous skits for Candid Camera. Concentrate on the places and people that you know. Example: Borrow a precocious six-year-old to masquerade as the principal of your school. Place the child in the principal's chair and have the school secretary take in visitors, one at a time. Imagine the facial expressions of the adults and their stammering speech as they see that "Dr. Jones" is a small girl or boy!

1 _____
_____
_____
_____

2 _____
_____
_____
_____

3 _____
_____
_____
_____

Animal Antics

Animals aren't funny—not in their natural state. Describe a poodle in a short story (almost everybody likes dogs!), and your readers will glow with interest but they won't laugh. Have the poodle don trousers and a top hat as it brings in its master's paper and your readers will chuckle! The reason? In the second case, the animal is aping a human—and that's always funny! It's incongruity again: someone or something doing what it doesn't normally do. Just for fun—and to hone your sense of the ludicrous—see if you can make each of the following animals funny by having each ape a human in appearance or action:

1 a turtle _____
_____

2 a monkey _____
_____

3 an elephant _____
_____

4 a mouse _____
_____

5 a bear _____
_____

This works with inanimate objects, too. A house becomes funny when its windows and door ape a human's grin; a garbage can becomes funny when its tipped lid reminds one of a rakish hat on a human head! Incongruity is the key; it will unlock many a laugh.

Comic Techniques

Now that you know how to spot the comic, the next problem is—how to express it. You have undoubtedly heard someone tell a hilarious story and tell it so ineptly that no one laughed. (And isn't that a horrible experience!) Here are a couple of techniques that should help you keep the humor in "humorous."

The Role of Repetition

Repetition is funny—sometimes. If thirty cars stop, one after another, at a stop sign, that's not funny. But if a woman in church takes off and then replaces her hat thirty times, everyone around her will be trying to smother their giggles. The woman's behavior is unexpected, abnormal, incongruous.

With words, the same rule works. You can repeat "the" or "and" or "a" one hundred times and it won't bring a chuckle; but the right word or phrase repeated half a dozen times will have your readers in hysterics.

You can do it with a pair of ordinary words like "orange juice."

> He awakened, stretched out his hand, and found his morning eye-opener . . . orange juice. He drank deeply. Ah, orange juice! How refreshing, how cool, how delicious. Outside, the sun burned with mid-summer intensity, its rays as dazzling and bright as . . . orange juice. He shook his head; he had to stop thinking about orange juice. Orange juice wouldn't solve his problem. The clock (orange like orange juice) shouted that it was ten-thirty. In a few minutes his boss would be calling. He got out of bed and shrugged his arms into an orange robe—almost the color of orange juice, he noticed irritably. He had to think. He had to have an answer ready.

The humor in that paragraph comes from the repetition of the two words, *orange juice*. Repetition as a humorous device is far more effective, though, when it occurs within a complete essay or short story. To see it at its best, read the essay "Pigs Is Pigs" by Ellis Parker Butler.

Try it anyhow. Choose a word or short phrase that you consider promising. Then build a paragraph in which you use that word or phrase at least five times. Aim for a mildly humorous tone.

_____

_____

_____

_____

_____

_____

_____

_____

_____

_____

_____

_____

_____

The Absurd Analogy

In Chapter 18, page 122, we talked about how the carefully developed analogy can clarify thinking and facilitate communication. An analogy that is absurd can do something else: it can add humor to your writing.

In the 1660's, Samuel Butler wrote a mock-heroic epic poem of more than 10,000 lines. His "hero" was Hudibras, a long-faced pedant whose pretentious speech made him a target for comic darts. Butler describes him as speaking Greek "as naturally as pigs squeak." Later he asserts that Hudibras is so clever he can measure pots of ale "by geometric scale," and can tell what hour the clock strikes "by algebra."

One of the most memorable comic touches comes, though, in Part II of the poem. You have read many descriptions of the rising sun—descriptions that dwell on its beauty and rest on lovely, even divine similes. Here's how Butler described it.

> And, like a lobster, boiled the morn
> From black to red began to turn.

Notice that the simile (or analogy) is strictly accurate. With the dawn, black does indeed turn to red; so does a lobster, with boiling. But we are not used to such a homely comparison. Instead of admiring, we guffaw—which is precisely what Butler wanted us to do.

One more example before you get to work. Many people (non-Germans) have noted with despair the great distance between the subject and the verb in a German sentence. Mark Twain, wishing to make the same comment, compared the German to a strange creature of the sea:

> Whenever the literary German dives into a sentence, that is the last you are going to see of him until he emerges on the other side of the Atlantic with his verb in his mouth.*

When an analogy is really a simile, a short sentence can pack long humor. To wit:

He felt like the symptoms on a medicine bottle. (George Ade)

His face fell like a cookbook cake. (Joseph C. Lincoln)

Futile as a tenor in a boiler shop. (Henry Irving Dodge)

His face looked like a face that had refused to jell and was about to run down on his clothes. (Irvin S. Cobb)

---

*From A CONNECTICUT YANKEE IN KING ARTHUR'S COURT by Mark Twain. Harper & Row, Publishers, Inc.

Now it's your turn. Try to complete the following similes so that they will be effective and funny. (Remember: the comparison must be valid, but it must also be far-fetched: that is, between two unlike objects.)

1 My head felt like _____

2 He was as punctual as _____

3 Her face was as expressionless as _____

4 He was as inflexible as _____

5 She was as motionless as _____

One step further. Witty definitions can be developed by using farfetched comparisons, too.

EXAMPLES: *Talent*, like gout, sometimes skips two generations. (Balzac)

A *committee meeting* is like a piggy bank in which the minutes are kept while the hours are wasted.

Adult . . . a person who has stopped growing . . . except in the middle.

Play the comic. Develop witty definitions for the following:

1 teen-ager _____

_____

_____

2 love _____

_____

_____

3 football _____

_____

_____

4 a teacher _____

_____

_____

5 a parent _____

_____

_____

You are now started on the road to comedy . . . and a long and painful road it is. But take heart. Like any proper road, this one has filling stations (try high-octane Thurber or low-lead Twain) and rest areas (relax with the daily newspaper: the graveyard for sick humor). Even so, before you arrive at your destination, you will be scratched by satire, pinched by parody, and made itchy by the incongruous.

It's all in a good cause, though . . . for fun!

27. ONCE OVER LIGHTLY

We Americans have a fondness for exaggeration. We exaggerate our virtues and we exaggerate our vices; we exaggerate our natural wonders and our human-made phenomena; we even exaggerate our joys and our griefs. It all begins with . . .

Telling Lies

Ask a three-year-old who broke Daddy's favorite reading lamp and she will answer with shocked awe: "It was a monster!" Ask a teen-ager where his term paper is and he will reply, with heartbreaking pathos: "Our dog ate it." Ask any experienced driver why he was fool enough to run out of gas on a superhighway, and he will play the indignant citizen and point at the treachery of Detroit.

Lying is as natural as breathing. We lie to get out of trouble, to avoid trouble, and—sometimes—to compound trouble. Unlike most skills, the ability to lie often deteriorates with age. The teen-ager's lie is more interesting than the adult's; and the child's lie is the most imaginative of all three. When we are little, we lie with daring and verve. We love our lies so well that the line between truth and falsehood grows blurred. Begin your in-depth study of telling lies by collecting (or remembering) half a dozen lies you have heard (or told). Rate each as F (dull); C (average); B (good); or A (excellent).

1 _____
  _____
2 _____
  _____
3 _____
  _____
4 _____
  _____
5 _____
  _____
6 _____
  _____

Now that you have some background in the art of lying, see if you can lie your way out of the following dilemmas. But—for comedy's sake—lie with imagination!

7 Your mother sent you to the store to buy milk and bread. Along the way you passed a new pizza parlor. You could not resist a couple of the chewy, lush-with-mushroom slices. As you wipe away the last dripping tomato from your chin, you wonder what excuse you will give. How *will* you explain that the money is gone?

_____
_____
_____
_____

8 Your boss owns a small ice-cream shop. On his anniversary he leaves you in charge. You promise faithfully to lock up and to deposit the money in the night-slot at the bank. As you leave for work the next morning, you realize you didn't lock up, and the money is still in the pocket of your jacket. How will you explain your dereliction?

_____
_____
_____
_____

9 Usually, after a date, you manage to get home by midnight or 1 a.m. This morning, though, you didn't get in until 2:30. Your parents pretended to be asleep, but you know they were just storing up ammunition for the breakfast-table assault. Arm yourself. What will you tell them?

_____
_____
_____
_____

Finished lying? Good. Go back and rate them. If you would give yourself all "A's", you're doing fine and are ready for the more advanced art of . . .

Hyperbole

Hyperbole is deliberate exaggeration used as a figure of speech. You are surely quite skilled in this already.

Examples:

> As you carry a ten-pound bag of potatoes from the car to the house, you complain: "This sack weighs a ton!"

> As you carry a much-wanted and heavy stereo set from the store to your home (five miles), you insist: "It's as light as a feather!"

Hyperbole never attempts to deceive; it is meant to startle, to emphasize, or to amuse. Many examples of hyperbole have been used so often they are trite, as are the two given above. Complete each of the following statements by adding a trite, hyperbolic phrase. (Usually this will be the first phrase that comes to your mind.)

1 I'm so tired I could sleep for _____ .

2 You're two hours late! I've been waiting for you _____ .

3 You see—you broke your neck. I've told you _____
not to wear those shoes with the flapping soles!

4 "I'll love you till the seas _____," he whispered persuasively.

5 Said one farmer to another: "Why, he's such a rotten shot he couldn't hit the
_____!"

Now do something you've probably never done before. Think carefully about each of those five examples of hyperbole. What does each mean? Imagine being so tired that you actually need *years* of sleep! The first time these phrases were used they were powerful *and* amusing; but overuse has left them threadbare and thin. If you want to startle your reader, you must seek new examples of hyperbole that will shake him from head to foot with amazement.

> Not—"I'm so tired I could sleep for years (or for a century)!"
> But—"I'm so tired I could sleep at a jet airport during the Christmas holidays!"
> Or—"I'm so tired I could sleep on the handle of a jackhammer!"

You try it. Create original hyperbolic phrases and then use them in sentences to describe each of the following:

6 A person who's extremely hungry.

_____

_____

7 A person who can run very fast.

_____

_____

8 A person who is 120 years old.

_____

_____

9 A person who wishes to promise unending love to another person.

_____

_____

_____

10 A person who is digging ditches in the sun when the temperature registers 120°.

_____

_____

_____

After you have become adept at hyperbole, you are ready for the major leagues—for joining the mainstream of American humor, for creating . . .

Tall Tales

The tall tale is so tall that the fellow who creates it needs 73 ladders to reach the top and finish it off. It's been knocking around in this country since one dinosaur told about his little cousin who was restless one night and wriggled so much in his sleep that he accidentally dug out the Grand Canyon. After the dinosaurs, the tall tale kind of went out of fashion until it got as skimpy as a licked postage stamp. But it came back with the Minutemen. Why, in one minute an untrained colonist with a pea-shooter could capture a whole regiment of British redcoats, tie 'em together with strips of bark, and toss them out to the West Coast. That's how the giant redwoods came into existence.

The Civil War helped too. One Johnny Reb down in Florida kidnapped the population of a New York city and buried them in the Everglades. He buried them so deep it took them over a hundred years to dig their way to the surface, and they were pretty old and tired by the time they succeeded. But they're stubborn, those New Yorkers. They rested for three minutes, then started right in building themselves clusters of homes. Retirement villages, they call them.

The tall tale's out of style now. Only the other day a sixteen-year-old kid told me he knew a student who was honest, hardworking, and interested in knowledge for its own sake. The way these kids lie!

✿   ✿   ✿   ✿   ✿

If any kind of humor is indigenous to America, it's the tall tale. There was the giant lumberjack, Paul Bunyan, who built a house so high "he had to put the last five stories on hinges to let the moon go by." There was Pecos Bill who grew up with the coyotes and could kill a deer by running it to death. And there was Davy Crockett who could *grin* a raccoon out of a tree. Once Davy grinned so hard even the bark fell off!

You have a right, by heritage, to create the tall tale, and all you really need is—a rollicking imagination. Before you create your own tall tale, make your imagination rollick by suggesting answers to the following questions:

Example: Why is the sky blue?

A workman was painting the wall of a building blue and had been promised he would be paid triple time until he was finished—so he just kept painting higher and higher until the whole sky was a pretty baby blue.

1   How did the Mississippi River come into existence?

_____

_____

_____

2   How could the national debt be paid off?

_____

_____

_____

3 Why does it snow?

_____

_____

_____

   Now that your imagination is leaping like an overactive salmon, you are ready to write a tall tale of your own. Start with your school. Look around you. How about the walls? For some reason, in most schools the walls are either dingy, or a sick yellow. Create a tall tale to explain *why* they are as they are. Is your school building a several-story-sandwich, or a one-story sprawler? Create a tall tale to explain its structure. Is your basketball team outstanding—or is it in the league cellar? Create a tall tale to explain its position. Three things to remember:

—*Use facts logically:* killing a deer by running it to death is funny; killing a tortoise by running it to death isn't.

—*Use details:* the redcoats forming the redwoods; the hinges on Paul Bunyan's house.

—*Combine fact and fiction:* the Civil War and retirement villages combined with the kidnapping of a city by one soldier.

   A Tall Tale about _____

_____

_____

_____

_____

_____

_____

_____

_____

   Read your tall tale to at least one person. Notice your listener's reactions—when he or she is amused, when bored. Revise as needed.

   Write one more tall tale on any topic. You will do best if you choose a topic about which you know quite a bit.

_____

_____

_____

_____

_____

_____

_____

Tall tales exaggerate *everything*. If, instead, you focus your exaggeration on distinctive features or objects, you are really creating . . .

Caricatures

Caricatures are often (but not always) visual. They take a person's most striking features and accentuate them. Below, at the left, is a picture of Washington Irving, lawyer, editor, and writer. At the right is a caricature of Irving drawn by Mark Summers when he was a senior at Yale University.*

Compare—in the picture and in the caricature—the long, straggled sideburns, the thick eyebrows, the dark deep-set eyes, the broad nose, the heavy lower lip, and the cleft in the chin. Summers then went a step further: in Irving's left hand, he placed a quill (a symbol of the writer), and—remembering the headless horseman in "The Legend of Sleepy Hollow"—in the right hand, he placed the author's own (detached) head. The caricature thus gives a capsule history as well as a portrait of the subject.

---

*From A STUDENT CARTOONIST'S VIEW OF GREAT FIGURES IN AMERICAN HISTORY by Mark W. Summers. Copyright 1972 by Mark W. Summers. Reprinted by permission of Simon & Schuster, Inc.; Pocket Books and Washington Square Press divisions.

But caricatures may also be verbal, as no one better knew than Irving himself. One of the most famous literary caricatures appears in "The Legend of Sleepy Hollow." Irving is describing Ichabod Crane, the schoolmaster:

> He was tall, but exceedingly lank, with narrow shoulders, long arms and legs, hands that dangled a mile out of his sleeves, feet that might have served for shovels, and his whole frame most loosely hung together. His head was small, and flat at top, with huge ears, large green glassy eyes, and a long snip nose, so that it looked like a weathercock perched upon his spindle neck, to tell which way the wind blew. To see him striding along the profile of a hill on a windy day, with his clothes bagging and fluttering about him, one might have mistaken him for the genius of famine descending upon the earth, or some scarecrow eloped from a cornfield.*

Irving wants his readers to get a sense of Crane's *physical structure*. All the details emphasize this: lank; narrow shoulders; long arms and big feet; small head and long neck; etc. (Notice, however, that Irving omitted irrelevant details like the sound of Crane's voice or the way he parted his hair.) Notice, too, the hyperbole: "dangled a mile out of his sleeves" and "feet that might have served for shovels." Notice the use of simile: a nose "like a weathercock"; and the use of analogy (the whole man compared to a scarecrow). Before the story even begins, poor Ichabod is a figure of fun, a target for mockery and insults, a ludicrous weakling.

You may not be able to create a second Ichabod Crane, but you can develop a good verbal caricature if you follow three steps: (1) select a *single* general impression you want the reader to receive; (2) conjure up a character complete with all relevant details; (3) imitate Irving's style.

Ready:

_____

_____

_____

_____

_____

_____

_____

_____

_____

_____

_____

_____

_____

---

*Washington Irving. "The Legend of Sleepy Hollow" in SELECTED WRITINGS OF WASHINGTON IRVING, edited by Saxe Commins. Copyright 1945, The Modern Library.

Litotes

The four techniques we've looked at so far—lying, hyperbole, tall tales, and caricatures—all emphasize bigness or exaggeration. Just the opposite of these is litotes. *Litotes* is the art of understatement. In its simplest form it occurs when you call a fat boy Skinny or a skinny boy Fatso. In a more sophisticated form it occurs when you affirm something by expressing the fact in the negative.

For example: a woman passes by. Your friend says, "Isn't she ugly?" You agree, but you don't wish to be blunt; so you answer, "Well, she's no great beauty."

In the following sentences, show *how* litotes is being used by explaining *why* it is being used.

EXAMPLE: You were *less than generous* in your donation to the Children's Fund.

EXPLANATION: The speaker wishes to censure, but not too sharply. "Less than generous" is kinder than "miserly," but it implies the same judgment.

1 Louis says: "Jim's a fool, isn't he?"
Maria replies: "Well, he's *no Einstein*, that's for sure."

_____

_____

_____

_____

2 A critic writes: "In her role as Lady Macbeth, she was somewhat *less than adequate*."

_____

_____

_____

_____

3 Reporter to golf champion: "You have a fantastic drive—one of the longest I've seen."
Champ, nodding: "Thanks. I think it's *fairly decent*."

_____

_____

_____

4 From a newspaper article: "The increase in the bank-loan interest rate will *not be trivial* in its effect."

_____

_____

_____

_____

5   Student: "I know I'm failing, but I don't want to drop the course."
      Counselor: "An F isn't *much of an asset* on your record."

_____

_____

_____

_____

> Every technique considered in this chapter—*lying, hyperbole, tall tales, caricature, litotes*—will animate your writing. But remember the title: "Once Over Lightly." Use these techniques sparingly, as though you had only a few dozen of each to last you a lifetime. As the cook admonished:
>
> > A heavy hand with spice
> > Is not nice.
> > A light hand
> > Is grand.

28. PARODY CAPER

Are you bored with your literature anthology? Furious at Longfellow, impatient with Poe? Do you dream at night of taking a sword to sonnets and of quartering quatrains? If you do, try Parody Caper, a panacea for paranoiacs. Each little parody pill carries a powerful punch, guaranteed to make literary greats disappear! Better yet, Parody Caper will improve your appearance—it will sharpen your teeth, strengthen your fingernails, and add terror to your tongue. Also useful for deflating politicians and prime ministers as well as poets.

As you no doubt have realized, the above is a parody of modern advertising. It uses rhetorical questions*, alliteration, and exaggerated promises to get you to buy something . . . and it may work because (like the ad it parodies) it is based on truth.

Max Eastman, an American humorist, defined parody as "the exaggerated imitation of a work or style of art." Note that word *exaggerated*.

You can parody almost anything: a walk, a way of speaking, even an idea. All you have to do is imitate—but imitate in an exaggerated way.

Parody can be sharp and critical (and then it hurts); or it can be casual fun. Parody a specific old man, crippled with arthritis, and you are cruel. Parody a specific old politician, who still tries to use a cane in menacing fashion, and you are critical. Parody an old man who is just any old man and you are funny.

If you wish to become a parodist, just amble (chuckling) through these four easy stages.

Pillaging Proverbs

Ambrose Bierce, master of sardonic humor, had fun parodying proverbs. Bierce loved to deflate the inflated, and he felt that proverbs—the moral sausages of the Respectable—were an attractive target. Watch how he parodies each wise saw into a wisecrack!

Proverb: A penny saved is a penny earned.
Bierce: A penny saved is a penny to squander.

Proverb: A bird in the hand is worth two in the bush.
Bierce: A bird in the hand is worth what it will bring.

Proverb: A man is known by the company that he keeps.
Bierce: A man is known by the company that he organizes.

Proverb: What is worth doing is worth doing well.
Bierce: What is worth doing is worth the trouble of asking somebody to do it.

---

*A rhetorical question is one that expects no answer. It is used only to catch interest and to emphasize a point.

You should be feeling sufficiently cynical now to try a few transformations of your own. See if you can Bierce-erize the following proverbs:

1 Children should be seen and not heard.

_____

2 Barking dogs never bite.

_____

3 Lost time is never found again.

_____

4 Strike while the iron is hot.

_____

5 If at first you don't succeed, try, try again.

_____

Priming the Primer

You know, of course, what a primer is: an elementary textbook, especially a book which helps children learn to read. Your generation, for the most part, struggled with Dick and Jane and their dog Spot. Remember? "See Dick run. See Jane run. See Spot run. Run, Spot, run!"

Because of the short sentences, the one-two-three rhythm and the monotonous tone, the primer is exquisitely easy to parody. The poet and humorist, Eugene Field, wrote a parody primer which was printed in the *Denver Tribune* in 1882. In these two choice excerpts, Field parodies both the primer style and the stinginess and occasional nastiness that seem to be part of our human nature.*

The Wasp
See the Wasp. He has pretty yellow Stripes around his Body, and a Darning Needle in his Tail. If you will Pat the Wasp upon the Tail, we will Give You a Nice Picture Book.

The Oyster
Here we have an Oyster. It is going to a Church Fair. When it Gets to the Fair, it will Swim around in a big Kettle of Warm Water. A Lady will Stir it with a Spoon, and sell the Warm Water for Forty Cents a pint. Then the Oyster will move on to the next Fair. In this Way, the Oyster will visit all the Church Fairs in Town, and Bring a great many Dollars into the Church Treasury. The Oyster goes a great Way in a Good Cause.

_____

*Eugene Field. "The Wasp" and "The Oyster"—later published in book form. Quoted in A SUBTREASURY OF AMERICAN HUMOR, edited by E. B. White and Katherine S. White. Copyright 1941, Coward-McCann, Inc.

Delightful, isn't it? Think for a minute. Isn't there something that annoys you in your family, school, or community? Select a minor annoyance, then write a parody about it in the primer style. Your parody should be amusing, but it should also make a point.

_____

_____

_____

_____

_____

_____

Nursery Logic

The nursery rhyme is also fine fodder for parody. You can attack it in at least two ways. The simplest approach is to keep the structure, rhythm, and first line, and then use the next few lines to comment on modern life.

You all know—

> Mary had a little lamb,
>   Its fleece was white as snow.
> And everywhere that Mary went
>   That lamb was sure to go.

Here's how it might be rewritten in times of inflation, depression, recession, unemployment, etcetera, etcetera.

> Mary had a little lamb,
>   It fattened as it grew.
> And when it died, poor Mary cried—
>   Then dined on mutton stew.

Try it with "Jack and Jill"—

> Jack and Jill went up the hill
>   To fetch a pail of water;
> Jack fell down and broke his crown,
>   And Jill came tumbling after.

YOUR PARODY _____

_____

_____

_____

Try one more:

> Humpty Dumpty sat on a wall,
> Humpty Dumpty had a great fall;
> All the king's horses
> And all the king's men,
> Couldn't put Humpty Dumpty together again.

_____

_____

_____

_____

_____

The second approach to parodying a nursery rhyme (or other literary work) is much more difficult. This time you keep the content but change the structure, rewriting in the style of some well-known author.

Carolyn Wells, a really fine parodist, one day had a challenging idea: she would create eighteen parodies of one four-line poem—and of a nonsense poem, at that! Below is her introduction and three of the parodies.* Read . . . with delight.

Variations (or Parodying a Quatrain to Death)

DIVERSIONS OF THE RE-ECHO CLUB

It is with pleasure that we announce our ability to offer to the public the papers of the Re-Echo Club. This club, somewhat after the order of the Echo Club, late of Boston, takes pleasure in trying to better what is done. On the occasion of the meeting of which the following gems of poesy are the result, the several members of the club engaged to write up the well-known tradition of the Purple Cow in more elaborate form than the quatrain made famous by Mr. Gelett Burgess:

> "I never saw a Purple Cow,
>   I never hope to see one;
> But I can tell you, anyhow,
>   I'd rather see than be one."

Mr. J. Keats:

A cow of purple is a joy forever.
Its loveliness increases. I have never
Seen this phenomenon. Yet ever keep
A brave lookout; lest I should be asleep
When she comes by. For, though I would not be one,
I've oft imagined 'twould be a joy to see one.

_____

*"Diversions of the Re-Echo Club" by Carolyn Wells in THE BOOK OF HUMOROUS VERSE compiled by Carolyn Wells. Copyright 1920, 1936 by Doubleday & Company, Inc.

Mr. W. Wordsworth:

She dwelt among the untrodden ways
   Beside the springs of Dee;
A Cow whom there were few to praise
   And very few to see.

A violet by a mossy stone
   Greeting the smiling East
Is not so purple, I must own,
   As that erratic beast.

She lived unknown, that Cow, and so
   I never chanced to see;
But if I had to be one, oh,
   The difference to me!

Mr. R. Kipling:

In the old ten-acre pasture,
   Lookin' eastward toward a tree,
There's a Purple Cow a-settin'
   And I know she thinks of me.
For the wind is in the gum-tree,
   And the hay is in the mow,
And the cow-bells are a-calling
   "Come and see a Purple Cow!"

But I am not going now,
   Not at present, anyhow,
For I am not fond of purple, and
   I can't abide a cow;
   No, I shall not go today,
   Where the Purple Cattle play.
   But I think I'd rather see one
   Than to be one, anyhow.

Continue where Ms. Wells stopped. Working alone or in a group, create a few more "Purple Cow Parodies." Rewrite Gelett Burgess' quatrain in the style of Walt Whitman or Rod McKuen, or Emily Dickinson or E. E. Cummings . . . or of anyone else.

After you have finished, swap parodies . . . and enjoy.

This parody-fest should have at least four results:

1 laughter,
2 appreciation of the art of parody,
3 heightened awareness of style, and
4 laughter . . . laughter . . . and more laughter.

Laugh on.

29. STRIKE WITH SATIRE

When you are furiously angry with someone, you can hang him, and go to jail; or slander him, and go to court; or drown him in ridicule, and go on the bestseller list. Drowning an opponent in ridicule is the forte of the satirist.

The satirist may be gentle; but the *satire* is often cruelly barbed. In *Brave New World*, Aldous Huxley mocked a scientifically operated way of life to death. With *Main Street*, Sinclair Lewis plunged the small town into a humiliation from which it has never fully recovered. And Orwell's *Animal Farm* exposed mercilessly the hypocrisy of communism with the quiet satire of—"All animals are equal; but some animals are more equal than others."

What exactly is satire?

Henry Carlisle, the editor of *American Satire in Prose and Verse*, claimed that satire "finds normal things abnormal, proper people odd, ridiculous, and sometimes even evil and outrageous. Worst of all, it is both fictional and true." And that's the first characteristic of satire: *it must be based on the real, and be exaggerated or distorted into the non-real.*

Leonard Feinberg, the author of *Introduction to Satire*, added: "Satire usually shows us familiar things in a new way." And that's the second characteristic of satire: *to awaken us to an awareness of the wickedness and the folly in human nature and in human society.*

David Worcester, in *The Art of Satire*, commented: "The laughter of comedy is relatively purposeless. The laughter of satire is directed toward an end." And that's the third characteristic of satire: *it must have a purpose—to make us condemn the evil, despise the stupid, or deflate the pompous.*

Remember—SATIRE must

> . . . be based on the real, but made non-real;
> . . . awaken us to the wickedness and folly of life; and
> . . . have a purpose.

You are ready now to begin your apprenticeship as a satirist.

Tampering With Tests

Start with something you know; and you certainly know a good deal about test-taking. Have you ever winced at this kind of question: "What kind of coat did Jim wear on page 43?" Or this kind: "Explain the significance of the author's tendency to use personification in describing ivy." If you have, you possess all the material you need to compose a satiric quiz.

Here's one to get you started. The "literary work" to be analyzed is the nursery rhyme, "Jack and Jill." The point of view is that of an active feminist. (Having a specific point of view is not necessary, but it will sharpen your satire.)

Jack and Jill went up the hill
To fetch a pail of water.
Jack fell down and broke his crown
And Jill came tumbling after.

1 Since Jack precedes Jill, is Jack a male chauvinist? Explain.

2 Notice that Jack and Jill *went up* the hill, not down it. Might this be an analogy for the upward struggle faced by a young couple who have just been married and are trying to be partners, rather than master and servant? Why, or why not?

3 Interestingly enough, these two young people are going to all of this trouble just to get some *water*. Why do they need water? So that Jill can scrub the floor? Jack may help her get the water, but will he help her scrub the floor?

4 "Jack fell down." What does this tell you about the propensity of males for accidents, especially when work is in the offing?

5 When he fell, Jack broke his crown. What does a crown signify? Why is Jill not described as wearing a crown? Is the broken crown of Jack a symbol for the coming breakdown of male supremacy? Give specific illustrations from history to support your answer.

6 Note that Jack "fell" but Jill "tumbled." Which verb is more dignified? What does this suggest about the author's attitude? The present participle, "tumbling," is carefully used to describe Jill's action. Does the use of the present participle belittle Jill's action? Does the use of the simple past tense maximize Jack's mishap? Explain in not more than 3,000 words the way verb tenses reflect human prejudices.

One could, of course, go on and make up at least twenty questions; but five or six are usually sufficient.

It's your turn now. Make up a five-question quiz on "Little Boy Blue." If possible, develop your questions from a particular point of view—and remember: you are *not* developing a serious test, but one that satirizes test-taking.

Little Boy Blue come blow your horn,
The sheep are in the meadow, the cows are in the corn.
Where's the little boy who looks after the sheep?
He's under the haystack, fast asleep.

_____

_____

_____

_____

_____

_____

_____

_____

_____

How to Write "How-to's"

Continue with the satiric "how-to." In this exercise, you begin with a simple process and make it incredibly complex by describing it as the federal government might (or a doctor, lawyer, politician, etc.).

For example, here is the beginning of a recipe for making a peanut-butter sandwich, as it might appear in a federal government directive. We won't give you the everyday recipe; *everybody* knows how to make a peanut-butter sandwich.

1 Extract from the breadbox (or any equivalent container) a loaf of bread. (It is not necessary to have a full loaf; half a loaf will do. Also, it is important to recognize that any kind of bread may be used: white bread; whole wheat bread; rye bread; even cracked wheat bread.) It is essential, however, that it be bread of some type (see appendix for definition of bread).

2 Return all bread to breadbox (or equivalent container) *except* two slices. One slice alone will not provide sufficient nutrient. More than two slices will result in an overabundance of caloric intake. Two slices (supplemented with peanut-butter) provide adequate vitamin and mineral material to ensure essential energy for four hours, or until the customary time for dinner in most households.

Complete the recipe.

_____

_____

_____

_____

_____

_____

_____

_____

_____

_____

Headlining History

The third step in your apprenticeship is to satirize history by headlining it. The familiarizing and sensationalizing of a headline strips even history of its dignity and impact.

Begin by taking almost any description of an important historical event from a textbook. (Some examples: Battle of Lexington; Landing of the Pilgrims; signing of the Emancipation Proclamation; etc.) Spray with a little melodrama. Then write a headline and lead (first) paragraph.

Here's one example, using the Boston Tea Party.

UNFAIR TEA TAX SENDS SIXTY "INDIANS"
TO DUMPING PARTY

340 Chests of Tea Make Boston Brew;
Parliament Shaken

December 17, 1773. Two ships from London suffered a rude surprise last night when they tried to have 340 chests of tea landed in defiance of the popular will. After an angry session at the Old South Meeting House, 60 Bostonians, disguised as Indians, boarded the vessels, tore open the hatches, and cast all 340 chests of tea into the waters of Boston Harbor—"a Boston brew," said one wag, "that would slake the thirst of Old England for many a month!"

YOUR HISTORICAL EVENT _____

_____

_____

_____

_____

_____

_____

_____

_____

_____

_____

(Suggested Group Project: If you enjoyed this experiment in headlining, explore the history of your town or city, write up the important events, with headlines, and "publish" a one-issue newspaper. It will be the "talk of the town" for a few days!)

Slaughter With Quatrains

You are ready for a more sophisticated challenge. Just add a touch of rhyme to the techniques of satire you have already mastered, and you can create a series of literary portraits that your entire school will enjoy! Of course, Dorothy Parker preceded you— with "A Pig's-Eye View of Literature."

Here's Parker on Tennyson:

> Should Heaven send me any son,
> I hope he's not like Tennyson.
> I'd rather have him play a fiddle
> Than rise and bow and speak an idyll.*

---

*From "A Pig's-Eye View of Literature" by Dorothy Parker in THE PORTABLE DOROTHY PARKER, copyright 1927, 1944. Reprinted by permission of The Viking Press, Inc.

And Parker on Walter Savage Landor:

> Upon the work of Walter Landor
> I am unfit to write with candor.
> If you can read it, well and good;
> But as for me, I never could.*

You can have a lot of fun with this. Start by listing below a few works (title and author) that you *didn't* enjoy. (We know this is difficult—you probably loved *Silas Marner* and adored *David Copperfield;* but there must be a few you found just a trifle boring.)

_____

_____

_____

_____

_____

Now choose one of those authors and think about his or her writing style. Use Parker's first quatrain—the one on Tennyson—as a model. (It's better because it mentions the author's name and refers to a specific work.) Or you may prefer to use the following quatrain (not by Parker) as a model:

> When Steinbeck *The Red Pony* wrote
> He doubtless little knew
> The boring tests and symbol hunts
> He'd make us gallop through!

YOURS   (author and title) _____

_____

_____

_____

_____

Now that you've written one slaughtering quatrain, write two more.

_____

_____

_____

_____

_____

_____

_____

_____

_____

*From "A Pig's-Eye View of Literature" by Dorothy Parker in THE PORTABLE DOROTHY PARKER, copyright 1927, 1944. Reprinted by permission of The Viking Press, Inc.

(Project for the Ambitious: as a group or as a class, collect as many of these slaughtering quatrains as you can. Edit them. Select the best. Type on ditto masters and run off 50 or 100 copies. Staple. Distribute (free or for a small charge). Instant hilarity!

Your apprenticeship as a satirist is now over (at least for the time being). Prove it—by writing a satiric fable in the style of Ambrose Bierce. Here are two of Bierce's fables to help you get started.*

Satirizing the graft and greed of legislators:

KANGAROO AND ZEBRA

A Kangaroo hopping awkwardly along with some bulky object concealed in her pouch met a Zebra, and desirous of keeping his attention upon himself [rather than on her and the object she was spiriting away], said:

"Your costume looks as if you might have come out of the penitentiary."

"Appearances are deceitful," replied the Zebra, smiling in the consciousness of a more insupportable wit, "or I should have to think that you had come out of the Legislature."

Satirizing the medical profession's interest in fees:

DOG AND DOCTOR

A Dog that had seen a Doctor attending the burial of a wealthy patient said: "When do you expect to dig it up?"

"Why should I dig it up?" the Doctor asked.

"When I bury a bone," said the Dog, "it is with an intention to uncover it later and pick it."

"The bones that I bury," said the Doctor, "are those that I can no longer pick."

YOURS _____

_____

_____

_____

_____

_____

_____

_____

> **Everybody loves satire, but nobody loves the satirist. Satirists have been called "merciless strategists," "wily diplomats," and "zealous urban missionaries." So if you decide to major in satire, acquire a crash helmet. You'll need it!**

——————

*Ambrose Bierce's "Kangaroo and Zebra" and "Dog and Doctor" from *Fantastic Fables*, as reprinted in THE SARDONIC HUMOR OF AMBROSE BIERCE, edited by George Barkin. Copyright 1963, Dover Publications, Inc.

30. A POTPOURRI OF WIT

"Good wits jump; a word to the wise is enough," said Cervantes. In this—the last chapter dealing with the comic, and the last in the workshop section—we intend to do just that: make your wits jump. Ready?

The Pun

Terrible things have been said about the pun. It has been belittled, sneered at, lampooned, and maligned. When a pun is uttered, the savant groans; but notice how said savant rushes to try it on the next person he meets! The truth is—quick-witted people love the quick wit of word play; and if the pun is the stepchild of humor (as some people claim), it is an enormously admired stepchild.

Lewis Carroll, in *Alice in Wonderland*, had a marvelous time with puns.

> "We called him Tortoise because he taught us," said the Mock Turtle angrily. "Really you are very dull!"

and

> "Reeling and Writhing, of course, to begin with," the Mock Turtle replied, "and the different branches of Arithmetic—Ambition, Distraction, Uglification, and Derision."

This is very superior word play from the maestro himself; but you can start with something a bit more elementary.

Try the *Occupational Hazard* approach, or—as some wit said somewhere—

> "I'm a *cabdriver*, and at times I can't *hack* the job."

Another example:

> "I'm a *floorwalker*, and at times I can't *stand* it."

Concoct three Occupational Hazard puns of your own.

1 _____

2 _____

3 _____

Try the *Animal Parts* approach: "The kinkajou is a great story teller: it enjoys a long *tail!*" or "The giraffe is a great *neck*er!" Dream up three Animal Parts puns.

4 _____

5 _____

6 _____

Try the *Medical Symptom* approach. You know, of course, that "the dermatologist shouldn't be *rash*" and that "an oculist shouldn't *eye* the ladies." Conjure up three Medical Symptom puns.

7 _____

8 _____

9 _____

Try the *Elegant Discharge* approach. You can just *fire* a worker from his job, but how much better to do it with style! The Elegant Discharge demands that only a rifleman should be *fired*, and only a battery salesman should be *discharged*. Lumberjacks should be given the *ax*, and garbage collectors should, of course, be *canned*. Help three other occupations to an Elegant Discharge.

10 _____

11 _____

12 _____

When you have acquired the habit of making puns (or near-puns), you can sneak an occasional one into your writing. It will amuse you, and may amuse a reader here and there. George Oppenheim, the drama critic, did it when he summed up someone who advocated drugs as a "drugged individualist." And Shakespeare did it, when he had the cobbler in *Julius Caesar* say: "I meddle with no tradesmen's matters, nor women's matters, but with awl."

If Shakespeare could get away with it, so can you!

The Paradox

If you had to strain your wit to jump over a mere pun, you will find the paradox a fearsome hurdle. For a paradox is a statement that seems to be self-contradictory and therefore absurd, but that really tells the truth. You have probably uttered a paradox or two without knowing it: "I hate being in love!" for example. And some teacher, trying to force you to make a choice, has probably quoted the proverb: "No choice is also a choice"—as it is, of course.

Ponder the following paradoxes; think about them; find the truth that shines through the apparent self-contradictions; and enjoy them.

Vision is the Art of seeing Things invisible.	(Swift)
Being natural is simply a pose.	(Wilde)
I am the slave of liberty.	(Robespierre)
There are some defeats more triumphant than victories.	(Montaigne)
What ruins mankind is the ignorance of the expert.	(Chesterton)
We are often obstinate through weakness and daring through timidity.	(La Rochefoucauld)

Now that you have *seen* truth through the paradoxes of others, try to *find* truth for yourself through some original paradoxes. Can you manage three?

1 _____

_____

2 _____

_____

3 _____

_____

One-Liners

After that tough mental struggle with paradoxes, you have earned some relaxation—and what better way to relax than by dreaming up one-liners. A one-liner is a wisecrack or gag about any subject. In fact, that's how you begin to write one: choose any subject.

One-way streets? How's this? One young driver I know likes them because on a one-way street you can be bumped only in the rear.

Open minds? Well, there was the conservative politician who believed that open minds should be closed for repairs.

Insomnia? Joe's insomnia is so bad the sheep are picketing for shorter hours.

The procedure for creating one-liners? Just play with a topic and explore related topics until a couple of ideas begin to mesh. Let's analyze that last one-liner. An insomniac is someone who has difficulty getting to sleep. When someone has trouble sleeping, everyone tells him to count sheep. Since an insomniac always has trouble falling asleep, the sheep would be jumping fences every night and all night. Hence they would be overworked. In America, if one feels one is working too long, one pickets for shorter hours. Result: the one-liner—Joe's insomnia is so bad the sheep are picketing for shorter hours.

Create three original one-liners on your own topics or on a few of the topics listed below:

a golf player	college
French bread	roadhogs
actors	income tax
down payments	movies
a nickel	beards

1 _____

_____

2 _____

_____

3 _____

_____

(*Dividend:* If you discover you have a knack for writing one-liners, consider sending them to comedians. Your best market will be the entertainers who play at local theaters and clubs since many of them cannot yet afford full-time writers. Imagine getting paid for a joke!)

The Insult

Everyone enjoys a clever insult, except the victim; and if it's clever enough, even the victim may chuckle. Since this is so, you—as a creative person—should abstain from the stupid insult. Learn to insult beautifully; make your barb a work of art.

Groucho Marx, when he resigned from the Friars Club, explained:

"I just don't want to belong to any club that would have me as a member."

Marconi told this anecdote.

He and his mother's gardener were working one day when a young count passed by and began bragging about his lineage. The gardener listened for a while and then said quietly: "So much the worse for you, sir; for, as we gardeners say, the older the seed, the worse the crop."[1]

The third insult—a real beauty—originated with Abraham Lincoln, one of the wittiest of our Presidents.

The Civil War was in progress, and General McClellan, the commander of the Union Army, was so fearful of making mistakes that he was doing nothing. Lincoln wrote him this brief letter: "My dear McClellan: If you don't want to use the Army, I should like to borrow it for a while. Yours respectfully, A. Lincoln."[2]

Each of the following anecdotes describes a situation that demands a clever insult. Sharpen your pen and complete each anecdote. You will have to be good; you are competing with some very clever people.

1 Near the end of an extremely dull evening, Dorothy Parker's escort said rather pompously: "I can't bear fools." Miss Parker replied:[3]

_____

_____

2 Max Baer was naturally a bit disgruntled after he lost the heavyweight title to Jim Braddock. A reporter asked Baer how long he thought Braddock would be champion. Baer replied:

_____

_____

[1,2]From Herbert V. Prochnow, THE PUBLIC SPEAKER'S TREASURE CHEST. Copyright 1942, Harper & Row, Publishers, Inc.
[3]From A TREASURY OF LAUGHTER, Louis Untermeyer. Copyright 1946, Simon & Schuster, Inc.

3   Sometime in the early 19th century, John Randolph and Henry Clay met on a narrow
    street. The two men despised each other, and Randolph said haughtily: "I never
    give way to scoundrels." Clay stepped into the gutter and replied:[1]

    _____

    _____

4   A young man asked Mozart how to write a concerto. The composer suggested that
    he wait until he was a little older. The youth protested: "But you composed when
    you were seven or eight." "Yes," Mozart agreed, "but[2]

    _____

    _____

5   Fritz Kreisler was once asked to bring his violin to a dinner party. He informed his
    hostess that if he did, the fee would be $1,500. Annoyed, the woman said unpleas-
    antly: "In that case, don't mingle with the guests." Kreisler replied:[3]

    _____

    _____

When you have finished, compare your insults with those actually spoken by the
people involved. You will find them below, and we are willing to bet that they are cleverer
than you thought they would be!

        1   Parker: "That's strange. Your mother did."
        2   Baer: "Until the next fight."
        3   Clay: "I always do."
        4   Mozart: . . . I didn't have to ask anyone how to do it."
        5   Kreisler: "In that case, my fee will be $500."

How does a writer use insults? Well, they work nicely in satires, are useful in parodies,
and (if clever enough) add spice to almost any piece of writing.

Irony

Irony is to language and literature as salt is to food. It is essential to life and sharpens
our palates, but is seldom satisfying when taken by itself. Irony results when you speak
with tongue-in-cheek. It enables you to express something clearly though you seem
to be saying the opposite.

You and a friend are playing checkers. His mind is on other things and he loses quickly.
You comment: "Your playing is superb tonight." Your tone of voice and your sentence,
in context, transform what seems to be praise into criticism.

[1,3]From A TREASURY OF LAUGHTER, Louis Untermeyer. Copyright 1946, Simon & Schuster, Inc.
[2]From Herbert V. Prochnow, THE PUBLIC SPEAKER'S TREASURE CHEST. Copyright 1942, Harper &
Row, Publishers, Inc.

In *Julius Caesar*, when Antony wants to arouse strong feelings against Brutus, he repeats a number of times: "But Brutus is an honorable man." Brutus (like everyone else in the audience) knew that Antony meant the opposite; but what could he do? Call Antony a liar? One characteristic of irony is that it renders the victim helpless: try to refute it and you end by looking ridiculous!

Not only words are ironic; an incident may be ironic also. The man who devised the guillotine died on the guillotine. In "The Gift of the Magi," O. Henry tells the story of Della who sells her beautiful hair to buy a watchchain for her husband, Jim, and of Jim who sells his precious watch to buy an expensive comb for Della. In Maupassant's "The Necklace" a couple slave for fifteen years to replace a necklace—only to find that the one lost had had little value.

As you can see, irony can be grim, amusing, or touching. It occurs in tragedy and in comedy, in satire and in simple humor. It plays a part in daily life. Yet many people find irony difficult to grasp.

Explain the use of irony in each of the following examples, and you should be one step closer to understanding this literary technique:

1 An IRS investigator has been sentenced to prison for five years for failing to report his full income on his tax return.

_____

_____

_____

2 During World War II the exercise period was called "Happy Hour" by the naval trainees.

_____

_____

_____

3 In the Bible, when the prophet Elijah saw the priests of Baal calling upon their idols, he shouted: "Cry louder! Baal is a god, but perhaps he is talking, or walking, or traveling, or perhaps he is sleeping and must be awakened."

_____

_____

_____

You are ready now to use irony. Create an ironic surprise ending (tragic or comic) for each of the following plot outlines. *Don't* choose the first ending you think of—that will be the obvious solution.

1 A young soldier has been involved in a major war for three years. He receives a leave of absence, flies across the Pacific Ocean to California, and then flies across the continent to New York. He lands at Kennedy Airport and takes a limousine to a Long Island suburb. He gets out of the limousine just one block from his parents' home.

_____

_____

_____

_____

_____

2 A businessman decides it would be a good idea to have a lawyer in the family, so he persuades his daughter to go to Harvard Law. The daughter does well and graduates with high honor.

_____

_____

_____

_____

3 A young secretary, intent on getting married, works hard for four years during which she saves every penny she possibly can. At the end of the four years, she makes a reservation on a cruise ship that will stop at many Mediterranean seaports and islands.

_____

_____

_____

_____

4 Jack Corcoran hates women. He has resolved to remain a bachelor to avoid being bound by female wiles. Because he is a reporter, Corcoran finds himself the only male at a lecture being given by Anne Morrison, a leader of the feminist movement.

_____

_____

_____

_____

You now possess a good many tools of the trade. Powered by ideas and armed with words, you are ready for battle. True, the battle for creation is a bloodless battle; yet it is a real battle. And the studio, though more elegant than the workshop, is a cruel arena. Enter at your own risk. If you are one of the fortunate (perhaps) few, you will find it a risk well worth taking. Writer, present arms . . .

Part Two
THE STUDIO

. . . wherein you will experiment with the writing of
serious and humorous short stories,
sonnets, limericks, and free verse,
plays for the stage, screen, and radio,
informal essays, and
thought-provoking articles.

Unit VI
The Essay

INTRODUCTION

The ESSAY is the oldest and the youngest . . . the most often used, the most abused . . . the easiest, the hardest . . . the most delicious and the dullest kind of writing.

It is almost impossible *not* to write essays. When, in a letter to a friend, you write at length about one incident, you are writing a miniature essay. If you are a nurse and describe in a report a patient's behavior and reaction to a sedative, you are writing an essay. On your income tax return, if you add a paragraph or two explaining why you should have the right to claim a certain exemption, you are writing an essay.

What *is* an essay? It is a discussion, in prose, of a particular topic. It may be one page long, or it may be book-length. It may be as formal and rigid as a rented tuxedo, as casual and comfortable as a pair of old jeans.

There are descriptive essays telling about strange and wondrous lands, like Frances Trollope's *Domestic Manners of the Americans*. Writing in 1832, Mrs. Trollope discussed the peculiar eating habits of Americans: "they consume an extraordinary quantity of bacon"; "they mix things together"—like eggs and oysters, salt fish and onions. They like "horrible half-baked hot rolls," and they are "extravagantly fond" of all kinds of sweets.

There are critical essays like Poe's "The Philosophy of Composition" in which the poet explains, in detail, exactly how he wrote "The Raven."

There are satirical essays, some—like Jonathan Swift's "A Modest Proposal"—designed to shake governments and consciences, and others—like Russell Baker's "Spaced Out"—designed to shake our heads with amusement and rueful self-recognition.

There are biographical essays like William Allen White's charming and agonized memorial to his young daughter, Mary White; and autobiographical essays like Graham Greene's "My Lost Childhood," a lovely journey into memory to find the boy he was who fathered the man he is.

There are aphoristic essays, full of "wise saws and modern instances," like those of Francis Bacon and Ralph Waldo Emerson; philosophical essays like John Locke's "Essay on Human Understanding"; personal essays like Charles Lamb's "A Dissertation on Roast Pig" or Leigh Hunt's "Getting Up on Cold Mornings."

In *Walden*, Henry David Thoreau wrote a series of essays, each reflecting on some aspect of nature: the cracking of ice in a pond, a battle between ants, the care of a woodcock for her brood. In *A Room of One's Own*, Virginia Woolf wrote a book-length essay exploring the value of solitude and independence to the woman writer. And, in "The Simple Art of Murder," Raymond Chandler analyzed the detective story—how it should (and should not) be written.

If it is any or all of these things, what then is an essay? It is a prose writing; it deals with one idea; it gives a writer's opinions. Such a simple recipe for such a charming literary form! Other ways of defining it: Crystallized conversation. (So converse.) Pointed opinions. (So opine.) Polished vignettes. (So write.) Enjoy.

1 *All About You*. Set yourself an impossible task: to run a block in ten seconds, to read a newspaper in five minutes, to make a bed in half a minute. Describe how you felt under pressure.

_____

_____

_____

_____

2 *Sense-less*. Two of our senses are sight and hearing. Stimulate your own awareness by giving up one of these for a half hour. (Do this experiment *only* with a trusted friend—never alone.) Close off your hearing (with plugs or cotton) and walk down the main street. Is it different in a *silent* world? Blindfold yourself in your own room. How is it different when you cannot see? Make a few notes of your reactions.

_____

_____

_____

_____

_____

3 *Coin-a-Word*. Start with an activity in which you are interested—perhaps skiing. Then make up a small glossary (three to five coined words plus definitions) of words that should exist, but don't. Two possibilities in the skiing category would be

    skiathon: a long-distance skiing competition (after "marathon")

    skisun: a person in charge of ski equipment at a lodge or during a competition (after "bosun")

_____

_____

_____

_____

4 *Create a Person*. Read again your description of the character you parsed in Chapter 17. Write a letter to yourself *from* that person. Your imaginary correspondent should have a speech style and interests different from yours. Show the letter to a real friend and see if s/he accepts the imaginary person as real.

REAL FRIEND'S REACTION _____

_____

_____

5 *Literary Anagrams.* Begin with the name of a well-known author. Rearrange the letters to make one or more words (an anagram). Then use the anagram in a meaningful sentence.

> EXAMPLE   EMERSON. Rearrangement: *mere son*. Sentence: To his mother, Ralph was a *mere son*, not a famous essayist.

Create at least two of these.

_____

_____

_____

_____

6 *Birth Announcement.* Find out (or, if you prefer, make up) information regarding your birth: date, exact time of day, place, vital statistics (weight, hair, etc.), doctor, and any memorable happenings. Use this information to compose an unusual announcement of your own birth.

_____

_____

_____

_____

_____

_____

7 *Improvisation.* Here is an ice-pop stick. List ten ways it can be used (excluding its purpose: to support an ice pop).

_____   _____

_____   _____

_____   _____

_____   _____

_____   _____

8 *Question the Answer.* All your life you have been answering questions; now try to question some answers.

> EXAMPLE   *Answer:*   Cautiously, very cautiously.
> *Question:*   How do you pet a skunk?

Here are some answers for you to question.

a. *Answer:* With great confidence.

   Question: _____

   _____

b. *Answer:* On tip-toe.

   Question: _____

   _____

c. *Answer:* One at a time.

   Question: _____

   _____

9 *Advanced Role-Play.* You are a mosquito. Describe the world as you see it through your mosquito eyes. Consider your size, purpose, and the probable reactions of people to your presence.

YOUR DESCRIPTION _____

_____

_____

_____

_____

_____

_____

10 *Positive Thinking.* Some time ago William Arthur Ward of Texas Wesleyan College suggested a new kind of ESP (extrasensory perception). For example, Ward said: "When deadlines are near, traffic is jammed and nerves are frayed, use your ESP—Express Something Patient." Or—"When you are surrounded by attitudes of pessimism and cynicism, use your ESP—Express Something Positive." Look up some "P" adjectives and create a few more new kinds of ESP.

_____

_____

_____

_____

_____

_____

_____

_____

31. THE BEGINNING: SIX VARIATIONS

According to the Bible, before Creation was chaos.

And—for the writer—before creation is chaos.

The only way to eliminate this chaos—to make sense out of nonsense—is to use *form* to structure your material. (If you doubt this, try baking a cake sometime without using a pan to provide shape!)

Naturally, the first step in the actual writing of an essay or article is to compose an introduction (although some authors write the introduction only after they have completed the body of the essay).

If you simply begin at the beginning, your reader may never get to the middle. Grab the reader's attention; rivet it on what *you* are saying. There are several ways to do just this.

The News Item or Ad Opener

One way to develop a dazzling introduction is to use an ad or news item as a springboard; then toss in a few statistics or a quotation.

OUR TURN   (for an article about the current home-repairs mania)

> Dear Gloria—Please come home. I'll call the plumber the next time a pipe bursts. No more home repairs, I swear! Love, Jack.

All over the United States men—and women—are hammering, tacking, welding, and drilling. The results? A lot of broken bits and a growing number of broken marriages. Ads like the above appear frequently, suggesting that a home repairer sometimes finds himself without a home to repair. As Jane Conover said recently, "I'm tired of being a workbench widow. Our marriage survived Roger's bouts with golfing and skiing—at least *they* are seasonal—but a workbench is forever!"

YOUR TURN   (Use a real ad or news item as a springboard, or create your own.)

_____

_____

_____

_____

_____

_____

_____

_____

The Rhetorical Question Gambit

Another way to snare your readers is to throw them a couple of rhetorical questions. This approach is especially effective if the questions concern *them*.

OUR TURN

What would you do if the pipes under the sink burst, sending a cascade of water across the kitchen floor? Or if all the lights went out fifteen minutes before Thanksgiving dinner? Ten years ago you would have reached for the telephone; but today—if you're a typical American—you'll probably reach for a wrench or a fuse instead.

YOUR TURN _____

_____

_____

_____

_____

_____

_____

The Suspense Hook

Then there's the suspense hook, good when you're dealing with danger—physical or otherwise. It's hard for any reader to stop reading when he's wondering what will happen next!

OUR TURN

It was 20° below zero, and the narrow mountain road leading to the hospital glittered with a fresh coating of sleet. The fan belt of my old pick-up truck had just snapped—leaving us in the middle of a white, frozen desert. Despairingly, I looked at my wife. If the baby were to come now....I shook my head. I couldn't accept that. But I couldn't make a broken fan belt whole again, either.

YOUR TURN _____

_____

_____

_____

_____

_____

_____

The Joke Beginning

The joke beginning is helpful when you are dealing with prosaic material; and what is more prosaic than some home repairs? Just take a joke that is roughly appropriate and change it to fit your situation.

OUR TURN

Have you heard the latest home-repair joke? It goes like this:

Homeowner: "It took me two years to realize I had absolutely no talent for fixing things."
Repairperson: "You gave up?"
Homeowner: (matter of factly) "I didn't. The house did."

Jokes like this have become increasingly popular as the home-repair mania sweeps across America. They are told (happily) by carpenters and plumbers, and (ruefully) by homeowners who discover that "repairing repairs" is often woefully expensive.

YOUR TURN _____

_____

_____

_____

_____

_____

_____

_____

The Favorite Quotation Formula

The familiar is always safe—that's why the favorite quotation formula still works. Use a one-sentence quotation, a nursery rhyme, or an excerpt from a poem to lead into your introduction. As long as most of your readers recognize it, they will follow you joyfully!

OUR TURN

Humpty Dumpty sat on a wall,
Humpty Dumpty had a great fall.
    All the king's horses
    And all the king's men
Couldn't put Humpty Dumpty together again.

Neither can the home repairer put Humpty Dumpty together again— as many people learn only after suffering severe blows to their egos and wallets. They are also learning that less shell-shattering problems than Humpty's *can* be handled by ordinary electricians and plumbers and carpenters . . . and handled quite well. Even so, the "do-it-yourself" mania shows no sign of abating.

_____

_____

_____

_____

_____

_____

_____

_____

The Anecdote Approach

Another safe starter is the anecdote. Doesn't everyone love a story? As with the *Joke Beginning*, you can take an almost-appropriate story and trim it to fit.

OUR TURN

> This morning my delicate and formerly helpless wife took one look at our spluttering toaster and called the electrician. After hearing his service fee, she rolled up her sleeves and shooed me out of the house. "It can't be *that* difficult to fix!" she said defiantly, a screwdriver in her clenched fist. I pulled out the plug and fled. My dear wife, my gentle Melissa, had joined millions of her fellow citizens and become a "do-it-yourselfer"!

YOUR TURN _____

_____

_____

_____

_____

_____

_____

_____

There are many other kinds of introductions, of course; but these six are proved achievers. Any one of them, skillfully handled, will catch your reader's attention. Your next job is to hold that reader as you plunge into the middle (or body) of your essay. On to Chapter 32. . . . .

32. THE MIDDLE: FOUR VARIATIONS

You have an eye-striking, mind-boggling introduction. Now what? How do you go about organizing a mountain of notes? What procedure should you follow?

You have four choices. Surely *one* of them will fit what you want to say and how you want to say it!

The Chronological Approach

This is the easiest organizing method, and sometimes the most natural. Suppose you decide to write an essay about snowmobiling for your school newspaper. You think about it and, after a little research, you have notes that include information about

1   early experiences of snowmobiling in the U.S.
2   present records for speed and distance
3   instances in which snowmobiles saved lives
4   who invented the snowmobile and when
5   mass production and sale of snowmobiles

If you choose the chronological approach, you will begin with the invention of the snowmobile (#4), go on to early experiences (#1), to popular use (#5), to saving lives (#3), and end with present records (#2).

Notice, however, that the "saving lives" paragraph is not really chronologically oriented. You might prefer to use this information in your introduction or conclusion.

One advantage of the chronological approach is that it almost guarantees that your essay will be easily readable.

Practice Session

Here are some notes made by a student for an essay on "The Death of the Amateur in the Olympic Games." Using the chronological approach, indicate the order (#1–6) in which the following points should be discussed:

(____) Olympics revived in 1894—indirect compensation paid to many athletes.

(____) Olympics began in ancient Greece—quadrennial (every four years) celebration of mind *and* body. Purpose: to encourage mental and physical fitness. Rewards: a garland, a medal, a statue.

(____) In the 1960's, some competing athletes were permitted to "win" large sums of money in silly bets; others received envelopes that just happened to contain hundreds of dollars.

(____) In ancient Greece, winning became all-important. Some city-states started to recruit professional athletes, calling them amateurs and rewarding them generously. Partly because of this, the Olympics came to an end in 393 A.D.

(____) In the late 1960's and '70's, some athletes had "cover" jobs: not much work but plenty of salary; some received dividends from manufacturers of sporting equipment; some received "gifts."

(____) Not many real amateurs are left. Modern Olympic competition almost demands full-time training for years. What direction will the Olympics take?

YOUR TURN

Choose a topic that lends itself to the chronological treatment. (The history of something, for example, or the biography of someone.)

Topic _____

Now do just enough research (an encyclopedia should be helpful) to determine five or six points for discussion. List them below.

_____

_____

_____

_____

_____

_____

Finally, study these five or six items carefully. Number them to indicate a correct chronological arrangement.

The Process (or Step-by-Step) Approach

If you want to explain how something is made or operated, the process approach should work well. It too is quite simple. Just break down the process into steps; then arrange the steps logically.

For example: collage-making is popular in many English and social studies classes. Suppose you decide to write a brief article (possibly for an educational journal) explaining exactly how junior high students can go about creating imaginative collages. Based on your own experiences, you intend to include the following steps (but not necessarily in the following order):

1 Paste pictures, sayings, etc. on cardboard backing.

2 Choose a theme or topic.

3 With magic markers or paints, add a proper heading and possibly some graffiti.

4 Arrange all items in a meaningful order—from upper left to lower right, or from the center outward.

5 Collect pictures, headlines, newspaper stories, cartoons—anything relevant.

Now you *know* that if you handed those directions to a seventh grader, you would end with chaos, not a collage. So you arrange them in logical order. You begin with #2, then continue with #5, 4, 1, and 3, in that sequence.

The organization is now complete. All that remains to be done is to write five paragraphs, each giving details about one of the five steps. The result is a logical, coherent essay.

Practice Session

Here are some notes for an article designed to teach readers how to take *good* slides of a child's birthday party. Using the process approach, indicate the order (#1–9) in which the following points should be discussed:

(____) Take a couple of slides of the children at the table, pulling party crackers or eating ice cream.

(____) Take a couple of slides of the "aftermath"—the paper-littered dining room, the crying birthday child, the exhausted mother.

(____) Take a closeup shot of the cake; this can serve as a title slide for the series.

(____) Plan. Develop a story line.

(____) Take a slide of at least one of the guests leaving.

(____) Take a few shots of the pre-party planning: decorating, fixing candy baskets, etc.

(____) Take slides of the children playing various games. Keep these slides informal.

(____) Take a slide of the young host or hostess welcoming guests.

(____) Take a slide or two of the "party child" cutting the cake.

YOUR TURN

Choose a topic that lends itself to the step-by-step treatment.

Topic _____

Now probe your memory (or do some research) to determine the essential steps in the process. List them below.

_____

_____

_____

_____

_____

_____

_____

_____

_____

_____

_____

Review the steps listed. If they are not already in a logical order, number them to indicate the proper sequence.

The "Map" Approach

When the *Chronological* or *Process* approaches won't work, maybe the "map" approach will. It's especially helpful when you want to describe something: your community, a house (exterior or interior), even a face. The "map" approach simply suggests that you think of the way items are located *in relation to each other*.

Do you want to describe someone's face? Start with the hair—progress to the brow, the eyes, the nose, the cheekbones, the mouth, the chin. Or do it in reverse, starting with the chin and ending with the hair. The important thing is that there be a logical progression in your description, not a haphazard one.

Practice Session

Here are five groups of sentences that describe a run-down house. Using the "map" approach, indicate the order (#1–5) in which the groups should appear.

(_____) The roof was like the shingles—in total disrepair—torn and discolored.

(_____) Bewildered, I backed up for a better view. The shades were drawn down to the sills, and three panes of glass were missing. From the window to the left, a narrow ribbon of light glittered through a rip in the shade.

(_____) The path leading to the house must have been attractive once. But now some of the flagstones were broken and others were sunk deep in the mud.

(_____) Over all, rose the chimney, like an emaciated old man, doddering, on the verge of falling. "No smoke," I said hoarsely. "No fire at all."

(_____) As I rapped twice with the knocker, the thin plywood door shook on its sagging hinges. I touched the knob warily—it was loose and came off in my hand.

YOUR TURN

Start with one room in your house: your own room, perhaps, or the kitchen. Decide first the overall tone you hope to achieve: Is it a happy room? A sad room? A chaotic room? An unlived-in room? Then, using the "map" approach, write groups of sentences, each group dealing with a description of one object. In each group include at least one detail that contributes to the overall tone or effect.

_____

_____

_____

_____

_____

_____

_____

_____

_____

_____

_____

_____

_____

The Categories Approach

If none of the other methods of organization work, this one will. It is the most flexible and easily the most popular.

After taking the notes you have accumulated for a particular essay, you spread them out on a desk. Then divide them into categories. (This will be easier if you use 3 × 5 cards for all note-taking.)

For example: if you are writing an article about *why* many young people go to college, you might end up with the following categories:

1 higher salaries in the future
2 fun
3 admission to a desired field of work
4 acquisition of knowledge
5 boredom
6 lack of jobs available to high school graduates
7 desire to live away from home

Fine! You have seven categories. Now what? Well, it's a good idea to begin with a high-interest item—probably #1. Everyone is interested in earning the highest possible salary. From there, you might go on to #3 and 4, dealing with the serious student. These two paragraphs will probably be the "meat" of your essay. Items 2 and 5 might be thrown together, followed by #7 and then by #6. (Ending with #6 is good because it also is a high-interest item and is related to #1, thus giving added unity to the structure.)

This isn't the only possible organization for this essay. You have to decide what sequence is right for you; and your decision should be based on your *purpose* and your own *thinking style*.

Practice Session

Here are a few notes for an essay about "How a Senior Class Can Raise Funds." How would you arrange them logically (#1–6)? Remember these three rules:

        (*a*)   start with a high-interest item
        (*b*)   end with a high-interest item
        (*c*)   group similar items, whenever possible

(____)   Sales: bazaars, rummage sales, candy sales

(____)   Dues from all members of the class

(____)   Benefits: dances, movies, variety shows

(____)   Donations from parents, storeowners, friends

(____)   Work details: car washes, lawn mowing, baby-sitting

(____)   Raffles: of donated articles

YOUR TURN

Suggest a possible *Categories* organization for one of the following subjects:

Tricks You Can Teach Your Dog

Finding a Job Is Difficult When You've Had No Experience

A Review of _____
   (any novel you have read)

Collecting _____
   (fill in stamps, bottles, whatever)

_____

_____

_____

_____

_____

_____

_____

_____

All clear? At this point, you know how to start an essay and how to organize the body of it. You are probably wondering how to end it effectively. If so, proceed to the next chapter . . . .

33. ENDINGS: THREE VARIETIES

An ending is not just a period.

An ending is not just a closing phrase like "That's all I have to say."

An ending must be satisfying. It must truly *complete* all that has gone before. The reader may chuckle with approval, or dash out to mail a furious letter. It doesn't matter which—as long as the circle is closed.

In a way, that sums it up—

Here is a story with no ending    Here is a story with a good ending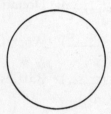

Closing the Circle: Variation I

The smoothest way to end an article is to go back to the beginning. Just—close the circle!

> **If you begin with this:**
>
> The biggest perennial source of senior headaches is raising money.
>
> **end with this.**
>
> Raising money will still cause senior headaches, but these six rules to financial success should eventually cure even the most stubborn migraines.

That ending not only closed the circle by swinging back to the introduction; it also summarized the body of the article: six rules for raising funds.

> **If you begin with this:**
>
> An amateur athlete is someone who plays for fun, not for money.
>
> **end with this.**
>
> With so many "amateurs" raking in bribes, dividends, and salaries for cover jobs, one wonders—is there a *real* amateur left in the world of sports? If there is, will he—or she—please stand up?

Here we provide the first sentence. You provide the last.

> **If you begin with this:**
>
> According to the most recent surveys, children spend more time sitting in front of the TV than they do sitting in the classroom.
>
> **end with this.**
>
> _____
>
> _____
>
> _____

This time you provide everything—the first sentence as well as the last—on any topic you choose.

> **If you begin with this:**
>
> _____
>
> _____
>
> _____
>
> _____
>
> **end with this.**
>
> _____
>
> _____
>
> _____
>
> _____

Closing the Circle: Variation II

Sometimes you may want to do more than just—close the circle. You can. You can redefine the problem and suggest a solution. Usually one sentence is not enough; you will have to work!

> **If you begin with this:**
>
> As unemployment sweeps across our country, more and more people are giving up. "Why keep trying?" they ask. "Why keep looking for jobs when none are to be had?"

end with this.

No matter what the economists say, *no* nation can long survive with high unemployment. The people are right. Jobs *must* be found—or created. Let our government soft-pedal everything else and concentrate on one thing: the bringing together of *what needs to be done* with the unwilling idle *who are eager to do it.*

YOUR TURN

If you begin with this:

Today's young people are bored. In their eternally frustrated quest for *meaning*, they worship gurus, collect in shabby communes, and venerate the unreal. What are they looking for? What is this *meaning* they seek so desperately?

end with this.

_____

_____

_____

_____

_____

Closing the Circle: Variation III

There is still a third way of closing the circle. You can end your essay or article by drawing a conclusion. This is especially good for a thoughtful or controversial piece of writing.

If you begin with this:

Once upon a time computers were just fancy machines. They could add or subtract, memorize, and give a report. Now something new has been suggested: tomorrow's computers may be able to make decisions!

end with this.

No doubt the decisions made for us by computers would be more logical—even better—than our own. But who wants to be ruled by a computer? Imagine asking a computer, "Shall I play tennis at 3 p.m.?" and being told, "No, stay home and study"! The computer can go on adding and memorizing, but it should leave decision-making where it belongs: in the finest computer of all, the human brain!

If you begin with this:

Most of our young people should stop being students when they are fourteen years old. They should leave school after eighth grade and go to work. If 20% go to high school and 10% go to college, there will be enough educated people to run this country. The rest should be doing what most people do best: following orders.

end with this.

_____

_____

_____

_____

_____

_____

_____

Endings are difficult, but a good one is as wildly satisfying to the writer as to the reader. It forces you to make decisions (_not_ computer ones!) and to take sides, firmly and un-equivocally. After you have finished, both you and your essay will be like perfect circles: complete and fulfilled, with no frayed edges. . . .

34. A PRIVATE GALLERY

Most private galleries are a conglomeration of hat rims, soles of shoes, and abbreviated heads. If you don't believe it, study your own family album. Better yet, listen while two other people browse through it, commenting all the way.

"That's Aunt Minnie behind the Lincoln Memorial. See—that's her hand sticking out at the right."

"This is Jim when he was three. You wouldn't guess it from this, but he had a beautiful smile. *You* know how kids are in front of a camera."

"That's Skip—the dog I had when I was little. Dad had a hard time getting Skip to stand still to have his picture taken. Skip was *never* still—always jumping and playing and having a ball!"

Sound familiar?

We are a nation of camera fiends. We carry cameras in our hands, over our shoulders, and around our necks; and we shoot everyone and everything. And a few days later we say sadly: "Well, Roger doesn't look *quite* like that."

The problem, of course, is that we shoot indiscriminately; we look (carelessly) with the lens and not with our eyes. To too many of us, the Grand Canyon is a thing of patches, a series of scraps glimpsed through the rangefinder. Because we haven't taken time to see the whole, to feel the whole, to understand the whole, our pictures are haphazard relics that carry little joy or meaning.

Our verbal pictures suffer from the same fault. Here's a typical student description of a mother:

> My Mom is sort of plump but still pretty. She has nice wavy brown hair and kind brown eyes. She cares about all of us, and she's always there when we need her. She likes to cook and to see us happy. To other people she may be just an average person, but to me she's beautiful.

What do we know about Mom? Nothing, really. She's the stereotyped mother of the stereotyped commercial. She's like every other mother in the world, and she's like none. For no one—not even a mother—is average, or ordinary. Each of us is an individual: eccentric and weird and wonderful; and a verbal picture must capture that "difference" if it is to be any good.

*   *   *   *   *

Before we actually start a character study, you have a decision to make. You can't create a character study without a character—so choose a subject to "photograph." It may be a parent or sister or brother, an uncle or aunt, a friend, or a neighbor. Choose someone who interests you and whom you know well.

YOUR SUBJECT _____

Physical Profile

The easiest part of any character study is physical details. "Mom," in the student description,

> is plump but pretty
> has brown wavy hair and brown eyes.

Fine—but what else? Does she have a mole to the right of her chin? Does she flush easily? Does she have the habit of flicking straggling hair from her brow with the pinkie of her right hand? (Review Chapter 17, "Parsing a Person," for additional suggestions.)

For "Mom," we might come up with a list like this:

—is plump and pretty

—hair is brown and wavy, but has a tendency to straggle

—while cooking, she has a tendency to use the pinkie of the right hand to flick hair from her brow

—is vigorous; does everything emphatically

—moves fast; can do several things at once

—has brown eyes that see everything—uses her eyes in frowning and smiling

—hands strong; long fingers; gentle

—voice strident, sometimes sharp, but always with an undercurrent of affection

Draw up a list of physical details suitable for *your* subject.

_____

_____

_____

_____

_____

_____

_____

_____

_____

Now let's see what happens when we *use* these physical details.

> My Mom is sort of plump but still pretty. She has nice wavy brown hair that has a tendency to straggle, and—especially when she's cooking—she's forever flicking it from her brow with the pinkie of her right hand. She moves vigorously, like an ambitious sergeant, organizing pots and pans, baking cookies, and ironing clothes. Her hands are strong enough to dig up a garden, gentle enough to comfort my little brother Jimmy. To other people, my mother may be just an average person, but to me she's beautiful.

YOUR TURN   (one word of caution: you don't have to use every detail you listed; use the ones that seem most important to you)

_____

_____

_____

_____

_____

_____

_____

_____

_____

_____

_____

_____

_____

_____

That's pretty good, isn't it? But it can be better. It needs something more—maybe unity, a touch of drama, *something!*

Caricature With a Difference

You tried your hand at writing a caricature in Chapter 27 (page 198), remember? A *good* caricature tries to create a single impression on the reader and does it dramatically. A *good* character study tries to do the same thing . . . but does it in a more gentle and honest fashion.

Consider again the revised description of "Mom." It needs unity, we said. Unity in a character study must come through the subject. What is Mom's salient characteristic—her outstanding trait? What do people remember years after they meet her? Her laughter? Her brisk practicality? Her bitter anger at injustice? Her green thumb?

Step 1

Now decide—what is your subject's salient (most striking) characteristic? Here are a few possibilities to trigger your thinking:

miserliness	optimism	orderliness
generosity	pessimism	impulsiveness
love of fair play	love for animals	self-pity
curiosity	love of cooking	egotism

There are dozens of others. Note below the trait you consider outstanding in your subject. Then add two other traits that the subject possesses, but to a lesser degree.

SALIENT CHARACTERISTIC _____

TWO LESSER TRAITS _____

_____

(Lesser traits are important: they will add depth to your character analysis. Using them, you can still create a single impression; but avoid turning your character study into a caricature.)

Step 2

The next step is to remember or create specific incidents that illustrate these traits. Let's say that "Mom," above all else, loves her family—that's her salient characteristic. She also loves to cook and is unusually generous. What does she do that *shows* she possesses each of these traits?

Mom's love for family: She smiles—and frowns—at us with vehemence. She really means it.

She has extraordinary faith in each of us, although she regularly condemns us for laziness.

When my little brother hurts himself, she comforts him with goodies.

Mom's love for cooking: She makes everything "from scratch"—it's better that way.

She's especially good at Italian cooking and sweet desserts.

Mom's generosity: She gives advice freely—to everyone.

She distributes food to friends and neighbors when they are ill or in trouble.

She gives *herself* to us.

Follow the same procedure with *your* subject. At the left, list the three traits you chose; at the right, list a few illustrations of each.

_____   _____

_____

_____

_____

_____

_____

_____

_____

_____

_____   _____

_____   _____

                                          _____

                                          _____

                                          _____

                                          _____

                                          _____

                                          _____

                                          _____

Step 3

This step isn't essential, but it will add a touch of drama to your character study. Probe your memory. Can you remember an incident in which your subject solved a problem or turned a difficulty into an advantage? If you can't, perhaps you can create one that *could* be true.

For the "Mom" study, it might be this:

> I remember once when I wanted to give up my pre-med course. Everything seemed too hard, too complicated. Mom threw the whole thing into perspective with a verbal slap and a coconut bar.

YOUR TURN _____

_____

_____

_____

_____

_____

_____

Even a mild conflict will give you a sort of skeleton on which to hang your description—as you will see in

Step 4

The final step is to weave the three traits, the illustrative material, and the dramatic incident together into an unmistakable portrait of your subject. The newly revised description of "Mom" might be something like this:

My Mom rules the kitchen as though it were a military base and she the only five-star general in the world. With one hand she stirs a huge cauldron of spaghetti sauce; with the other, she slaps around some dough for a pizza shell. With still another (she has an infinite number of hands that she can summon at will) she washes and bandaids Jimmy's bruised knee and stops his crying with a coconut bar. Every few seconds the pinkie of her right hand impatiently leaps to her forehead to flick away an undisciplined wisp of brown hair.

I slam my books shut and invade her empire. Mom frowns. "Pat, why aren't you studying?" she demands.

"I'm going to quit pre-med, Mom. It isn't worth it. My memory isn't big enough for all those bones and muscles."

She ignores me, scoops up a big pot of lamb stew from the stove and dumps it into a large casserole. "Sometimes I think you're just a lazy loafer, that's all. Here!" She thrusts the dish at me. "Make yourself useful for once. Take this to the Martins. With Jen in the hospital having an operation, and Lou out of a job, and one of the children sick with the flu, they *really* have trouble!" As I start for the door, I can still hear her calling—"Be careful! It's hot! Don't burn yourself!"

"And, Pat!" With the door half open, I turn to look at her. She's grinning, half angel, half Groucho Marx. "When you get back, Mr. Doctor, sir,—maybe you can have *two* coconut bars!"

I'm a pre-med student and coming up tomorrow is a final in anatomy; but suddenly I'm five years old again, and carefree. If my mother can cure bruised knees *and* the pre-med horrors with just a coconut bar, becoming an ordinary doctor should be a cinch!

YOUR TURN   You can use dialogue or not, as you like, but be sure to include your subject's major traits and some physical details—not by telling about them but by showing them through illustrative materials and a small dramatic incident. Good luck!

_____

_____

_____

_____

_____

_____

_____

_____

_____

_____

_____

_____

_____

_____

_____

_____

_____

_____

_____

_____

_____

_____

_____

Opening and Closing the Circle

As it stands, you have now a rather long anecdote that is also a character study. To become an essay, you need a beginning and an end.

The Beginning

Your beginning depends on your purpose. If you are writing this essay as an assignment—"The Most Unforgettable Person I've Ever Known"—you might use an introduction like this:

> If I had ever met George Washington or Eleanor Roosevelt, perhaps one of them would be *my* most unforgettable person. But I doubt it. A person doesn't have to be "public" to be memorable. I know. I have an "unforgettable" mother.

Determine your purpose; then write an introduction. (If you need some ideas, consult Chapter 31: "The Beginning.")

_____

_____

_____

_____

_____

_____

_____

_____

The Ending

The ending, remember, circles back to the beginning. Like this:

> I've never heard a sermon from my mother, but everything I know about courage and perseverance I've learned from her. I'll never forget her pizzas, or her stories about the Martins, or her proud but sarcastic "Mr. Doctor, sir!" In fact, I'll never forget *her*.

YOUR TURN   Review your introduction, recall your character study, then write your conclusion. (Chapter 33, "Endings," may be helpful.)

_____

_____

_____

_____

_____

_____

_____

_____

_____

This is a good time to start a special section of your journal: one for longer pieces of writing. Make this your first entry after combining your introduction, body, and conclusion.

If this seems like a lot of trouble, you should learn now about P. G. Wodehouse, the British-American humorist. Wodehouse wrote each page of each novel nine or ten times. He once told someone that after he was dead, probably everyone would talk about what a rotten writer he was. Then he added: "I hope at least one voice will be heard piping up: 'But he did take trouble.'"

If you emulate Wodehouse and "take trouble," you should soon have a satisfying anthology of which you can truly be proud.

35. JOURNEY TO THE KNOWN

Some writers sign up for a safari; others shiver in the Antarctic; and still others pull themselves, inch by inch, up the treacherous side of Mount Everest. Why? For most of them, it is the call of the unknown: the desire for a new experience, or for a promising subject for travel articles and books.

Yet it is not necessary to travel thousands of miles to find the unknown. Often the unknown lurks within the known. Often you can stumble upon it within a mile or two of your home . . . or even closer.

Here's the formula:

```
1  Select the place you want to write about.
2  Collect details.
3  Determine purpose and mood.
4  Select and organize details.
5  Write.
```

Select the Place

Select a place that really interests you . . . one you are curious about . . . or one that played a part in your childhood . . . or one that fascinates or appals you.

Some possibilities:

> a haunted house
> a nearby factory
> your first-grade classroom
> a cemetery
> the kitchen of a restaurant in town
> a historic landmark
> the house you lived in several years ago
> a hospital room

Before you make a decision, be sure you have access to the place. (You can't describe a particular kitchen unless you have permission to spend some time exploring it—or unless you happen to work in it!)

OUR CHOICE   Sleepy Hills Cemetery

YOUR CHOICE _____

Collect Details

Drumming up details is absolutely the first step. Try the library; talk with people; explore the place itself. (For additional help, see Chapter 15: "Research.")

Sleepy Hills Cemetery was founded in 1833.

The oldest marker reads:

> Daughter of Gen. William and Mrs. Mary Parker
> who died April the 4th, 1833,
> aged 2 years.
> "She died before she could live."

The Parkers (one of the founding families of Sleepy Hills) are well represented: Gen. William Parker, Col. Joseph Parker, Sgt. William Parker, Private William Parker, and a dozen or so others.

Sleepy Hills Cemetery includes some wooded areas, meadows, hills; newest plots near river.

Ten acres—head caretaker, Phil Tucker—been here for sixty years, is 76 years old. Said: "This place is really buzzing! The Parker plot is full up, but over there, there's lots of growing room. We have 3,400 bodies already. What do you think of that?"

Town of Sleepy Hills—once river port; now dying. Population 2600. Young people hate it.

Other markers in cemetery: ballerina; several millionaires; Ben Knolls; Sarah Chilton; pirate; many infants; one for 106-year-old woman.

YOUR DETAILS _____

_____

_____

_____

_____

_____

_____

_____

_____

_____

_____

_____

_____

_____

_____

Clarify Purpose

This may seem a strange time to think about your purpose—but it's a logical time. You now have plenty of "info" about a particular place. How can you use it?

> . . . To boost your community?

> . . . To arouse people to action?

> . . . To express some important but abstract idea?

> . . . To entertain or amuse?

OUR PURPOSE   to write an article about Sleepy Hills Cemetery that will make the people aware that the town of Sleepy Hills is rapidly deteriorating.

YOUR PURPOSE   _____
_____
_____

Determine Mood

Next comes mood—what mood are you aiming for? Will your essay be serious or humorous? Argumentative or expository? Nostalgic? Sentimental? Sarcastic? The mood should be determined by *two* factors: your purpose, and the details that you have accumulated.

Our *purpose* is to emphasize the deterioration of Sleepy Hills.

Our *details* support the idea that the whole town (with the exception of the cemetery) is dying.

Our *mood* (almost necessarily) will be a combination of the nostalgic and the sarcastic.

Your *purpose* is to _____

Your *details* _____
_____

Your *mood* will be _____
_____

Select and Organize Details

This step is highly personal. Every writer handles it in his or her own way.

- You may want to cross out notes you are not interested in, and underline others.

- Or you may want to scrawl memos to yourself: "good for introduction," "use in ending," etc.

- Or you may want to study your notes until they are part of you, then begin writing.

We recommend the first or second approach until you have done quite a bit of writing; eventually the organization becomes almost automatic.

Write

Now is the moment of truth!

- Remember your purpose.
- Remember the mood or tone at which you are aiming.
- Use your details to create the mood and to fulfill the purpose.

If you have trouble with the organization, the introduction, or the ending, review the first three chapters of this Unit (Chapters 31–33).

Here's our essay. Notice how, in the first paragraph, a few details emphasize the contrast between town and cemetery. The second paragraph describes the town as it was. The next three paragraphs concentrate on the "excitement" of cemetery life. And the last two paragraphs draw a conclusion and offer the reader a shocking choice between town and cemetery.

But we still have no title. Something short, something with a punch . . . how about

EPITAPH FOR A TOWN

In the village of Sleepy Hills, the storekeepers stopped taking inventory ten years ago, and sullen parents watch as the last of their young people leave for the "city." The liveliest place in town is at the end of Main Street—in the outskirts, really. Here rolling green hills are "home" to gallant soldiers, men who made and lost millions, the builder of a school, the creator of a court system, and a famous ballerina. It's the Sleepy Hills Cemetery.

In 1833, when the cemetery was founded, Sleepy Hills was a bustling river port with a population of almost 15,000. Ships waited in line to take on cargo. On Main Street, farmers and their wives stared in wonder at the new emporium, and speculators swaggered about, ostentatiously consulting huge gold timepieces. On town meeting night, the schoolhouse was jammed— everyone had something to say, everyone was deeply concerned about the present and the future of Sleepy Hills. That was in 1833.

In the ten-acre cemetery, you can still feel much of that early excitement. Here is the marker for Benjamin Knolls: a man of honor who placed the education of ALL children before his own welfare. Ben, single-handed, raised the money and supervised the building of the school. (Take a look at it now, but hurry: it's collapsing.) Here's another marker, this one for Sarah Chilton: "No one loved justice more; no one understood mercy better." Remember hearing about Sarah? She fought fiercely to establish a *good* court system in Sleepy Hills. While she was alive, no bribes were taken, no judges corrupted, no citizens unwilling to serve on juries. We need Sarah today.

The Parker plot is a capsule history of the town . . . from General William Parker who died in the Civil War "a gallant leader of gallant troops"; to

Colonel Joseph Parker who was a Roughrider under Teddy Roosevelt; to Sergeant William Parker who recruited soldiers during World War I; to Private William Parker who went AWOL during World War II and six years later drank himself to death. There's no one left in the Parker family now . . . and not much left of the town the old General helped to found.

Phil Tucker has been the head caretaker at Sleepy Hills for sixty years. He keeps the lawn trimmed, the flowers watered, and the gravestones shining. He has little time for pessimistic conversation about hopelessness and immorality and resignation. "This place is really buzzing!" he says enthusiastically. "The Parker plot is full up, but over there—" he gestures to a new section he has just opened—"over there, there's lots of growing room. We have 3,400 bodies already! What do you think of that?"

What do I think of that, Phil Tucker? Here, you have a population of 3,400; in town, we're down to 2600 and losing another hundred every year. Here, everything is in order, looking forward to the future; in town, everything is seedy, and nobody believes in any future at all. What I think, Phil Tucker, is that it's time for a change. Maybe you should become mayor of Sleepy Hills. It's time to make the town hall ring with protests and projects again; time to rebuild our school from the inside out; time for another Ben Knolls and another Sarah Chilton.

There's an alternative, though. We can just change signs: put the Sleepy Hills Cemetery sign here on Main Street, and put the Town of Sleepy Hills sign next to the very first grave:

Daughter of Gen. William and Mrs. Mary Parker
who died April the 4th, 1833,
aged 2 years.
"She died before she could live."

YOUR ESSAY

_____

_____

_____

_____

_____

_____

_____

_____

_____

_____

_____

_____

36. GARAGE SALES AND GARBAGE TRUCKS

Do you realize that every day has 24 hours, that every hour has 60 minutes, that every minute has 60 seconds, and that in every one of those 86,400 seconds daily something is happening? The chances are good that every day there are at least 86,400 different stories knocking at your brain, pleading for attention. (Remember *that* the next time you "can't think of anything to write about!")

We're not talking about big events now—like wars, or murders, or even birthday parties . . . but about the small things that occur almost without our noticing them.

You are lazily glancing out the window as a garbage truck goes by. On the side of the truck is painted: "Your garbage is our lunch." You shudder a little and go back to drying the dishes. But whether you realize it or not, several articles also just went by. An article about the men who collect garbage—how they feel, how they got into this line of work. An article about odd sayings on trucks. An article about garbage disposal and the environment. A philosophical inquiry into the meaning of "Your garbage is our lunch."

Your mother goes to a garage sale and you decide to accompany her. Stand a little to one side; watch, listen, and make mental notes. Ask yourself questions: Is your mother-at-a-garage-sale different from your mother-at-home? Who holds garage sales? Why? When did they start? What kinds of people go to them? What sort of stuff do they sell? What prices do they charge? Notice the often expensive cars that prospective customers drive up in. Listen to the bargaining. Consider the one-interest buyers: the men interested only in tools, the women interested only in books. There are at least a dozen articles here.

Move to still smaller events. Accidentally you sprinkle nutmeg instead of cinnamon on a slice of toast. It tastes different. You wonder where nutmeg comes from, what it's used for. You wonder how many people each day accidentally reach for the wrong container; and you wonder what the results are.

Play Detective

One of the best ways to develop a writer's mind is to become a story detective. Try your hand at finding the "hidden" stories in everyday life.

Begin with school. Think about it. Where might a hidden story lurk?

Some possibilities:

bake sales	paintings and portraits in classrooms
band practice	ball-point pen vending machines
school colors	visitors to the school

Choose one topic: _____

List at least five questions that would be helpful in exploring the topic. (If you need help, check questions about garage sales.)

_____

_____

_____

_____

_____

Now try it at home.

Some possibilities:

report card day	a pet hit by a car
dental appointments	loss of electricity for four hours
family TV viewing	the family car

Your topic: _____

Five questions: _____

_____

_____

_____

_____

_____

Choose one of the school or home topics and consider this your current project.

Topic: _____

Acquire Answers

You already have a list of five questions about your topic. Go out now and get answers. You may have to visit the main office or the school dietitian. You may have to interview people—even members of your own family. However you do it, get the answers and write them below.

_____

_____

_____

_____

_____

_____

_____

_____

_____

_____

_____

_____

Add a New Dimension

Most of the "info" you now have is basic. Start digging—find something new, something different.

Are you writing about a dog hit by a car? Call a veterinarian and find out how often injured dogs are brought to his office. Or call a police station: find out how many dead dogs are reported weekly.

Are you writing about a vending machine for ball-point pens? Write to the manufacturer of the machine. Who thought up the machine? Where are most of the machines placed? How many machines of this type are in operation? Are there any major problems?

Get the idea? Dig. Add this special, different information below.

_____

_____

_____

_____

_____

_____

_____

_____

_____

Collect Quotations

Quotations are vitality boosters (see "Drama Through Dialogue," page 162). Collect a half dozen that you can use or not use as you see fit. Get quotations from a variety of people.

For example: for a bake sale, get a quotation from the student who baked cookies, from her or his parent, from the school dietitian, from the owner of a bakery, from a customer.

List the quotations below. Be sure to identify each one.

_____

_____

_____

_____

_____

_____

_____

_____

_____

_____

_____

Garnish With the Off-Beat

People love odd facts. (Note the recurring trivia craze.) Find something different, unusual . . . something that will make your reader say to a friend, "Hey, did you know that—?"

Like what?   Like—what did the very first vending machine dispense?
              Like—did kids in ancient Greece get report cards?
              Like—how old are false teeth?

Where do you find "off-beat info" of this type?

Explore a few of the following:

> Any good encyclopedia
> *The People's Almanac* by David Wallechinsky and Irving Wallace
> *Famous First Facts and Records* by Joseph N. Kane
> *Guinness Book of World Records* by Norris McWhirter and Ross McWhirter
> Almanacs of all kinds

Write below at least one odd fact that is relevant to your topic and can be included in your essay.

_____

_____

_____

Complete the Catechism

1   What is your purpose in writing this article?

_____

_____

2   What mood are you aiming for?

_____

_____

3 List below the 3 to 5 major points, in order, that you will be discussing:

_____

_____

_____

_____

_____

You're ready. Start writing. Refer, if necessary, to Chapter 31 (introductions), Chapter 32 (organization), and Chapter 33 (endings). And don't forget to top the essay with a brilliant, scintillating title!

_____

_____

_____

_____

_____

_____

_____

_____

_____

_____

_____

_____

_____

_____

_____

_____

37. ON YOUR MARK!

Big, flashy events lead to good articles, too. They don't occur as frequently as minor events, but they provide dozens of "spin-off" ideas.

The Big Story

First choose a topic for your "big story." And choose carefully: you are going to be working with it for quite a while!
Some possibilities:

> a specific athletic event
> a community celebration (e.g., for Fourth of July)
> a covered-dish supper or church picnic
> an auction or bazaar
> a visit to your school or community by a well-known
> politician or entertainer

YOUR CHOICE _____

Now be a reporter. Get the facts . . . *all* the facts. And don't forget to collect a few quotations and anecdotes.
Use this material to write a feature article for a newspaper. This means

(*a*) start with a lead paragraph that gives the most important information *and* catches the reader's attention;

(*b*) give a straight chronological rundown on the event itself, but "spice" with quotations, statistics, and anecdotes;

(*c*) end with a brief conclusion that is also forceful.

Work on scrap paper. When you have finished, check your work and copy the polished feature below. It should be about 200 words.

_____
_____
_____
_____
_____
_____
_____
_____
_____

_____

_____

_____

_____

_____

_____

_____

_____

_____

The Spin-Off

More fun than the basic big story, for many writers, is the spin-off. This is an article suggested by the main topic.

Suppose you wrote about a cross-country ski competition that took place in your town. You've already written the big story—the feature. But before and during and after the event, there are dozens of possible spin-off stories.

To wit:

Interviews with the skiers . . . why they took up cross-country skiing . . . what they get out of it . . . why they compete . . . how they train.

Interviews with coaches . . . what aspects of training are most important.

Interviews with sporting goods storeowners and manufacturers of cross-country skiing equipment . . . "secrets" about best equipment . . . maintenance.

Famous cross-country ski trails.

History of cross-country skiing . . . when it started . . . where.

Cross-country skiers as life savers.

Present popularity of the sport . . . why it is popular . . . how many people go out for it.

Cross-country skiing in the Olympics.

What doctors think of cross-country skiing.

Comparison of speed and techniques for men and for women in cross-country skiing.

Children and cross-country skiing.

Fashion outfits for cross-country skiing.

What to eat . . . and where . . . when you're cross-country skiing.

Sections of this country in which it is popular . . . other parts of the world.

You see? We've barely glided over the surface of the topic and we already have at least two dozen possible spin-off stories.

Take your "big story"—examine it from every possible angle—find and list at least ten spin-off stories coming from the original story.

_____

_____

_____

_____

_____

_____

_____

_____

_____

_____

Now choose *one* of your spin-off topics and write an introductory paragraph for a new feature story. (Refer to Chapter 31 to review writing an introduction.)

_____

_____

_____

_____

_____

_____

_____

_____

_____

If you're pleased with your introduction and you're interested in the topic, why not write the rest of the story? If you do, copy it into your journal—the section for longer, completed works.

The Remote Spin-Off

The most challenge, though, lies in the remote spin-off—usually a general commentary of some kind. Before you can begin, you must have a strong point of view and have done some thoughtful thinking about the topic.

Let an example be your guide. George Sheehan, a middle-aged cardiologist (heart specialist), was also a devoted sports fan. For years, he watched professional sports, and the longer he watched, the more he realized that professional athletes no longer "played" at sports; they worked at it. He wondered if they had lost the ability to play "just for fun."

After much pondering, Dr. Sheehan wrote an article called "Play Is Where Life Lives, Where the Game Is the Game" which was printed in *The Physician and Sportsmedicine* and later in the New York *Times*. It's a perfect "remote spin-off" story. We'll come back to it in a few minutes, but first let's set up our own remote spin-offs.

Finding Ideas for a Remote Spin-Off

After working and thinking about cross-country skiing, we might wonder if the growing emphasis on winter sports is humanity's subconscious attempt to prepare for a coming Ice Age. Now there's a remote spin-off story that would be fun to write!

Or (more practically) we might become interested in Tourism as an industry and explore its influence on sports like cross-country skiing. Are motels, restaurants, etc. coming into existence to serve recreational athletes, or are motel and restaurant owners deliberately creating an appeal for recreational sports? If the latter, is this a service or a disservice?

That should be enough to get you started. Think about your own big story topic and your own spin-off suggestions. Then broaden your thinking base to include health, or education, or economic measures. Think, examine, and muse until you come up with at least one strong remote spin-off story on your basic topic.

YOUR REMOTE SPIN-OFF _____ .

_____

_____

_____

_____

Writing the Remote Spin-Off

Writing this kind of story is a greater challenge because it covers a broader field. But it's also more fun because you can put more of yourself into it.

George Sheehan, for example, in his essay on "playing," equated sports and life. In the very first paragraph he zoomed in on the role of "play" in life itself. (Notice how neatly he twisted Shakespeare's "to be or not to be" to construct an eyecatching introduction.)

> Shakespeare was wrong. To play or not to play: that is the real question.
> Anyone with a sense of humor can see that life is a joke, not a tragedy. It
> is also a riddle, and like all riddles has an obvious answer: play, not suicide.*

_____

Write an introduction for your own remote spin-off:

_____

_____

_____

_____

_____

_____

_____

_____

Dr. Sheehan then went on to regret the way professional athletes work at their playing; and at the way politicians—and all of us—have followed their example. Peace of mind, he claims, comes only from playing at life for its own sake, not from playing (or working) to win.

Near the end of his essay, Dr. Sheehan cites phys. ed. as a perfect example of play turned into work.

> What happened to our play on our way to becoming adults? Downgraded by the intellectuals, dismissed by the economists, put aside by the psychologists, it was left to the teachers to deliver the coup de grace. "Physical education" was born and turned what was joy into boredom, fun into drudgery, pleasure into work. What might have led us into Eden led us into a blind alley instead, and simply changed our view of the universe.*

List below the major points you will cover in your remote spin-off essay. Include at least one concrete example as proof of your idea—as Sheehan included the phys. ed. example.

_____

_____

_____

_____

_____

_____

_____

_____

_____

_____

In his concluding paragraph, Dr. Sheehan swings back to his introduction. But he does considerably more: he expands and deepens and broadens the very concept of play so that, as we finish the story, we are almost forced to weigh our own actions—one by one—against this exciting new measure. Watch the way he does this:

> Play, of course, says otherwise. You may already have found that out. If you are doing something you would do for nothing, then you are on your way to salvation. And if you could drop it in a minute and forget the outcome, you are even further along. And if while you are doing it you are transported into another existence, there is no need for you to worry about the future.*

Write your own conclusion now, following Dr. Sheehan's general approach.

_____
_____
_____
_____
_____
_____
_____
_____
_____
_____

Now complete the essay and make a clean copy. If several other students have participated in this exercise, try this: keep swapping papers and reading rapidly until each of you finds one paper with which you violently disagree. Write a short essay, in answer; and return both to the original author ... who will then write a short essay to answer your answer, and return all three to you ... who will then— You see? You can keep it going forever! George Sheehan's original essay started a year-long controversy in the New York *Times* as people with different points of view joined the battle.

Maybe that's another reason the remote spin-off story is so popular in our time: it gives us a chance to tell everyone what is wrong with the world. Now, if only someone will listen. . . . . .

---

38. SHARPENED SWORDS

Here's a chance to combine the creative and the practical.

Every newspaper prints reviews: reviews of books, plays, concerts, movies, even TV shows. And—here's good news!—it's not too difficult to get a review printed, especially in small local newspapers. It's also a chance to thrust a sword or two, as you will see.

Selecting a Subject

Begin by choosing the subject you are going to review. For this practice session, select something you have already seen or read.

Some possibilities:

> a novel read as a class assignment
> an admired (or much-disliked) movie
> a school play (if presented recently)
> a TV drama seen recently (or a weekly drama)
> a favorite record

Choose a specific work to review.

YOUR CHOICE _____

Accumulating Data

Now scurry about collecting data until you have enough to complete all the items below that are applicable to your choice.

Title _____

Author (or composer) _____

Date (of publication, release, or performance) _____

Names of major characters _____

_____

_____

Setting _____

Director _____

Actors _____

_____

_____

Other works by same author or composer _____

_____

Mastering the Storyline

Summarize the storyline, in detail. (For a recording, summarize the overall theme, in detail.) Be sure to include the beginning, the development, and the ending; one or two major scenes; and at least one interesting incident.

_____
_____
_____
_____
_____
_____
_____
_____

Establishing Your Point of View

As a critic, you must have a definite point of view. Are you for, or against, your subject? You will find that the following questions will help you to determine particular aspects of your point of view. Answer briefly all that apply to your subject.

1 Was the storyline strong? Did it grip you? Is it believable?

_____
_____
_____
_____

2 Are the characters rounded, rather than one-dimensional? Are they realistic?

_____
_____
_____

3 Is the setting clearly described or shown? Is it subtly related to the storyline?

_____
_____
_____

4 What is the mood of the work? Is the mood sustained throughout?

_____
_____
_____

5 Comment briefly on anything else that you especially liked or disliked (e.g., the author's style, the lighting, the closeups, the sets, etc.).

_____

_____

_____

_____

_____

_____

Collecting Supplementary Information

There are other kinds of information that, while not essential, will help to make your review more interesting.

For example:

— for a recording: Has this recording star made other records? How did they sell? How were they received?

— for a novel: Did this author write any other books? Name a couple of titles. How did they sell?

— for a movie: Are there any Oscar winners in the cast? What other pictures are credited to the director?

— for all: Have you heard any anecdotes about the writing or producing of this specific work?

List below any supplementary information you can find.

_____

_____

_____

_____

_____

_____

Identifying the Purpose

While it's not always possible to determine an author's or composer's purpose in creating a particular work, you can at least make an educated guess. Is the work primarily designed to entertain? Or is it supposed to make us think about a particular problem or point of injustice? Be as definite as you can about the writer's or producer's probable purpose.

_____

_____

_____

Playing the Prophet

Here's a chance to do a little predicting. Will this play or record or book be popular? Will it make money? Will it win any awards? *Should* it? Have a little fun here, take a risk or two. No one can hang you for making a prediction that doesn't come true!

_____

_____

_____

Special Preparation: You have enough material now, but you may still feel a touch uncertain. Even professional critics often do. Turn to a few professionals before you begin writing. If you are reviewing a novel, read a few reviews of other novels. If you are reviewing a recording, read a few reviews of other records. Use them to help you to organize your material. Then list below the five major points you will discuss, in the order in which you will discuss them.

_____

_____

_____

_____

_____

Sharpen Your Sword

The critic has a special prerogative: to slash and lash without mercy. After seeing a play, for example, you may criticize the storyline, the characterization, the acting, the directing, the sets, even the structure of the theater. This is, according to the rules of the game, fair play. But there's a hitch: you must do it cleverly.

> *Don't* say: "The acting was rotten."
> *Do* say: "The best acting appeared after the final curtain."

Even if you love the play or novel you are reviewing, there must be one or two things about it that you don't like. For a moment, focus on one of them. Then sharpen your verbal sword by taking a thrust or two at it.

_____

_____

❖   ❖   ❖

Write

With your brain sharpened (as well as your sword), you couldn't be more ready. Write a review that will delight *or* horrify—not one that will leave the reader wondering how you really feel about the subject. Be definite; be specific; be emphatic. GO!

_____

_____

_____

_____

_____

_____

_____

_____

_____

_____

_____

_____

_____

_____

_____

_____

_____

_____

_____

_____

_____

Now that you know *how* to write a review, you may enjoy repeat performances. If you get really good at it, try submitting your work to your school or local newspaper. And if that doesn't work, try the back door: write your review as a Letter to the Editor. They will almost *have* to print it, then!

One word of caution: if your judgments and predictions are printed, *you* become a fair target; and you may have other critics thrusting verbal swords at you. Pity the poor 19th century reviewer who liked *The Adventures of Tom Sawyer*, the new novel by Mark Twain, but who found it a bit too violent, with too much emphasis placed on the wicked deeds of Tom and his friends. His final judgment—it's a good story but probably shouldn't be read by children!

39. IDEAS AND YOU

Have you ever had an interior light bulb flick on, and felt like crying "Eureka!" If you have, you know that was the moment an idea was born.

For a writer, an idea is priceless: something to foster, to strengthen, to become the pearl around which an essay or poem can grow. Where do you find such pearls? You already possess them; you only have to find them, deep within yourself.

Your Past, Present, and Future

In one of James Joyce's novels, a character realizes that since all of his body cells change every seven years, he has, in a sense, already been several different people and will probably be several more before he dies. It is a fascinating idea . . .

The Past You

Start with the past—the *you* of the first two seven-year periods—up to the age of 14. Be as detached as you can.

> What kind of child were you?
> What did you like and dislike?
> What values, if any, did you already have?

(Be brutally honest. After all, this was a different *you* that you are examining so critically . . . a *you* that no longer exists.)

> Did you have a terrible temper?
> Were you stubborn?
> Or were you almost unbearably sweet and docile?

Describe this earlier *you* in detail. Consider starting with an anecdote: one that sums up that early self.

_____

_____

_____

_____

_____

_____

_____

_____

_____

_____

_____
_____
_____
_____

The Present You

This will be harder—it is almost impossible to be objective about ourselves *as we are*. But try.

> What are you like now? (Ignore physical appearance unless it really matters to you.)
> What kind of person are you?
> What values do you cherish?
> Which aspects of life seem important to you?
> Which seem unimportant?
> How do you relate to other people: to your family, to your friends?

Describe yourself, as you are now, in detail. Include a brief comparison with the earlier self described in "The Past You."

_____
_____
_____
_____
_____
_____
_____
_____
_____
_____
_____
_____

The Future You

Here is a chance to dream. What will you be like in the year 2000?

> Will your present values still be meaningful to you?
> What will you be doing?
> What will you have accomplished?
> What will you think of your teen-age children?
> How will the future *you* be different from the present you?
> How will it be the same?

All of this is hypothetical, of course. Life handles all of us in different ways—opens and shuts unexpected doors—twists us and straightens us in an apparently meaningless alternation. But you can make an educated guess, based on the present you and the past you. Describe that future self in detail.

_____
_____
_____
_____
_____
_____
_____
_____
_____
_____
_____
_____
_____
_____

A Wrap-Up

Now with all this under your belt, try one more experiment. Write a letter from your present self to your future self. Tell that future self (circa 2000 A.D.) what you think it should know; what you think it should remember. Take your time with this. Remember—you are creating a letter of advice to the person you may become. This is your last chance to remind that person how you feel *now*.

_____
_____
_____
_____
_____
_____
_____
_____
_____
_____
_____

_____

_____

_____

_____

_____

_____

_____

_____

_____

When you have finished the letter, copy it, place the copy in an envelope, seal it, and address the envelope to yourself, the year 2000. Then place it in a jewelry box, a Bible, an album—some place where it will not easily get lost. On your birthday, in the year 2000, open the letter . . . and read. If you were totally honest, the contents of that letter may mean more to you than the wisest teaching of the wisest philosopher.

                 *   *   *

What does all that have to do with you as a writer? The answer is that it has everything to do with it.

Reread your descriptions of your three selves and your letter to your future self. What ideas run through all four pieces of writing? Are you concerned with religious ideas, like faith in God, immortality, the existence of a soul? Or with political ideas, like liberty and equality? Or with economic ideas, like the right to earn a living? Or with generally humane ideas like loyalty and concern for others?

If one idea trails through all four selections, you can be pretty certain that this idea is a part of you—that it will shape your thinking and your behavior in the years ahead; that it will, to some extent, determine your point of view.

Let this new knowledge of yourself serve you in two ways: as a storehouse of the ideas especially important to you, and as an indicator of your own angle of vision.

                 *   *   *

Russell Baker, a syndicated columnist and satirist, has written hundreds of essays about his ideas. One of them, "Spaced Out," is worth close examination. It is really a kind of prose-poem.

Baker starts with an idea that is not new, but which most of us keep forgetting. The *idea:* that though world-wide catastrophes threaten, the only thing truly important to most of us is our present, individual state. The idea is important, but it is the way Baker expresses the idea that makes us realize its importance.

And this is the reason writers exist: *to turn an old idea into a new idea, to make us think and feel.*

Read "Spaced Out"—preferably aloud.

SPACED OUT*

by Russell Baker

I am sitting here 93 million miles from the sun on a rounded rock which is spinning at the rate of 1,000 miles an hour,

and roaring through space to nobody-knows-where,

to keep a rendezvous with nobody-knows-what,

for nobody-knows-why,

and all around me whole continents are drifting rootlessly over the surface of the planet,

India ramming into the underbelly of Asia, America skidding off toward China by way of Alaska,

Antarctica slipping away from Africa at the rate of an inch per eon,

and my head pointing down into space with nothing between me and infinity but something called gravity which I can't even understand, and which you can't even buy anyplace so as to have some stored away for a gravityless day,

while off to the north of me the polar ice cap may,

or may not,

be getting ready to send down oceanic mountains of ice that will bury everything from Bangor to Richmond in a ponderous white death,

and there, off to the east, the ocean is tearing away at the land and wrenching it into the sea bottom and coming back for more,

as if the ocean is determined to claim it all before the deadly swarms of killer bees,

which are moving relentlessly northward from South America,

can get here to take possession,

although it seems more likely that the protective ozone layer in the upper atmosphere may collapse first,

exposing us all, ocean, killer bees and me, too,

to the merciless spraying of deadly cosmic rays.

I am sitting here on this spinning, speeding rock surrounded by four billion people,

eight planets,

one awesome lot of galaxies,

hydrogen bombs enough to kill me 30 times over,

and mountains of handguns and frozen food,

and I am being swept along in the whole galaxy's insane dash toward the far wall of the universe,

across distances longer to traverse than Sunday afternoon on the New Jersey Turnpike,

so long, in fact, that when we get there I shall be at least 800,000 years old,

provided, of course, that the whole galaxy doesn't run into another speeding galaxy at some poorly marked universal intersection and turn us all into space garbage,

or that the sun doesn't burn out in the meantime,

or that some highly intelligent ferns from deepest space do not land from flying fern pots and cage me up in a greenhouse for scientific study.

So, as I say, I am sitting here with the continents moving, and killer bees coming, and the ocean eating away, and the ice cap poised, and the galaxy racing across the universe,

and the thermonuclear 30-times-over bombs stacked up around me,

and only the gravity holding me onto the rock,

which, if you saw it from Spica or Arcturus, you wouldn't even be able to see, since it is so minute that even from these relatively close stars it would look no bigger than an ant in the Sahara Desert as viewed from the top of the Empire State Building,

and as I sit here,

93 million miles from the sun,

I am feeling absolutely miserable,

and realize,

with self-pity and despair,

that I am

getting a cold.

Isn't that last section incredible? So many ways of destroying our world, so many terrors we may have to face—yet all sink to nothing compared to the simple fact that I, the individual human being—wrapped in my ego, concerned only with my own existence—*am getting a cold*. Beautiful.

You are probably eager to start expressing *your* idea in a new and startling way; but before you do, spend a few minutes analyzing some aspects of Baker's style.

Sharpen your own style by extracting from Baker's essay examples of the following techniques. (If you need help, refer to the page number following each technique.)

piling up of details for effect (p. 166): _____

_____

_____

hyperbole (p. 193): _____

_____

litotes (p. 199): _____

vivid strong verbs (p. 158): _____

_____

parallelism (p. 144): _____

_____

_____

You're ready. Use the all-prose, or the prose-poem, approach—whichever you prefer. Take an idea from one (or all) of those four mini-essays you wrote at the beginning of this chapter. Then think, for a long time, about *how* you can express it in a new and different way—so startling, so unexpected that it will shock your reader into paying attention and reacting.

This is—granted—a difficult assignment; but if you do it well, you will have a richly satisfying experience. You will be exhausted, but cleansed. You will have truly created. And, best of all, you will have in your hands a non-violent weapon to influence the thinking of your own section of humanity.

Begin. . . .

_____

_____

_____

_____

_____

_____

_____

_____

_____

_____

_____

_____

_____

_____

_____

_____

_____

_____

_____

_____

_____

_____

_____

Unit VII
The Poem

INTRODUCTION

A poem is. . . .Well, what do the *poets* say a poem is?

Edgar Allan Poe said: *With me poetry has not been a purpose, but a passion.*

Emily Dickinson said: *If I read a book and it makes my whole body so cold no fire can ever warm me, I know that it is poetry. If I feel physically as if the top of my head were taken off, I know that is poetry. These are the only ways I know it. Is there any other way?*

Percy Bysshe Shelley said: *Poetry is the record of the best and happiest moments of the happiest and best minds.*

Robert Frost said: *Poetry is a fresh look and a fresh listen.* And he also said: a poem *begins in delight and ends in wisdom.*

What all of these poets seem to be saying is that they write poems because what they want to say is too passionate, too tenuous, too supernal to be expressed in prose.
But maybe that's too "highfalutin'." One might say, simply . . .

A poem is an itch.

It teases and torments you; it will not go away; *it will not let you be.*
If a boy in second grade learns "I have a little shadow that goes in and out with me . . .," the lines will pop up to haunt him decades later in the middle of an important business meeting.
If a fourteen-year-old girl memorizes "Out of the night that covers me/ Black as the pit from pole to pole . . . ," she will find the words surfacing a half century later when despair threatens.

A poem is an itch.

It asks—who am I? and who is God? and *why* is the world? A poem never asks simple questions, like "What are we going to have for dinner?" It always asks absurd questions, like "What is a friend?" (impossible to answer) or "Tell me, exactly what is love?" (blasphemous even to ask!)

A poem is an itch.

It will never let you be. It wants you to do outrageous things like imagining that the strokes of a clock are really apples falling from a tree, and the tree is life's time, and you can't ever, ever pick up those apples once they have fallen ("A Harvest to Seduce" by Melville Cane, page 284). It wants you to place failure, and insults, and the contempt of the world on one side of the scale and love on the other, and find *love* the weightier ("Sonnet 29" by William Shakespeare, page 328). It wants you to endure the death of one loved by discovering within yourself the ribs and beams of the structural pattern underlying life ("Patterns" by Amy Lowell, pages 330–332).

A poem is an itch.

It gives you insomnia; it appears suddenly in a vagrant cloud; it makes the mind rock; it plants a seed of discontent that can shatter smugness; it contradicts—freezing and burning simultaneously. It lulls, and agitates, and maddens, and soothes.
Never mind. Let Archibald MacLeish say it:

> *A poem should not mean*
> *But be.*

---

*From Archibald MacLeish's "Ars Poetica" from COLLECTED POEMS OF ARCHIBALD MACLEISH. Reprinted by permission of Houghton Mifflin Company.

1 *Re-creation*. The time is now. God, disillusioned with humans, has decided to re-create them. He advertises for an assistant. You wish to apply, and you know you should be ready to suggest possible revisions. List five changes that you think would be helpful in humans in today's world. (Example: Automatic ear flaps that would descend when a jet plane is overhead or while snowmobiling.)

_____

_____

_____

_____

_____

_____

_____

_____

_____

_____

2 *Tantalizing Titles*. Create some story titles with appropriate authors that should exist but don't; for example: the TV chiller, *Blizzard*, by I. C. Snow. Try for three.

_____

_____

_____

3 *Rhyme Time*. Divide into two teams. Team A offers a line; Team B must come up with a second line that rhymes with it.

> TEAM A Once upon a June day *dreary*,

> TEAM B Home I came completely *weary*.

If Team B is successful, it gets a point and gives a new first line. If it is not successful, it challenges Team A to provide a line. If Team A can do so, *it* gets a point and once again gives a first line.

Before you begin, jot down a few words that may offer trouble.

Examples: *trouble* (possible rhymes: *double*, *bubble*)
  nightingale (possible rhymes: *biting hail*, or *writing mail*)

_____

_____

_____

_____

4 *Taste Treat*. Make up an alphabetical list of things you like to eat: A—avocado; B—beans; C—candy, etc. Try to find something you really like for every letter of the alphabet.

A _____   H _____   O _____   U _____

B _____   I _____   P _____   V _____

C _____   J _____   Q _____   W _____

D _____   K _____   R _____   X _____

E _____   L _____   S _____   Y _____

F _____   M _____   T _____   Z _____

G _____   N _____

5 *Wastebasket Wizardry*.   Take an old wastebasket. Transform it into a gift for someone you know well. Use paint, contact paper, decals, anything. Add bits of poetry and/or short quotations appropriate for the person. Describe the wastebasket as it looks (or would look) after this "restoration."

_____

_____

_____

_____

6 *The Ice Age Cometh*.   You suddenly find yourself and a friend sitting on the roof of your house. The sun is bright and hot, and the two of you are wearing just shorts and shirts. But from the north sweeps a horizon-wide glacier, inexorably and rapidly. Already the ice around the house is ten feet deep. The new ice age is here. Write either a brief description of the scene or a description of your thoughts.

_____

_____

_____

_____

7 *City Census*.   Take the name of a city. Divide into syllables. Define each syllable and see if someone else can identify it from your definitions. Keep the definitions in the order of the syllables.

Examples: half golden + half silver = DEN VER
            beret + my father = TAM PA

Prepare three. Then test each one.

_____

_____

_____

8 *Easel Time.* Draw a monster, depending on your imagination, not on monsters already created by others. Then invent a name for this monster. Write a few lines of doggerel verse describing the monster and his actions.

9 *Recipes for Recycling.* As our natural resources are used up, it becomes more and more important that we recycle as many things as possible. Some recycling is being done commercially—as with paper. But much can be done by individuals. Plastic detergent bottles, for example, can be washed, marked with numbers from *one* to *ten*, and used as bowling pins in a game for children. Exercise your ingenuity by dreaming up a practical *second* use for each of the following articles:

egg boxes _____

cereal boxes _____

small juice cans _____

stale bread _____

a bent spoon _____

10 *Sound-Vision.* Borrow a small tape recorder and record half a dozen unusual noises: the hum of a refrigerator, rain falling on a cake tin, etc. Swap tapes with another person. Play the new tape, listening to each sound until you *see* it. Record briefly what you *see* through your ears. For example, from the first sound, you might quite literally see a refrigerator that is humming, but with a little imagination you might see a bee buzzing on the window pane, or a fellow student hissing softly during an exam, or a large balloon slowly being deflated. Be as imaginative as you can.

40. A POEM IS BORN

Some poems spring into existence, fully formed. Others begin as a single word or the sprig of an idea, and grow with painful slowness. It matters not.

"Kubla Khan" by Coleridge came in a dream and the poet had little to do but write it down.

"Rudolph the Red-Nosed Reindeer" began as a work assignment. In 1939, Robert May wrote catalog copy for Montgomery Ward. One day his boss asked him to write a Christmas story that could be given away to children during the holiday season. Eight months later, May submitted a story in verse about Rudolph and his red nose. Millions of copies were distributed, it was rewritten as a song, and became an animated cartoon . . . the rest is "tradition."

Another poem "written to order" (request, really, in this case) is "On the Finish of the Sailing Ship Race" by John Masefield. In 1963, the Long Island marine historian, Frank Braynard, was working on plans for an international race of square-rigged ships in conjunction with the World's Fair. He wrote to Masefield, then the Poet Laureate of England, and asked him to write a poem for the occasion; and he visited President Kennedy asking him to review the sailing ships as they entered New York Harbor. Both agreed; but a few months later the President was assassinated. Masefield continued with his poem, dedicating it to the former Navy officer. He included these lines:

> ". . . He has gone . . .
> Among the radiant, ever venturing on,
> Somewhere, with morning, as such spirits will."

Most poems, however, come neither in a dream nor as an assignment or request. Most poems come because a poet *wills* them to. Melville Cane in *Making a Poem*, one of the few books on this subject, suggested one recipe. Make yourself quiet, he said, receptive and willing. When an idea comes, or a word, write it down quickly until words pile up, helter-skelter, on the page. During this process the first line will appear, almost by accident. Play with it, develop it, letting the form of the poem and the fulfillment of the idea *grow* as the poem grows.

Cane described how one poem, "A Harvest to Seduce," evolved from this recipe. Night after night he found himself disturbed by the midnight striking of an old-fashioned bedroom clock. He found himself waiting for it, listening to it, thinking about it. Gradually the strokes changed. They took on a "globular shape," then turned into twelve apples falling from an apple tree. That image gave birth to the phrase, "the tree of time."

Cane thought some more, realized he had been brooding overmuch on the things he had left undone and on the irrevocable passing of time. Such brooding, near self-pity, is seductive. At this point, the poet knew the poem he had to write.

A HARVEST TO SEDUCE[*]
by Melville Cane

Upon the tree of time
The fruit looms high,
The fruit so fair to pluck.
The hour's late and black.
The time-tree quivers,
Loosens and delivers
The midnight crop.

Twelve drop,
A harvest to seduce,
Lacking joy or juice.

Beware the vain lament,
The hunger for what's spent.
This is dead-sea fruit
And ashes to the taste.
Quash it with your foot.
What is past is past.

This is Cane's favorite recipe; but there are others.

**** At a time of anger or other emotional stress, release that emotion into a poem, freeing it to create rather than to destroy.

**** Keep a dictionary always at hand; sometimes a word or a definition will trigger a poem.

**** Take notes—of things, facts, words. When you're in the mood to write, read them over until one "clicks."

**** Above all, write . . . write every day . . . and if you can think of nothing to write about, scrawl words at random on a piece of paper. Such scribbling often leads the way to sense.

Another poet, Edith Segal, once walked lonely in the night. A familiar face approached, and her heart beat faster: a chance to walk, a chance to talk . . . But the friend had an appointment; and—doubly lonely, now—Edith returned to her apartment and wrote two lines in her notebook:

Take my hand and walk with me,
Be my friend and talk to me.

There they stayed until, years later, they suddenly burst into the title poem of her first collection of poetry for children.

What both Cane and Segal seem to be saying is that any poem, any good poem anyway, must come from within us—from our own experience—from our hurts and dreams and fears.

---

[*]"A Harvest to Seduce" by Melville Cane. © 1956 by Melville Cane. Reprinted from his volume, MAKING A POEM, by permission of Harcourt Brace Jovanovich, Inc.

It is time now to consider giving birth to some poems of your own.

I Remember . . .

Several poets (and who should know better?) suggest that you start with "I remember . . ."

> I remember a school carnival where I pitched pennies and won a silver whistle.
>
> I remember a green frog, chopped to pieces in Daddy's lawn mower.
>
> I remember a pink and frilly dress I ripped to shreds, sliding down a stone balustrade.
>
> And I remember the thunder in my mother's eyes when she saw it.

You try it. Plunge into memory. Go back as far as you can; and rescue your earliest "I remembers . . ."

_____

_____

_____

_____

_____

_____

_____

_____

_____

_____

_____

_____

_____

_____

If you have been honest, you have there the beginning of a poem . . . for you have resurrected the true, and that is the source of poetry.

Definition: Level I

Another road to poetry is to define something—not as the dictionary would define it, but through specific memories. Consider *childhood*. How would *you* define it? Here's what one student wrote:

Childhood is walking along the street on the fifth of July,
    looking for unspent firecrackers.

Childhood is waking up early to read *Tom Sawyer* in the
    first light,
  and taking a flashlight to bed to read *Little Women*
    under the covers.

Childhood is selling lemonade, and falling off a swing,
    and getting lost in the woods called Bloody Hollow.

Childhood is cotton candy.

Childhood is playing Monopoly on rainy afternoons, and
    hearing grownups say *no* a thousand times,
    and *never, never* stepping on a crack because
    it'll break your mother's back.

Childhood is jumping rope,
  and playing Red Rover at dusk,
  and beating up the boy down the block because his
    three-wheel bicycle is bigger than yours and
    he won't give you a turn.

Childhood is saying, "Star light, star bright, first star
  I see tonight; I wish I may, I wish I might, have the
  wish I make tonight"
    and believing it.

YOUR TURN   (Be honest; use real memories; and be specific.)

_____

_____

_____

_____

_____

_____

_____

_____

_____

_____

_____

_____

_____

_____

Definition: Level II

Now define something in a different way. Hold to your remembering, and to the (unaccustomed) taste of honesty in your mouth; but go a step beyond. Bring in all five senses to help you. Melissa Rowland of Cincinnati, Ohio, defined "loneliness" like this:

> Loneliness is grey.
> It sounds like a cold wind in winter.
> It smells like an attic in autumn.
> It tastes like bitter aspirin.
> Loneliness feels like a tear gently running
> down your face.*

Notice that each line takes off from a different "sense" and that the first line is almost a metaphor, while the remaining four use similes. (Review pages 117–121.)

YOUR TURN _____

_____

_____

_____

_____

_____

* * * *

A few more quick ways to get the poetic juices flowing:

Word Harvest

Jot down a dozen or so words that you find interesting: words like dragonet or helicopter or mitten. Then write a short poem using one or more of these words (it can be a nonsense poem).

YOUR WORDS

_____ _____ _____ _____

_____ _____ _____ _____

_____ _____ _____

YOUR POEM _____

_____

_____

_____

_____

_____

_____

*Special permission granted by *Read Magazine*, published by Xerox Education Publications, © Xerox Corp., 1975.

Petty Theft

"Steal" the first line of a children's rhyme or well-known poem. Then toss the original aside and complete the poem in a totally different spirit and with different content.

MODEL: Twinkle, twinkle, little star
How I wonder what you are.
Up above the world so high
Like a diamond in the sky.

NEW VERSION: Twinkle, twinkle, little star,
How you resent what you are!
Wanting fame and glory bright,
Doomed to chorus lines at night.

MODEL: _____

_____

_____

_____

NEW VERSION: _____

_____

_____

_____

Color Serenade

Write a color poem. Start each line like this:

        Red is . . .
        Green is . . .   etc.

Let the rest of each line be literal (e.g., "red is the color of a frostbitten nose") or figurative ("red is a rhino, mad from the sun"). Include at least five colors.

_____

_____

_____

_____

_____

_____

Right now, before you go any further, start a new section in your journal. Note any words that daze or delight you. Note any smell that appeals, any sight that appals. Note cloud formations and the ways people smile and the sound of an angry fly. Note ideas. Note phrases that come to you out of the blue; and phrases you create laboriously between two math problems. Note bits of dialogue, how a tear falls, your last thought before falling asleep.

41. TIME. MIME. LIME. RHYME.

Rhymes are for children and minor poets. So say the savants, and they should know it. The fact remains (as everyone knows) that rhyming is fun, even in prose.

A well-placed rhyme will keep you in time. It will brighten your words into swift silver birds. It lends a neat charm to an essay on farms; gives a dignified air to a sonnet on hair. It lingers (once said) like a tune in your head; teases memory till sadness has fled. So please, won't you try? To terse verse, rhyme apply.

Terse Verse

Make your title long, and your verse short but strong:

To a Jazz-Loving Friend at the Concert's End

Scat,
Cat!

From an Ungrammatical but Concerned Mother to Her Often Sloppy and Ravenous Brother

Eat
Neat.

It's your turn now; just take a bow.

TITLE _____

VERSE   _____

               _____

TITLE _____

VERSE   _____

               _____

Terse Verse Made Worse

Play the game just the same, but use polysyllabic rhymes.

What the Sharp-tongued Music Critic Said of the Pianist Whose Playing Was Heavy as Lead

Malingering
Fingering.

How the Captain Described His First Mate, Who Went to Bed Early and Got Up Late

Cruiser
Snoozer.

Your turn to churn:

TITLE _____

_____

VERSE _____

_____

TITLE _____

_____

VERSE _____

_____

Strain Your Brain

Another thing that's fun to do is to rhyme one word with two ... perhaps perverse, but good for light verse.

> Danny had a little tan doe,
> For whom he liked to play the banjo.

Got it? Transmit.

_____

_____

Rhyme Time

This time select a word you love and list all the rhymes you can think of: e.g., for *like*, there's mike and spike, bike, hike, and strike, and even tyke.

YOUR WORD SUBLIME _____

YOUR RHYMES

_____	_____	_____	_____
_____	_____	_____	_____
_____	_____	_____	_____
_____	_____	_____	_____

Now mix them up; combine anew. Try a four-line stanza rhyming stew.

_____

_____

_____

_____

❋　❋　❋　❋　❋　❋　❋

Kinds of Rhyme

There are three kinds of end-rhyme (an end-rhyme is simply one that occurs at the *end* of a line):

> Single (also called masculine or strong)
> Double (also called feminine or weak)
> Triple

The *single* rhyme is the most common: a one-syllable rhyme, like *night* and *sight*, or *June* and *tune*. It is illustrated in the following limerick:

> There was an obliging young *snail*,
> Who wished to deliver the *mail*;
> And he said that though **slow**
> He was sure he could **go**
> Once a week to each house without *fail*.[1]

The *double* rhyme is a two-syllable rhyme: like *fighting* and *biting*, or *daughter* and *water*.

> There was once an absurd Allig*ator*,
> Who wanted to serve as head-*waiter*,
> And was greatly **enraged**
> When they said they'd **engaged**
> One whose outward attractions were *greater*.[2]

Lines 1, 2, and 5 end with true double rhymes. Lines 3 and 4 *seem* to end in double rhymes but really end in single rhymes since the first syllables in "*en*raged" and "*en*gaged" are identical (rather than rhyming).

The *triple* rhyme is a three-syllable rhyme: like *hungering* and *blundering*.

> To them it was *glorious*,
> To march home *victorious* . . .

Double and triple rhymes are especially useful in writing light verse. Look at what Hilaire Belloc created with the help of triple rhymes:

THE HIPPOPOTAMUS
by Hilaire Belloc

> I shoot the Hippopotamus
> With bullets made of *platinum*
> Because if I use leaden ones
> His hide is sure to *flatten 'em*.[3]

[1,2]"The Kind Snail" and "The Absurd Alligator," by Isabel F. Bellows, in *St. Nicholas*, July and June 1887 respectively.
[3]"The Hippopotamus," by Hilaire Belloc, from CAUTIONARY VERSES. Copyright 1931, Alfred A. Knopf, Inc.

Try your hand at a couplet (two lines) or quatrain (four lines) employing double or triple rhymes. You'll enjoy it more if you follow Belloc's example and aim for a "far-out" second rhyme.

_____

_____

_____

_____

Internal Rhyme

A different kind of rhyme is the *internal rhyme* which occurs between two or more words in the same line of verse, or between two words, other than end words, in different lines of verse. Poe used the first type when he wrote—

Once upon a midnight *dreary*, while I pondered weak and *weary* . . .

Thomas Hood used the second type:

> *Lizzy!* go down and open the street-door;
> *Busy* I am to any one but him.
> *Know* him you must—he has been often here;
> *Show* him upstairs, and tell him I'm alone.*

Internal rhyme, especially as Poe used it, is excellent if you are writing a poem that needs a strong swinging rhythm. Try a quatrain; it can be as simple and nonsensical as this:

> With his hat in his *hand*, the cat took a firm *stand*
> Defending his saucer of milk . . .
> "It's mine, it's all *mine*! and I think it's di*vine*
> Drinking *milk* in a hat made of *silk*!"

YOURS _____

_____

_____

_____

Almost-Rhymes

There are two more techniques, more subtle than rhyme, that will add a smoothness and a hidden music to your poetry. The first is **assonance**. Assonance is a repetition of *vowel* sounds. For example, *bone* and *cone* are rhymes: but *bone* and *home* illustrate assonance. Below, label each pair of words as rhyme or assonance.

_____

*Thomas Hood. "The Double Knock," in POEMS OF THOMAS HOOD, selected by William Cole, copyright 1968. Reprinted by permission of Thomas Y. Crowell Company, Inc.

a	true and blue	_____
b	fate and lake	_____
c	ice and five	_____
d	mellow and yellow	_____
e	hungry and month	_____

The second kind of almost-rhyme is *consonance*: a repetition of *consonant* sounds. The repeated sound may be at the beginning of words (as in alliteration, page 71) or in the middle or at the ending of words. Some examples from Tennyson's "In Memoriam":*

O yet we trust that somehow good	(alliteration and consonance)
Will be the final goal of ill	(consonance)
To pangs of nature, sins of will	(consonance)
Defects of doubt, and taints of blood . . .	(alliteration and consonance)

This time indicate whether each line below includes alliteration or consonance, or both.

"A pin or a pen?"	_____
Implored a plump pup.	_____
"It's a sin not to spin,"	_____
Quipped the plate to the cup.	_____

Rhyme Scheme

The rhyme scheme is simply the pattern of rhymes in a particular poem or kind of poem. Letters of the alphabet are used to indicate different word endings.

Words that have the same ending (that rhyme) are represented by the same letter.

In June	a
he tolled	b
a tune	a
so bold.	b

The rhyme scheme for this "poem" is, then, a, b, a, b.

But if we change the lines around—

In June	a
he tolled	b
so bold	b
a tune.	a

the rhyme scheme changes too; this time, it's a, b, b, a.

---

*From "In Memoriam," by Alfred Lord Tennyson, in THE POEMS AND PLAYS OF ALFRED LORD TENNYSON. Copyright 1938, The Modern Library.

More letters of the alphabet can, of course, be used. If we revise our poem slightly, to this—

In June	a
he tolled	b
a bell	c
so bold	b

we have still a third rhyme scheme: a, b, c, b.

It is possible to write doggerel to any rhyme scheme. Suppose someone suggests this one: a, a, b, b, a. Something like this would fit:

At sea	a
The bee	a
Found flies,	b
Two pies,	b
And me.	a

It's practice time for you. Write nonsense verses to fit the following rhyme schemes:

_____ a

_____ b

_____ a

_____ b

_____ a

and

_____ a

_____ b

_____ c

_____ b

_____ a

Today fashion dictates that poetry should not rhyme. That's incorrect; it would be more accurate to say that poetry *need* not rhyme. Some fine poets use no rhyme at all: the King James translation of the Bible (most notably, the "Psalms") is without rhyme; so is the best of Whitman's work. But some other fine poets have (and still do) use rhyme: Shakespeare did, and Keats, and Emily Dickinson; and Leonard Cohen still does. The important thing is that you know how to use it.

That is true of rhyme, but not of assonance and consonance; these techniques, less familiar, are essential. The most modern poetry (if it is to be poetry) must have flow and liquidity and grace—and these are almost unattainable without assonance and consonance. Learn to use them deliberately, and you will soon be using them automatically . . . in prose as well as in verse.

Besides—this whole gallery of rhyming tricks (and in a sense that's what techniques are) is tremendously helpful in writing light verse. Light verse can be pure fun, but it can also be a severe teacher, pointing a satirical finger at our faults or rapping our knuckles with ironic comment. For a delightful closing, relish this poetic tidbit by Richard Armour, a master of light verse.

PERSONNEL OPINION
by Richard Armour

You can't keep a good man down.
    The times I have heard this are myriad.
In fact, as employers know,
    You can't keep a good man, period.*

---

*Richard Armour's "Personnel Opinion," in WRITING LIGHT VERSE AND PROSE HUMOR. Copyright 1947, The Writer, Inc., Boston. Reprinted by permission of Richard Armour.

42. RHYTHM LESSON

One, two, three . . . *one*, two, three . . . *one*, two, three, . . . *one*, two, three.

Sound familiar? It's the dancing teacher's attempt to pound rhythm into reluctant feet and sullen heads. If you have any sense of rhythm at all, you will *feel* that first long step, followed by two shorter ones.

Recognizing—and putting—the rhythm into poetry is not much different. There are six basic *metrical feet*[1] (of which you will want to know two well) and eight *metrical lines*[2] (of which you will wish to master five).

If you are a free-verse addict, you are probably moaning about "destruction of creativity" and "regulations" and "the end of spontaneity." As Scrooge would say, *Humbug!* Spontaneity is the result, not the means. It takes brutally hard work to hammer out a line that looks easy and flowing. Knowledge of the traditional rhythms, skill in handling the different rhythms are as vital to the writer of free verse as to the writer of the sonnet. In the latter, the pattern is obvious. In the former, the pattern is hidden. But in both cases, there is, there must be a rhythmical pattern.

Metrical Feet

Every language has its own innate rhythm; and the innate rhythm of English is the iambic foot. Walt Whitman wrote whole paragraphs of prose using iambic feet. You can *dream* in iambic with only a little effort!

The Iamb

Try this. With a pencil, drum lightly on a book or desk. For the first beat, hit lightly and quickly, moving on to the second beat. For the second, hit a little harder and dwell on it. Pause. Repeat. Pause. Repeat. If we use this sign (˘) for the short first beat, and this sign (—) for the longer, second beat, your drumming can be charted like this:

$$\smile\ -/\smile\ -/\smile\ -/$$

Before we go any further, master the iambic rhythm thoroughly.

a Below, mark the second line, indicating iambic feet.

$$\overset{\smile}{\text{She}}\ \overset{-}{\text{went}}\ \Big/\ \overset{\smile}{\text{to}}\ \overset{-}{\text{town}}\ \Big/$$

To buy a gown.

---

[1]A *metrical foot* is a unit consisting of some stressed and unstressed syllables.
[2]A *metrical line* consists of a specific number of metrical feet.

b   This time write a second line in iambic to match the first.

$$\breve{H}e \;\; \overline{bought} \;\Big|\; \breve{a} \;\; \overline{fan} \;\Big|\; \breve{cy} \;\; \overline{car} \;\Big|$$

_____

c   Finally, write two rhyming lines in iambic, on any topic, of any length. Mark the iambic feet.

_____

_____

The iambic foot is the basic foot in English. It is used for serious poetry, light poetry, even prose. A second popular foot is the *anapest*.

The Anapest

This time, with your pencil, drum a different tune: hit two light, short strokes, followed by one harder, longer one. It would look like this:

$$\breve{} \;\; \breve{} \;\; \overline{} \;\Big|\; \breve{} \;\; \breve{} \;\; \overline{} \;\Big|\; \breve{} \;\; \breve{} \;\; \overline{} \;\Big|\; \breve{} \;\; \breve{} \;\; \overline{} \;\Big|$$

This is the *anapestic* line. It's excellent for light, sprightly verse—to convey action—to provide a stronger, more pronounced rhythm. But it is less natural and less versatile.

Master the anapest.

a   Below, mark the second line, indicating anapestic feet.

$$\breve{I} \;\; \breve{will} \;\; \overline{walk} \;\Big|\; \breve{with} \;\; \breve{an} \;\; \overline{air} \;\Big|$$

Of a man with green hair.

b   This time, write a second line in anapestic to match the first.

$$\breve{In} \;\; \breve{a} \;\; \overline{land} \;\Big|\; \breve{far} \;\; \breve{a} \;\; \overline{way} \;\Big|$$

_____

c   Finally, write two rhyming lines in anapestic, on any topic, of any length. Mark the anapestic feet.

_____

_____

The other four metrical feet are less often used, but you should be familiar with them.

The *trochee:* the trochaic foot is a two-syllable foot, the opposite of the iambic: one long syllable, followed by one short syllable.

$$- \smile \ | - \smile \ | - \smile \ | - \smile \ |$$

You may recognize one of the opening lines from *Macbeth:*

$$\overline{\text{Dou}} \breve{\text{ble,}} \ \big/ \overline{\text{dou}} \breve{\text{ble,}} \ \big/ \overline{\text{toil}} \ \breve{\text{and}} \ \big/ \overline{\text{trou}} \breve{\text{ble}} \ \big/$$

The *dactyl:* the dactylic foot is a three-syllable foot, the opposite of the anapestic: one long syllable, followed by two short syllables.

$$- \smile \smile \ | - \smile \smile \ | - \smile \smile \ | - \smile \smile \ |$$

For example (from Tennyson):

$$\overline{\text{Love}} \ \breve{\text{a}} \breve{\text{gain,}} \ \big/ \overline{\text{song}} \ \breve{\text{a}} \breve{\text{gain,}} \ \big/ \overline{\text{nest}} \ \breve{\text{a}} \breve{\text{gain,}} \ \big/ \overline{\text{young}} \ \breve{\text{a}} \breve{\text{gain.}} \ \big/$$

The *spondee:* the spondaic foot is a two-syllable foot, with both syllables long. (This metrical foot is usually used only for variation within a line.) Compound words are usually spondaic: e.g., football.

$$- - \ | - - \ | - - \ |$$

The *pyrrhic:* the pyrrhic foot is a two-syllable foot, with both syllables short. (Like the spondee, the pyrrhic is usually used only for variation within a line.)

$$\smile \smile \ | \smile \smile \ | \smile \smile \ |$$

You can, almost completely, forget the last two; just remember they are there to provide variation and to prevent a singsong quality. It is the first four—and especially the first two—on which you should concentrate.

Metrical Lines

Part of metrical rhythm is the metrical line: it may be very short or very long. Here are the eight basic metrical lines. If you notice the prefix in each name, you will find them fairly easy to remember.

*mono*meter	one foot per line
*di*meter	two feet per line
*tri*meter	three feet per line
*tetra*meter	four feet per line
*penta*meter	five feet per line
*hexa*meter	six feet per line
*hepta*meter	seven feet per line
*octo*meter	eight feet per line

These metrical lines combine with metrical feet in all sorts of fascinating combinations. For example, monometer and iambic (i.e., iambic monometer) will give you a rapid, often amusing verse.

> To town
> I went
> To buy
> A tent.
> But tents
> Were high.
> I'd buy
> A pie.
> Still pies
> Cause fat.
> Perhaps
> A hat?   etcetera, etcetera.

You can keep this kind of rhyming going almost indefinitely. In fact, it could make a fun kind of game in class or at a party.

Try a different combination: some dimeter, some trimeter, both mostly anapestic. The limerick form is a good one for practice of this kind.*

> There was/a small boy/of Woonsock/et
> Who fas/tened himself/to a rock/et.
> He went/up quite straight/
> But 'tis need/less to state/
> That he did/not return/to Woonsock/et.

Notice that the first, second, and fifth lines are trimeter; the third and fourth are dimeter. Although most of the feet are anapestic, the first syllable of each of the first three lines is an iamb. Most interesting, though, is the short "homeless" syllable at the ends of lines 1, 2, and 5. These leftover syllables occur frequently in limericks (usually, as here, in lines 1, 2, and 5) and provide an additional touch of humor.

---

*"There Was a Small Boy of Woonsocket," by Margaret Vandegrift, in *St. Nicholas*, July, 1887.

Try a limerick of your own now. Follow the metrical line-metrical foot pattern closely, and adhere to the rhyme scheme: a, a, b, b, a. Remember: nonsense is not only permitted; it's preferred!

_____

_____

_____

_____

_____

Non-metrical Rhythm

Not all rhythm is metrical, or measured. Often it is irregular, and hence impossible to pattern. Rhythm demands recurring accents or stresses but not at specified intervals. There is rhythm in the trotting of a horse, in the jingling of bells, in a heartbeat. It is far more difficult than metrical rhythm to analyze, to understand, and to use—*because* it is irregular. No one can show you how to incorporate this kind of rhythm into your writing. You must *feel* it (though practice with metrical rhythm will often increase this more natural rhythm).

Read aloud this excerpt from "Out of the Cradle Endlessly Rocking" by Walt Whitman. Though there is no pattern of meter, there is a strong, insistent rhythm.

> Once Paumanok,
> When the lilac-scent was in the air and Fifth-month
>   grass was growing,
> Up this seashore in some briers,
> Two feathered guests from Alabama, two together,
> And their nest, and four light-green eggs spotted with brown,
> And every day the he-bird to and fro near at hand,
> And every day the she-bird crouched on her nest, silent,
>   with bright eyes,
> And every day I, a curious boy, never too close, never
>   disturbing them,
> Cautiously peering, absorbing, translating.*

The rhythm lies, in part, in the recurring *-ing* words; in the repetition ("And every day"; "never"); in the frequent use of "and" to merge and blend; in small patterns of phrases ("in the air" and "up this seashore" and "in some briers"). It lies in all of these, in word-choice, in a piling of emotion on emotion until the culmination in the final two lines. Do you see why this kind of rhythm is almost impossible to analyze? Listen to your heartbeat. Now pretend to be frightened; frighten yourself. Listen to your heartbeat change—grow faster, pound a little, skip a beat, pound again. Let it taper off. Listen to it slow down, hop occasionally, slow some more. It *cannot* be charted; it cannot be thoroughly analyzed; but the rhythm is there, unmistakable and powerful.

_____

*Walt Whitman's "Out of the Cradle Endlessly Rocking" in THE COMPLETE POETRY AND PROSE OF WALT WHITMAN. Copyright 1954, Doubleday & Company, Inc.

It is this rhythm you will find in the finest poems—sometimes with, sometimes without metrical rhythm. If you hope to acquire it, you will have to learn to listen to your heartbeat, to the movement of ocean and wind, to the cadence of birdsong and cicada, to the inaudible rhythm of sun, moon, and stars. And after you have listened, and absorbed, you may (and only *may*) be able to get that rhythm into your own writing.

Meanwhile—while you are listening and absorbing—play with metrical rhythm. Before you can fly, you must run; and before you can run, you must toddle. So "toddle" with iambic monometer or anapestic dimeter. You did—when you were a baby, with nonsense sounds. Do it again, delight in it and in yourself, and feel rhythm grow in your blood and bones.

43. TROPE REVIEW

When a general reviews his troops, he is simply making sure they are in good working condition: that, if needed, they will be alert, prepared, and ready to spring into action. This is precisely the purpose of this chapter: to give you a chance to review your *tropes* (troops) so that they will be there, waiting, when you need them.

You are already familiar with most of these tropes; you have both played and worked with them. The few new ones are marked with an asterisk (*). So assume a military bearing, straighten your poet's cap, and pass in leisurely fashion before the ranks. After each trope, a small lighthearted example (in verse) is given. Respond with one of your own. Restrict yourself to nonsense verse; it's more fun and less blasphemous. For greater challenge (but this is optional) try to use the metrical foot-metrical line pattern illustrated in each example.

Alliteration

Alliteration is the recurring of initial sounds.

> Review pages 71–73.

EXAMPLE   (anapestic tetrameter)

> When _t_wo-_t_iming _T_essie _t_rips _t_o _t_own,
> She wears _g_rim, _g_rey _g_loves and a _g_ossamer _g_own.

YOUR TURN   _____

_____

*Antithesis

Antithesis is the deliberate contrasting of two terms for effect. A well-known example is Alexander Pope's "Man proposes, God disposes." "Proposes" (offers) and "disposes" (settles) are opposites, placed together; because they rhyme, they are doubly effective. But rhyme isn't necessary as you can see in Shakespeare's "Fair is foul and foul is fair"—another example of antithesis.

EXAMPLE   (iambic dimeter)

> When credit's *high*
>   And debts are *low*
> From *work* to *play*
>   We're apt to go.
>
> When credit's *low*
>   And debts are *high*,
> From *play* to *work*
>   We're apt to fly.

_____

_____

_____

_____

_____

_____

_____

_____

*Apostrophe

Apostrophe occurs when we address the dead (as if they were living), the inanimate (as if they were capable of understanding), the absent (as if they were present). Shakespeare used it when Macbeth, after killing King Duncan, heard a bell and said mournfully: "Hear it not, Duncan; for it is a knell/That summons thee to heaven or to hell." John Donne used it memorably when he wrote "Death, be not proud . . ." And children use it when they chant tearfully: "Rain, rain, go away/Come again another day."

EXAMPLE   (iambic trimeter)

> O *Rain*, withhold your tears!
> Shine gently, gentle *Sun!*
> Dear *Wind*, try not to blow!
> (I just had my hair done.)

YOUR TURN _____

_____

_____

_____

Hyperbole

Hyperbole is an exaggeration so wild that no one is expected to believe it.

| Review pages 193–194. |

EXAMPLE   (alternating lines of anapestic tetrameter and trimeter)

> She appeared in a hat, such a glorious hat
>   That the passersby fainted in awe.
> Made of satin and steel, trimmed with bright
>   orange peel,
>   It drooped past her brow to her jaw.

YOUR TURN _____

_____

_____

_____

Litotes

Litotes is understatement whereby you convey what you mean by saying the opposite . . . as when you call the 6′10″ basketball player "Shorty" or the two-month-old infant "Tiger."

Review pages 199–200.

EXAMPLE (anapestic dimeter and trimeter)

"How lovely!" she thumped,
As she glanced at the dump,
   "So fragrant, so neat, and so—nice.
I hadn't realized before
That they had a free store
   And a luxury home for the mice."

YOUR TURN _____

_____

_____

_____

_____

_____

Metaphor

A metaphor is an implied comparison. It does not use *like* or *as.* "He's a lion in a fight" we say admiringly; or "he's chicken" we say un-admiringly.

Review pages 119–121.

EXAMPLE (iambic tetrameter)

The world's a stage; the people in it
   Are actors who have muffed their lines.
The set's collapsed, the costumes rotted.
   Close the curtain. (Tea at nine?)

YOUR TURN _____

_____

_____

_____

Metonymy

Review pages 68–70.

Metonymy occurs when you substitute the name of one object for the name of another closely associated with it. It's metonymy when you whisper softly, "The kettle is boiling" when you really mean that the water in the kettle is boiling.

EXAMPLE (iambic tetrameter and trimeter)

> The White House called, the Senate sat,
>   The House refused to vote.
> The Capitol is seeking funds.
>   (Construction crews, please note.)

YOUR TURN _____

_____

_____

_____

Onomatopoeia

Review pages 49–51.

Onomatopoeia occurs when a word sounds like its meaning: *pop* or *crackle* or *hiss*.

EXAMPLE (trochaic tetrameter)

> Siren-like, she booms and buzzes,
>   (Boo or whistle when you see 'er.)
> Sizzling, munching, hissing, crunching . . .
>   That is ono-mato-poeia.

YOUR TURN _____

_____

_____

_____

Oxymoron

Review pages 73–74.

Oxymoron occurs when two apparently contradictory terms are brought together to form a sharper perception. You know all about it—why falling in love is "bitter-sweet."

EXAMPLE (anapestic dimeter and tetrameter)

> "Run slowly," she warned,
> "Or you'll fall up the hill,
>   And make a nice mess of your face!"
> So like a wise fool,
> I rushed snail-like to school,
>   Displaying rhinoceros grace.

_____

_____

_____

_____

_____

_____

Personification

Personification occurs when you attribute human character- | Review page 121.
istics to ideas, or to inanimate objects, or to animals. Wordsworth
used it when he talked about "wander[ing] lonely as a cloud," and
again, when he suggested that waves "danced."

EXAMPLE   (anapestic tetrameter and trimeter)

> The "call of the wild" is to stillness, you say?
> Then what of the brooklets that babble in May?
> And what of the north winds that whistle and neigh?
> That roar? It's the surf, in the bay.
>
> What of the pine trees that murmur in aisles?
> What of the ice that crackles when riled?
> And what of the whispering flowers so mild?
> *These* are the "call of the wild"!

YOUR TURN _____

_____

_____

_____

_____

_____

_____

_____

_____

Simile

A simile, as you already know, is a comparison using *like* or *as*. "Like a rose," we say—or "swift as a deer."

Review pages 117–119.

EXAMPLE (anapestic trimeter and tetrameter)

She runs like a deer, swift and sure,
She plays, like a kitten with thread;
She yelps like a puppy when she bruises her knee,
She coos, like a dove, in bed.

She dives like a swan, deep and true,
She eats like a bird (all day).
She cries like a banshee, and sings like a lark,
But she's really a Ms. in May.

YOUR TURN _____

_____

_____

_____

_____

_____

_____

_____

Synecdoche

Synecdoche results when you let a part of something represent the whole. Remember? . . . all *hands* on deck.

Review pages 67–68.

EXAMPLE (iambic tetrameter)

I do not like sy nec do che:
A part is not enough for me.

"Give us this day our daily bread—"
No—make that hot roast beef instead.

"A sail! a sail!" the drowning gloat.
When drowning, *I* prefer a boat.

"All hands on deck!" Nightmarish yen . . .
I like the hands attached to men.

I do not like sy nec do che:
The whole—not just the part—'s for me!

_____

_____

_____

_____

_____

_____

_____

_____

_____

_____

Review finished? Then, about face—march. . . .

44. FORMS IN CONCRETE

A poem is a statue is a mobile is a painting.

Crazy? Not if you're talking about *concrete poetry*. Concrete poetry can be seen as well as read. The meaning comes through the words *and* through the appearance. Verbal merges with graphic, and something brand new appears. Want to try it?

Step I (just a warm-up)

Begin by making a word *look* like its meaning. You can use printing or writing or even typing; but remember—you're allowed only one word, and the letter arrangement should suggest the meaning. Here are a few examples to get those creative juices flowing:

FLY   BROKEN   TOUCH   stream

YOUR TURN

Step II (just a bit more difficult)

This time choose a couple of words or a phrase. Combine illustration and words into a picture poem.

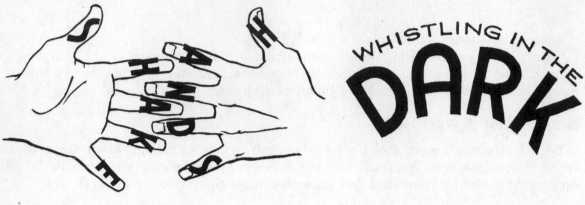

YOUR TURN

Step III (this is it!)

You are ready now to try a full poem "in concrete." The simplest type is the outline poem. Decide what you want to write about (make it a visible thing: like a dog or skyscraper); then decide what you want to say; finally, let the words outline the subject. Like this:

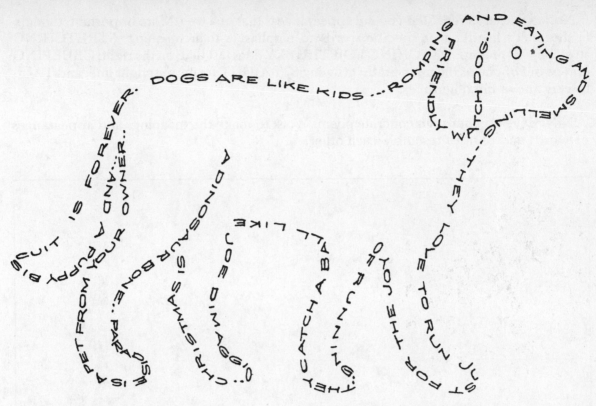

Or—if you doubt your drawing (or tracing) ability and you would like to be a bit more sophisticated, you might try a concrete poem in which the appearance and meaning merge tightly. Like this one, written by a student:*

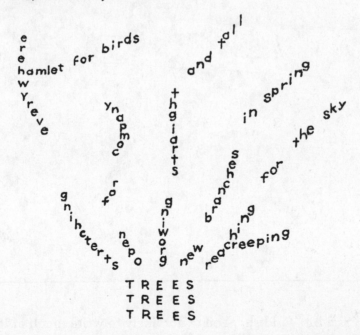

---

*"Trees" by Denise F. in Shirley Auerbach's "The Shape's the Thing," in *The English Journal*, April, 1973, p. 607. Copyright © 1973 by the National Council of Teachers of English. Reprinted by permission of the publisher and the author.

Notice that in "Trees" the general appearance is that of a tree. More important, though, is the poet's handling of specific words to emphasize their meaning. STRETCHING stretches left and up; REACHING FOR THE SKY does just that, on the right; CREEPING creeps out of one of the main limbs; growing STRAIGHT forms a straight line; and TALL towers above the other lines.

Now develop your own concrete poem. Work to make the meanings and appearances of words and phrases resemble each other.

Concrete poetry is a bit "faddish." You're not likely to write much of it; but if you play occasionally at being a "concretist," you will find you are growing increasingly aware of structure and sound, and increasingly sensitive to the correspondence of the senses and of the arts.

45. SHORT-ORDER FORMS

The long poem is complete and therefore satisfying. The short poem has a different purpose: it stirs the curiosity, unsettles the mind, and sets free the imagination. It asks questions and near-questions (unanswered); poses problems (unsolved); hints at ideas (undeveloped).

Short poems come in all structures—from the monosyllabic couplet (you can't get any shorter!) to the traditionally comic limerick to the strange, sometimes haunting triolet. In this chapter are nine short forms. Amble your way through them, stopping briefly at each to experiment and evaluate. At the end, you should have found at least two or three forms that are comfortable for *you*, suitable for *your* inner rhythm.

The Versatile Couplet

The couplet—two lines that rhyme—can do almost anything. In a series, it can become a long poem. Often, though, it chooses to stand alone. You are probably familiar with the shortest poem ever written; it has been frequently reprinted.

PHILOSOPHER
I?
Why?

Pondering the meaning of this monosyllabic couplet could take you the rest of your life! It leads to theology, suggests existentialism, turns determinism into a shambles. Try your hand at a monosyllabic couplet. All you need are two words that rhyme and that can be given meaning when topped by the *right* title. Work hard at finding that right title: it's the key to the independent couplet.

_____

_____

_____

Although one of the characteristics of the couplet is that the two lines rhyme, there are exceptions. Here is a lovely dual image by Charles Wharton Stork. Again the title is all-important, making the observation far more than an observation.

STANDARDS
White is the skimming gull on the somber green of the fir-trees,
Black is the soaring gull on a snowy glimmer of cloud.*

_____

*"Standards," by Charles Wharton Stork, in Mary J. J. Wrinn's THE HOLLOW REED, 1935, McGraw-Hill Book Company.

Try a non-rhyming couplet that is based on observation and uses just the right title to turn it into an idea.

———————————————

———————————————————————————————————

———————————————————————————————————

Couplet linked to couplet linked to couplet can make a marvelously funny poem, as George Martin Lane proved in this excerpt written in 1855.

ONE FISH BALL
The waiter he to him doth call,
And gently whispers—"One Fish Ball."
The waiter roars it through the hall,
The guests they start at "One Fish Ball!"
The guest then says, quite ill at ease,
"A piece of bread, sir, if you please."
The waiter roars it through the hall:
"We don't give bread with one Fish Ball!"

This bit of nonsense verse, written in iambic tetrameter couplets, depends on repetition for much of its humor. Try a George Martin Lane production. Just choose a phrase that amuses you (but make sure it has plenty of rhymes). Then go to it.

———————————————

———————————————————————————————————

———————————————————————————————————

———————————————————————————————————

———————————————————————————————————

———————————————————————————————————

———————————————————————————————————

———————————————————————————————————

The Conventional Quatrain

The quatrain, like the couplet, is extraordinarily versatile. It can be used in light verse or in serious philosophical writing. It can rhyme (favorite rhyme schemes are a, b, a, b; a, b, c, b; and a, b, b, a); or it can abjure rhyme. It can follow a regular meter (like iambic trimeter); or it can follow its own felt rhythm.

Here are a few quatrains well worth a little thought.

The first is by William Blake, the English poet and mystic. Notice how much Blake packs into four brief lines.

AUGURIES OF INNOCENCE[1]

To see the world in a grain of sand;
And a heaven in a wild flower;
Hold infinity in the palm of your hand,
And eternity in an hour.

The second quatrain is really a poetic definition of the title—by John Pierpont, lawyer, teacher, businessman, and minister of the early 19th century.

THE BALLOT[2]

A weapon that comes down as still
As snowflakes fall upon the sod;
But executes a freeman's will,
As lightning does the will of God.

The third quatrain, by Emily Dickinson, is less enigmatic than most of her poems. Short, apparently simple, it yet says a great deal about human nature.

PEDIGREE[3]

The pedigree of honey
Does not concern the bee;
A clover, any time, to him
Is aristocracy.

Having read these three, you should be ready to try a quatrain or two of your own: metrical or non-metrical, rhyming or non-rhyming.

_____

_____

_____

_____

_____

---

[1]"Auguries of Innocence" in SELECTED POETRY AND PROSE OF WILLIAM BLAKE, edited by Northrop Frye. Copyright 1953, The Modern Library.
[2]"The Ballot" in AN AMERICAN ANTHOLOGY, 1787–1900, edited by Edmund C. Stedman. Reprinted by permission of Houghton Mifflin Company.
[3]"Pedigree" in THE COMPLETE POEMS OF EMILY DICKINSON, edited by Thomas H. Johnson. Reprinted by permission of Little, Brown and Company.

The Late Lamented Limerick

Limericks, claim the critics, are out of date. Maybe . . . but what the critics don't realize is that a great many people thoroughly enjoy them still. The limerick is poetry for parties, picnics, and pie contests. It demands (and receives) no reverence, inspires no awe, causes no tears; but it is almost always good for a chuckle or a belly-laugh.

President Woodrow Wilson was fond of quoting this limerick. It is one that many of us find comforting.

> As a beauty I'm not a great star,
> There are others more handsome by far,
>   But my face I don't mind it,
>   Because I'm behind it—
> 'Tis the folks in the front that I jar.

As you undoubtedly have realized by now, the limerick is basically anapestic. The first, second, and fifth lines are trimeter; the third and fourth are dimeter. The rhyme scheme is a, a, b, b, a. The last line is usually the important one—the shocker, the twister, that makes the preceding four amusing in retrospect.

Probably the most familiar limerick is the one even children chant with delight:

> There was a young lady from Niger,
> Who smiled as she rode on a tiger.
>   They came back from the ride
>   With the lady inside,
> And the smile on the face of the tiger.*

If you wish to join the ranks of limerick-writers, follow the pattern given above, begin with "There was . . .," and write about anything—preferably, something silly and trivial.

_____

_____

_____

_____

_____

---

*From THE BOOK OF HUMOROUS VERSE compiled by Carolyn Wells. Copyright 1920, Doubleday & Company, Inc. Reprinted by permission of Maurice O'Connell, Jr.

The Elucidating Epigram

Fun to write (if you happen to be witty) is the epigram: a short poem (usually a couplet or quatrain) developing one idea in witty fashion.

TO WIT John Donne to a "friend":

> Thy flattering picture, Phryne, is like thee,
> Only in this, that you both painted be.[1]

TO WIT William Blake's recipe for greatness:

> Great things are done when men and mountains meet;
> These are not done by jostling in the street.[2]

TO WIT Alexander Pope's epigram that makes all of us grin ruefully:

> You beat your pate, and fancy wit will come.
> Knock as you please—there's nobody at home.[3]

YOUR TURN Dream up your own epigram, couplet or quatrain. Polish it well. It must be terse, witty, and pointed.

_____

_____

_____

_____

The Sad Tale of the Epitaph

For some reason that's never been determined, the epitaph (really a tombstone inscription) has joined the epigram as the home of witty (and often malicious) verse. The transformation happened a long time ago.

There was John Dryden who showed himself a right, royal husband:

> Here lies my wife: here let her lie!
> Now she's at rest—and so am I.[4]

---

[1]From *Poems* of John Donne. Published in the United States by E. P. Dutton & Co., Inc., and reprinted with their permission.
[2]From SELECTED POETRY AND PROSE OF WILLIAM BLAKE, edited by Northrop Frye. Copyright 1953, The Modern Library.
[3]From "Epigrams. An Empty House," as quoted in THE OXFORD DICTIONARY OF QUOTATIONS, Second Edition. Copyrights from 1941 to 1955, Oxford University Press, Oxford, England.
[4]From "Epitaph Intended for Dryden's Wife," as quoted in THE OXFORD DICTIONARY OF QUOTATIONS, Second Edition. Copyrights from 1941 to 1955, Oxford University Press, Oxford, England.

There was John Wilmot, Earl of Rochester, who showed himself a right, royal subject of Charles II:

> Here lies our Sovereign lord, the King,
>   Whose word no man relies on.
> He never said a foolish thing,
>   Nor ever did a wise one.

And there was Alexander Pope's epitaph for Isaac Newton, witty and terse, but without a touch of malice:

> Nature and Nature's laws lay hid in night:
> God said, "Let Newton be!" and all was light.

If you have learned to laugh at yourself, try an epitaph for yourself. If that's too hard, try one for a friend, or even a celebrity. Couplet or quatrain will do, but be terse and be witty.

_____

_____

_____

_____

The Elegant Cinquain

Just before World War I, a strong though frail woman found herself, by doctors' orders, at Saranac Lake, N.Y. But it was too late; she was dying, and she knew it. Walking, dreaming, thinking, in that dry, brisk mountain air, she put together a new kind of poem. The woman was Adelaide Crapsey; the poem was the cinquain. Even now, more than half a century later, the cinquain has some of the durability and some of the poignancy born in Adelaide Crapsey's year of awareness.

The cinquain consists of five lines:

> Line 1—two syllables
>   2—four syllables
>   3—six syllables
>   4—eight syllables
>   5—two syllables

The metrical foot is usually (but not necessarily) iambic; end rhyme occurs seldom, but internal rhyme, assonance, and consonance appear frequently.

Here are two cinquains by Adelaide Crapsey.

TRIAD[1]

These be
Three silent things:
The falling snow . . . the hour
Before the dawn . . . the mouth of one
Just dead.

THE WARNING[2]

Just now,
Out of the strange
Still dusk . . . as strange, as still . . .
A white moth flew: why am I grown
So cold?

Start with an observation of nature; think about it; relate it tentatively to something human. Then write, never stating, only suggesting the destination of your idea.

_____

_____

_____

_____

_____

_____

The Elusive Haiku

One of the most fleeting forms—as delicate under pressure as the snowflake—is the haiku, a creation of long-ago Japan. Haiku comes from the word *hokku*, meaning "beginning phrase." It makes a statement, paints a picture . . . and through the careful choice of words, provides a moment of illumination. Bashō, a 17th century master of the haiku in Japan, said of it: "Let your hokku resemble a willow-branch struck by a light shower and trembling a little in the wind." His best known hokku was, at one time, memorized by every Japanese schoolchild.

The old pond, aye! and
The sound of a frog leaping
Into the water.[3]

[1,2]From VERSE by Adelaide Crapsey. Copyright 1932 by Algernon S. Crapsey and renewed 1950 by The Adelaide Crapsey Foundation. Reprinted by permission of Alfred A. Knopf, Inc.
[3]Bashō's hokku reprinted in Mary J. J. Wrinn's THE HOLLOW REED, 1935, McGraw-Hill Book Company.

The formula for writing a haiku is simple: a first line of five syllables, a second line of seven, and a third line of five. What could be simpler? Except that to say something significant in seventeen syllables is no easy task.

As you prepare to write a haiku, dig first into your own life. Choose an experience that is still vividly real to you; extract from that experience a single detail that somehow sums up both the experience and its significance (as the sound of a single frog leaping into the water sums up the silence and solitude associated with meditation). Then manipulate a description of that single detail until you have compressed it (and a suggestion of the total experience) into seventeen syllables.

_____

_____

_____

The Terse Tonka

You will remember that *hokku* means "beginning phrase." Once upon a time the *hokku* was the first three lines of the *tonka*. It broke away to become a separate form; but the tonka persisted. Simply take a haiku, add two 7-syllable lines, and you have a tonka. Its 31 syllables allow a little more elaboration. Witness this tonka by Okura, a Japanese writer who lived more than a thousand years ago.

> Since he is too young
> To know the way, I would plead:
> "Pray, accept this gift,
> O Underworld messenger,
> And bear the child pick-a-back."*

Notice the intensity of grief here, for the death of a little boy: the evoking of family play, and the father's need to offer continuing protection. Like the haiku, the tonka is an intense form of poetry working through suggestion rather than statement.

YOUR TURN _____

_____

_____

_____

_____

The Dancing Triolet

To end this chapter of short forms, we have chosen the triolet, a French poem with a tricky refrain. Any kind of metrical foot is permissible, as well as any kind of metrical line. The eight-line stanza that is the triolet makes only two demands: the first line must also be

---

*From POETRY HANDBOOK by Babette Deutsch. Copyright © 1974, 1969, 1962, 1957 by Babette Deutsch. Reprinted with permission of Harper & Row, Publishers, Inc.

the fourth and seventh, while the second line is also the eighth; and only two end-rhymes may be used. It sounds complicated, but a glance at the following triolet by William Ernest Henley should clarify.

> Easy is the Triolet,
> If you really learn to make it!
> Once a neat refrain you get,
> Easy is the Triolet.
> As you see!—I pay my debt
> With another rhyme. Deuce take it,
> Easy is the Triolet,
> If you really learn to make it![1]

The triolet is light and gay, lending itself easily to word play and romantic teasing. Perhaps the best-known triolet is "The Kiss" by the English poet, Henry Austin Dobson.

> Rose kissed me today.
> Will she kiss me tomorrow?
> Let it be as it may,
> Rose kissed me *today;*
> But the pleasure gives way
> To a savor of sorrow;
> Rose kissed me today;
> *Will* she kiss me tomorrow?[2]

The two refrains add mightily to the cheerful lilt of the poem; and Dobson's subtle emphases (*today* in line 4, *will* in line 8) keep the refrains intact but increase the suggestiveness. How better could one express the silly but real restlessness of the lover who has barely enjoyed one kiss before he is wondering if there will be a repeat performance?

Choose a lighthearted topic. Create the first two lines carefully, and copy them below. Then copy the first line on lines 4 and 7, and the second line on line 8. You will discover that only lines 3, 5, and 6 are bare. Fill them in cleverly, and presto—a triolet!

(1) _____

(2) _____

(3) _____

(4) _____

(5) _____

(6) _____

(7) _____

(8) _____

---

[1]"The Triolet," in THE BOOK OF HUMOROUS VERSE, compiled by Carolyn Wells. Copyright 1920, Doubleday & Company, Inc. Reprinted by permission of Maurice O'Connell, Jr.

[2]"The Kiss," a stanza from "Rose-Leaves," as quoted in THE OXFORD DICTIONARY OF QUOTATIONS, Second Edition. Copyrights from 1941 to 1955, Oxford University Press, Oxford, England.

> *The short poem is perfect for light or serious thoughts. Its briefness suits our modern pace; its suggestiveness teases us to an unsatisfied-satisfaction (paradox!).*

Any one of these short forms could be used to create clever place-cards for a party; or—to create gentle-torturous expressions of your deepest emotions. You cannot possess them, but you can borrow them. Use them with tenderness. . . . .

46. THE LONGER POEM

The short poem is like the single diamond. It must provide its own radiance. It must be sufficient unto itself. The poet, like the diamond cutter, must have a steady hand: the slightest flaw will mar the beauty of the poem.

The long poem is like an elaborate necklace. The diamonds are supported by emeralds and rubies. The setting enhances. Many stones emit glittering rays. Perfection is still important, but is diminished by power. An occasional flaw is unnoticed under the barrage of sparkles.

The long poem is like a necklace in a second way. As the necklace is a series of stones, each linked to each, so the long poem is a series of short poems, each linked to each. Since you have already "mastered" the short poem, you should have little trouble with the long poem.

The Narrative Poem

The narrative poem tells a story. Sometimes it celebrates a historical person or event; sometimes it describes a shattered romance, or the death of a pet, or a criminal's nefarious deeds. It may be serious or comic, factual or fictitious, lilting or pedestrian. But always, above all else, it tells a story.

The Ballad

The ballad is one of the oldest forms of narrative poetry. Long before scholarly poets wrote down poems, balladeers created and chanted stories in verse. These "stories" were about love and hate, death and war, courage and superstitition. Because they were meant to be chanted, they possessed a strong rhythm and frequently used one or more refrains.

This is especially true of "Bonny Barbara Allan" which has been a favorite for centuries. In the 17th century, Samuel Pepys raved about the "perfect pleasure" he received when he heard it. In Virginia, ballad-lovers developed 92 different versions. In 1945, in "Dark of the Moon," a poetic drama, "Bonny Barbara Allan" made her debut on the Broadway stage.

Read it aloud so that you can hear the strong rhythm and the frequent modifications of the refrain. (The spelling and diction have been modernized to facilitate reading.)

BONNY BARBARA ALLAN

It was in and about the Martinmas time,
  When the green leaves were a-falling,
That Sir John Graeme, in the West Country,
  Fell in love with Barbara Allan.

He sent his man down through the town
  To the place where she was dwelling:
"O haste and come to my master dear,
  If you be Barbara Allan."

O slowly, slowly, rose she up,
  To the place where he was lying,
And when she drew the curtain by,
  "Young man, I think you're dying."

"O, it's I'm sick, and very, very sick,
  And it's all for Barbara Allan";
"O the better for me you'll never be,
  Though your heart's blood were a-spilling.

"O don't you remember, young man," said she,
  "When the red wine you were filling,
That you made the healths go round and round,
  And slighted Barbara Allan?"

He turned his face unto the wall,
  And death was with him dealing;
"Adieu, adieu, my dear friends all,
  And be kind to Barbara Allan."

And slowly, slowly, raised she up
  And slowly, slowly left him,
And sighing said, she could not stay
  Since death of life had reft him.

She had not gone a mile but two,
  When she heard the dead-bell ringing,
And every stroke that the dead-bell gave,
  It cried, "Woe to Barbara Allan!"

"O mother, mother, make my bed!
  O make it soft and narrow!
My love has died for me today,
  I'll die for him tomorrow."

NOTE

1 The dramatic storyline based on rejected love and death.

2 The main refrain—"Barbara Allan"—occurring in all but three of the nine stanzas.

3 The repetition *within* stanzas: e.g., "slowly, slowly" in stanza 3, and "round and round" in stanza 5.

4 The recurring sounds that link stanzas: e.g., "a-falling" in stanza 1, "dwelling" in stanza 2, "a-spilling" in stanza 4, etc.

5 The sadness of the closing stanza as the scale of justice comes into true balance.

As you can see, the ballad is not a difficult form: some quatrains, a lot of repetition both of phrases and sounds, and a dramatic storyline. Before you try one of your own, you should read a few modern ballads. Try some of these:

Rudyard Kipling.   "Gunga Din" or "Danny Deever"
Bret Harte.   "Jim Bludso"
Anonymous.   "Jesse James" or "Frankie and Johnny"
Edna St. Vincent Millay.   "The Ballad of the Harp-Weaver"
Alfred Noyes.   "The Highwayman"

As you begin your own ballad, think of a good storyline. It may be serious: the rejection by a young man of a young woman, or the death of a fellow student; or it may be frivolous: the mock account of a basketball game that was lost, or the tragicomical ending of an old but much loved car. Next, decide on a good, rhythmical refrain. Then write your quatrains, telling the story and remembering to emphasize drama and repetition. (If it will help, use "Bonny Barbara Allan" or one of the modern ballads as a model.)

When you have finished, polish it well and try it out on your family and friends. Then copy it into your journal.

A possible bonus: If you play the guitar, you will find that the ballad rhythm is easily "caught." Create a musical accompaniment for your ballad, and who knows? You may have a hit on your hands!

Other Narrative Poetry

The ballad is not the only type of narrative poetry. Given a strong story, you can tell it in almost any kind of verse form from the quatrain to free verse.

Read at least three of the following narrative poems:

Oscar Wilde.   "The Ballad of Reading Gaol"
Robert Frost.   "The Death of the Hired Man"
Amy Lowell.   "Patterns"
Robert Browning.   "The Pied Piper of Hamelin"
E. A. Robinson.   "Richard Cory" or "Mr. Flood's Party"
Henry Wadsworth Longfellow.   "Paul Revere's Ride"
Samuel Coleridge.   "The Rime of the Ancient Mariner"

After you have read three, choose a story that interests you. It may be from history, from the newspaper, from personal experience. It may be important to only one individual (like the young man's death in "Patterns") or it may be important to a country (like "Paul Revere's Ride"). Then begin telling the story, playing with various first lines until the right rhythm emerges. Once you have the rhythm, you can forge straight ahead to the story's end. Revise. Copy in your journal.

The Lyric

The lyric is a poem, usually brief, more interested in emotion, melody, and imagination than in narration. It may be two lines long, or five, or fourteen, or twenty—or even more. It may be an ode, an elegy, a cinquain, a sonnet, a triolet—or any one of a dozen other forms. But it must be melodic; it must be subjective; it must seek to create only one impression in the reader's mind.

The Ode

One kind of lyric poem is the *ode*. It is, as Louis Untermeyer once said, "a profound treatment of a profound subject." John Keats, for example, wrote "Ode on a Grecian Urn" in which he considered the enduring quality of beauty; Thomas Gray wrote "Ode on a Distant Prospect of Eton College" in which he remembered his own school days and pondered on the fate of the boys at Eton then and now. Gray ended the ode with this stanza:

> To each his sufferings; all are men,
> Condemned alike to groan,
> The tender for another's pain,
> The unfeeling for his own.
> Yet ah! why should they know their fate?
> Since sorrow never comes too late,
> And happiness too swiftly flies,
> Thought would destroy their paradise.
> No more; where ignorance is bliss,
> 'Tis folly to be wise.

Gray's ode consists of ten stanzas. As you have seen, this particular ode uses iambic trimeter and iambic tetrameter, and has an unusual rhyme scheme.

The same poet, Thomas Gray, wrote another ode: "Ode on the Death of a Favorite Cat," using a profound treatment of a *non*-profound subject.

> 'Twas on a lofty vase's side,
> Where China's gayest art had dyed
> The azure flowers that blow;
> Demurest of the tabby kind,
> The pensive Selima reclined,
> Gazed on the lake below.
>
> Her conscious tail her joy declared;
> The fair round face, the snowy beard,
> The velvet of her paws,
> Her coat, that with the tortoise vies,
> Her ears of jet, and emerald eyes,
> She saw; and purred applause.

Still had she gazed; but 'midst the tide
Two angel forms were seen to glide,
   The genii of the stream;
Their scaly armor's Tyrian hue
Through richest purple to the view
   Betrayed a golden gleam.

The hapless nymph with wonder saw:
A whisker first and then a claw,
   With many an ardent wish,
She stretched in vain to reach the prize.
What female heart can gold despise?
   What cat's averse to fish?

Presumptuous maid! with looks intent
Again she stretched, again she bent,
   Nor knew the gulf between.
(Malignant Fate sat by, and smiled)
The slippery verge her feet beguiled,
   She tumbled headlong in.

Eight times emerging from the flood
She mewed to every watery god,
   Some speedy aid to send.
No dolphin came, no nereid stirred:
Nor cruel Tom, nor Susan heard.
   A favorite has no friend!

From hence, ye beauties, undeceived,
Know, one false step is ne'er retrieved,
   And be with caution bold.
Not all that tempts your wandering eyes
And heedless hearts, is lawful prize;
   Nor all that glitters, gold.

   Write your own ode . . . serious or mocking. You may wish to follow either of Gray's as a model, or one by Keats or Shelley; or you may prefer to develop your own stanza form and rhyme scheme. Remember to use a *profound* treatment: be a little stiff, a little formal; be a little lush with your diction; toss in a Greek or Roman allusion to the gods; incorporate a moral. Your ode need not be long; but it should have dignity and a sort of self-confidence.

   Note below the topic and the verse form you intend to use; but copy the ode itself into your journal.

SUBJECT ——

VERSE FORM ———

The Sonnet

A favorite lyrical form during the last five centuries is the sonnet. The sonnet is a fourteen-line poem written in iambic pentameter. There are several types of sonnet but the two most important are the Petrarchan sonnet and the Shakespearean sonnet.

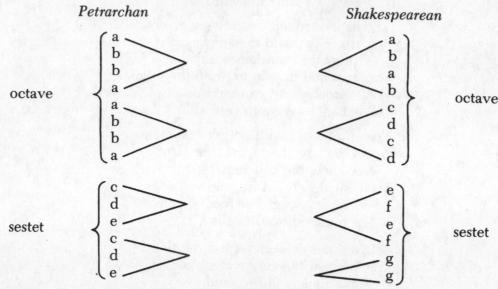

In each case, the octave (8-line stanza) describes a situation, while the sestet (6-line stanza) applies it. For example, in Longfellow's "Nature," the octave describes a mother's disposition of her child's toys after he is asleep, and the sestet compares this to Nature's disposition of our "playthings" in the adult world.

One of the best-loved sonnets of all time is Shakespeare's sonnet #29. You will find it not only a good model for writing sonnets of your own, but also a fine mental and emotional crutch. Memorize it. When people don't appreciate you, when you fail a test, when you feel you are going nowhere fast—shout it to the wind. You will find your mind cleared of confusion, and your heart of its burden. Read it.

> When, in disgrace with fortune and men's eyes,
> I all alone beweep my outcast state
> And trouble deaf heaven with my bootless cries
> And look upon myself and curse my fate,
> Wishing me like to one more rich in hope,
> Featured like him, like him with friends possessed,
> Desiring this man's art and that man's scope,
> With what I most enjoy contented least;
> Yet in these thoughts myself almost despising,
> Haply I think on thee, and then my state,
> Like to the lark at break of day arising
> From sullen earth, sings hymns at heaven's gate;
>   For thy sweet love remembered such wealth brings
>   That then I scorn to change my state with kings.*

---

*"Sonnet 29," from SHAKESPEARE: THE COMPLETE WORKS, edited by G. B. Harrison, published by Harcourt Brace Jovanovich, Inc.

Notice the easy transition from the octave to the sestet, as the poet first feels sorry for himself, then realizes that love is "all."

Sonnets can be written about almost anything of interest to humans. There are sonnets about the dead in war, about love successful and love unsuccessful, about Nature as a teacher, about God, about fear, and hate, and frustration. Milton wrote one about his blindness, and Keats wrote one about a new translation of Homer.

Select a topic—one emotionally important to you *right now*. Then begin. You will find the rigid structure both a help and a hindrance: a help because you already know the form you are using and do not have to think about it; a hindrance because you will have to chisel your thoughts and words to fit the form. Remember: fourteen lines of iambic pentameter, following either the Petrarchan or Shakespearean divisions.

When you have completed it, try it on a few choice friends; then copy into your journal.

Blank Verse

Like the sonnet, blank verse is written in iambic pentameter but with no rhyme. Iambic pentameter is the natural rhythm in English; if you read a little of it, you will find it easy to capture. You can talk in iambic pentameter; review your school notes in iambic pentameter; even dream in it!

Shakespeare's plays are written in iambic pentameter; several biblical translations rely on it heavily. An important thing to remember if you would write *good* blank verse is to let line run into line, rather than having each line end with a period or comma. Watch how Shakespeare did it in this brief passage from *Romeo and Juliet*:

> But, soft! what light through yonder window breaks?
> It is the east, and Juliet is the sun.
> Arise, fair sun, and kill the envious moon,
> Who is already sick and pale with grief
> That thou, her maid, art far more fair than she.

One more reminder: while iambic pentameter is the rule for blank verse, the good poet never follows it slavishly. When rhythm and sense demand, use occasional anapests or trochees; drop a syllable or add a syllable. Violating the rule at the right time is as important as abiding by the rule at the right time.

It's your turn now to try a little blank verse. Whether it is four lines or twenty when you have completed it, follow the established procedure: read it to a few friends, revise if necessary, and copy in your journal.

Free Verse

Many young writers favor free verse; and there is much to be said for it. With no metrical demands to be met, with no rhyme scheme to follow, words and thoughts flow freely. The problem is—sometimes they flow *too* freely. Words that flow from you, even when you are emotionally stirred, are not necessarily poetry; sadly, they are seldom poetry. Both words and phrases must be worked and reworked. The structure must be there, though hidden; the rhythm must be there, though not able to be scanned. Students often rebel; but most fine free verse poets spend an apprenticeship first working within strict, metrical forms. Only so could they develop their own *felt* forms.

Let the two-line poem, "In a Station of the Metro" by Ezra Pound, illustrate:

The apparition of these faces in the crowd;
Petals on a wet, black bough.[1]

The poem is really just one metaphor. Yet it is more. To prove this to yourself, try changing one word. Change "apparition" to "look," and the poem loses much of its effect. "Apparition" is longer, softer, more haunting; and is necessary. Change "faces" to "people"—and humor inappropriately enters. Change "crowd" to "mob," and you lose the assonance in "crowd" and "bough." Change "wet" to "dampish," and you lose the clipped rhythm of the second line plus the assonance in "petals" and "wet."

You see? Free verse poetry is harder to write than poetry with a pre-determined structure . . . immeasurably harder. It demands that the poet know well the tropes, the meters, and the stanzaic forms; the figures of speech and the ambiguity of words. It demands that the poet read long and lovingly the poems of the fine poets who have gone this way before. And it demands that the poet combine acquired knowledge with *felt* knowledge in new expression that is rhythmic and implicit.

If you still want to write free verse, practice all of the skills that have been introduced in this unit; then read "Patterns" by Amy Lowell. Read it aloud, slowly, as you sit alone in a room or loll against a tree. *Feel* the rhythm; *feel* the way the structure twines around the subject; feel *and* understand what Lowell is saying about structure in life and in poetry.

PATTERNS[2]
by Amy Lowell

I walk down the garden paths,
And all the daffodils
Are blowing, and the bright blue squills.
I walk down the patterned garden-paths
In my stiff, brocaded gown.
With my powdered hair and jewelled fan,
I too am a rare
Pattern. As I wander down
The garden paths.

My dress is richly figured,
And the train
Makes a pink and silver stain
On the gravel, and the thrift
Of the borders.
Just a plate of current fashion
Tripping by in high-heeled, ribboned shoes.

Not a softness anywhere about me,
Only whalebone and brocade.
And I sink on a seat in the shade
Of a lime tree. For my passion
Wars against the stiff brocade.
The daffodils and squills
Flutter in the breeze
As they please.
And I weep;
For the lime-tree is in blossom
And one small flower has dropped upon my bosom.

And the plashing of waterdrops
In the marble fountain
Comes down the garden-paths.
The dripping never stops.
Underneath my stiffened gown
Is the softness of a woman bathing in a marble basin,
A basin in the midst of hedges grown
So thick, she cannot see her lover hiding,
But she guesses he is near,
And the sliding of the water
Seems the stroking of a dear
Hand upon her.
What is Summer in a fine brocaded gown!
I should like to see it lying in a heap upon the ground.
All the pink and silver crumpled up on the ground.

I would be the pink and silver as I ran along the paths,
And he would stumble after,
Bewildered by my laughter.
I should see the sun flashing from his sword-hilt and buckles on his shoes.
I would choose
To lead him in a maze along the patterned paths,
A bright and laughing maze for my heavy-booted lover.
Till he caught me in the shade,
And the buttons of his waistcoat bruised my body as he clasped me,
Aching, melting, unafraid.
With the shadows of the leaves and the sundrops,
And the plopping of the waterdrops,
All about us in the open afternoon—
I am very like to swoon
With the weight of this brocade,
For the sun sifts through the shade.

Underneath the fallen blossom
In my bosom,
Is a letter I have hid.
It was brought to me this morning by a rider from the Duke.
"Madam, we regret to inform you that Lord Hartwell
Died in action Thursday se'nnight."

As I read it in the white, morning sunlight,
The letters squirmed like snakes.
"Any answer, Madam?" said my footman.
"No," I told him.
"See that the messenger takes some refreshment.
No, no answer."
And I walked into the garden,
Up and down the patterned paths,
In my stiff, correct brocade.
The blue and yellow flowers stood up proudly in the sun,
Each one.
I stood upright too,
Held rigid to the pattern
By the stiffness of my gown.
Up and down I walked.
Up and down.

In a month he would have been my husband.
In a month, here, underneath this lime,
We would have broken the pattern;
He for me, and I for him,
He as Colonel, I as Lady,
On this shady seat.
He had a whim
That sunlight carried blessing.
And I answered, "It shall be as you have said."
Now he is dead.

In Summer and in Winter I shall walk
Up and down
The patterned garden-paths
In my stiff, brocaded gown.
The squills and daffodils
Will give place to pillared roses, and to asters, and to snow.
I shall go
Up and down,
In my gown.
Gorgeously arrayed,
Boned and stayed.
And the softness of my body will be guarded from embrace
By each button, hook, and lace.
For the man who should loose me is dead,
Fighting with the Duke in Flanders,
In a pattern called a war.
Christ! What are patterns for?

Still challenged? Still think you can write *good* free verse? Then write.

47. A FANTASIA OF THE ARTS

No human exists as an independent being, isolated from other humans; and no art exists as an independent discipline, isolated from other arts. No one knows exactly which art leads the way with particular techniques or approaches, but it may go something like this:

From sculpture, the painter, musician, and writer learn to portray both outer and inner characteristics through attention to physical details.

From painting, the musician, writer, and sculptor learn to depict emotions through blending and contrast; and learn the importance of shadow and nuances.

From music, the writer, sculptor, and painter learn to pay attention to the innate rhythm of both animate and inanimate things and to use this innate rhythm to portray them meaningfully.

From literature, the sculptor, painter, and musician learn to tell a story, making the story illuminate the characters, as the characters from their own beings create the story.

The important thing to remember is that the arts, because they are the products of human imagination, are interrelated. You can learn about one art from the others; you can respond to one form in another form; you can be inspired by the others; and you can combine some or all of them in new and significant ways.

Inspiration Point

Now and then, let the other arts act as guides. Listen; look; *feel* . . . then let the song or the painting inspire your own writing of poetry.

Music

Borrow a recording of Beethoven's *Ninth Symphony* (or if that is too awesome, borrow something by the Beatles). Play it. First indulge in passivity: let the music sweep over and around you. Feel it. Enjoy it. Then begin participating actively. Think about it . . . about what the music is saying . . . about how mood is built and destroyed . . . about how melodies wander in and out, appearing, disappearing, reappearing.

When you are steeped in it, when it has been absorbed into you mentally and emotionally, put pencil to paper and begin writing. At first only single words may come, then phrases, then at last a line. Let the poem evolve until its form and purpose are clear. At that point, become the active poet, molding, shaping, creating.

Your poem may be a tone-poem, more interested in sound than in statement. Or it may duplicate the mood that Beethoven created. Or it may follow, inquisitively and curiously, one soft strain that meanders through the musical composition. Or it may be none of these—something apparently divorced from Beethoven, on a different subject, handled in a different way, yet retaining some of the power and strength of its origin.

In the space below, write the title and composer of the music that will be your "inspiration point." Add notes—words—even doodlings, as you listen. The completed poem should go, of course, into your journal.

_____

_____

_____

_____

_____

_____

_____

_____

_____

_____

_____

_____

_____

Painting

Go to the library and choose a book of European or American or Japanese paintings. (Better yet, if possible, go to an art museum and wander.) Browse—until you find a painting that is special, for you. Perhaps *The Land of Cockayne* painted by Pieter Bruegel in 1567. Study it for awhile. Notice the stuffed scholar, the slothful farmer, the lethargic knight. Notice their equipment (the book, the flail, the lance), now useless, lying at their sides. The pies, the jugs, the roast meats suggest the cause of their stupor. The boar, a knife stuck in its side, runs away. In the upper right corner, ominous yellow-dark clouds roil. The browns are strong, the greens weak and discolored.

Think about it. This is one man's picture of one type of human being—perhaps a more common type than we like to admit. It is a narrative painting in that it tells a story. It is a didactic painting in that it teaches a moral. It is a psychological painting in that it analyzes human behavior.

Put pencil to paper. Let the words come. Let the ideas form. Your poem may be a poem on gluttony; or a poem based on our relationship with nature; or a poem on abundance. It may be a narrative poem, told in enthusiastic quatrains; or a free verse poem filled with somber images and a weighty rhythm.

Below, write the name of the painting and the artist. Add notes. Place the completed poem in your journal.

_____

_____

_____

_____

_____

_____

_____

_____

_____

_____

_____

Sculpture

From an art book or in a museum, select a piece of statuary that appeals to you. It may be an elaborate portrayal—like Michelangelo's *Moses*; or it may be just a wood carving, beautifully shaped, lovely to the eye and to the touch.

Ponder for awhile—and meditate. With the *Moses*, one is caught first by the fierce, strong hair, by the incredible muscles and veins. Then the right hand attracts as it grasps lightly the two tablets containing the Ten Commandments. The eyes draw: sad with a touch of bewilderment, yet with calmness, too. Let your eyes pass slowly, thoughtfully, over the lines of the piece of sculpture you have chosen until you *feel* the sculptor's intent.

Then write.

_____

_____

_____

_____

_____

_____

_____

_____

_____

_____

The Companion Approach

Sometimes the *idea* behind a painting or a concerto will capture you. *Yes*, you think—*I've thought that many times ... well, almost that. But the artist didn't say quite what I mean*. At such times you may find a sense of completeness in writing a companion piece: a poem that says in words what another artist said in another medium.

One of the finest examples is what W. H. Auden did with the Icarus legend. Icarus was a Greek lad who tried to fly. His father Daedalus made him wings fastened with wax and warned him not to soar too close to the sun; but Icarus was young and impulsive and he flew higher and higher until the sun melted the wax and Icarus plunged to his death. In 1558, Pieter Bruegel painted *The Fall of Icarus*, based on the old legend. Examine the painting. In the foreground, a farmer plows, turning over the soil; and a bored shepherd tends his sheep. At the water's edge, an angler waits, hoping for a fish for his lunch. And off shore, ships sail by, intent on their own destinations and fortunes. Everyone is busy, too busy to notice the strange and marvelous sight of a boy falling from the heavens. In the lower righthand corner only flailing legs can be seen as Icarus disappears into the Aegean Sea. Ambition has been cut off by tragedy ... and nobody (except possibly Icarus) seems to care.

Fascinated by the universal implications in Bruegel's painting, the twentieth century poet Auden wrote "Musée des Beaux Arts" (Museum of the Fine Arts). He describes the picture, always adjusting the focus so that the *idea* behind the scene becomes clearer and clearer. We nod, recognizing that idea. Disaster is important only to the one it happens to. That earthquake in Guatemala? It took over 13,000 lives. Dreadful, isn't it? And we reach for a cookie and take another sip of coffee.

As the painting and the poem stand side by side, we realize something else: that human nature hasn't changed much in 400 years, that possibly it hasn't changed at all.

Choose your own painting or piece of sculpture or musical selection. Write a companion poem. Then present both in class—the original, and *your* original, though related, poem. You will find yourself growing more aware of the other arts; and of the universality of human virtues and faults.

_____

_____

_____

_____

_____

_____

_____

_____

_____

_____

_____

_____

Illustrate Your Own Poem

Another way in which you can bring the arts together is to illustrate your own poem. Check your journal. Is there a poem that you are especially proud of? If there is, use that; if not, write one. Then think about illustrating it.

If the poem is for children (or even if it is not) and if you have some talent in drawing, you might work with cartoon figures.

If the poem is about nature, and your drawing talent is slim, browse through some magazines and albums until you find pictures that "fit" it. Depending on what you are trying to say, you might choose pictures that correspond directly with your words; or pictures that reflect the opposite, for contrast; or pictures that symbolize rather than state. To make this clearer: if you wrote about a winter scene, you might choose pictures of snow and ice; or pictures of a summer day at the beach; or pictures of a refrigerator, a snobbish person, even a smile devoid of warmth.

You can use other things than drawings to illustrate your poem. You can use tiny figures shaped of clay; a statue; five minutes of taped music; even a few minutes of an 8 mm film sequence. Use your imagination. A carefully shaped, iced cake can be an illustration (and an always successful class project!). A tiny box theater with a "frozen" scene can be an illustration. A collage made of headlines, bits of cotton, and egg shells can be an illustration. Explore your own interests to find the one that is right for you.

Use the space below to explain, note-fashion, what you are planning, and how you intend to go about doing it. Present the final project to the class. This may seem like "play" rather than work; but a project or two of this type will add dimension to your own creative efforts. Besides—to an artist, there is no clear line between work and play. The two merge.

_____

_____

_____

_____

_____

_____

_____

_____

_____

_____

_____

_____

_____

_____

_____

A Fantasia

A fantasia, according to most dictionaries, is a medley of familiar themes. Why not end this brief dip into the arts with a suitable fantasia? Here's how.

Select a poem you have written; or write a new one.

If you have a camera, take some slides that will illustrate your words. If you don't have a camera, you should be able to find some slides in the library or film center of your school. Select some—perhaps fifteen or twenty. Arrange them to match certain phrases and ideas in your poem.

Listen to some music that is similar in mood. Tape a few bars here, a melody there. (Cassette tape is best, because it is the most portable.)

Now put the music, the slides, and the poem together. You will read the poem, of course—usually on tape, although you can read it live. The key to a successful presentation is timing: bringing all three arts together into a logical, smoothly running, and effective program.

A few hints:

Keep the presentation short: three to five minutes.

Use only slides that "fit"—better to have fewer, and to have those few of high quality and relevance.

Keep the music low while the poem is being read; although you may wish to raise the volume between stanzas or during an important pause.

Rehearse! Know how to operate the tape recorder and the slide projector. Have each one ready to start. Practice until your timing and procedures are perfect.

The creation of poetry is a lonely job (most writing is). You can probe your inner self only when you are encased in solitude—a solitude of silence or of noise. But with a project of this kind, you move from creation to communication.

As you watch others reacting to your poem, it will become a new and strange thing to you. It may seem better, or it may seem worse. As you listen to others talking about your poem, you will find yourself growing protective: defending it if it is attacked; beaming with pride if it is praised. Either way, the poem is moving away from you. It is beginning to take on a life of its own. *Your* part is finished; it must fail or succeed by itself.

And perhaps that is the last thing that you as a poet have to learn—to let it go. If it needs explanation, reclaim it quickly; and revise or destroy. For a poem—like every other work of art—must be complete in itself. After it leaves your worktable, it belongs to each reader, not to you.

It is a sad and proud thing . . . to be a poet.

Unit VIII
The Script

INTRODUCTION

Is scriptwriting a dying art? Some people claim it is. Below is a script that considers the present state of scripts: their usefulness and their variety. Notice that the format is prescribed: the video (what can be seen) is outlined on the left, and the audio (what can be heard) is outlined on the right.

In this script the video includes closeups, animated filming, stills, and regular filming. The audio includes dialogue between two characters, Doom and Lovely Young Woman (LYW); plus a musical theme (directions italicized). If you have not read many scripts, you may find it easier to read the audio column completely before looking at the video activities.

VIDEO	AUDIO
1 High angle shot of mountain of scripts. The time is late evening; the only light is from a few flickering candles.	*MUSIC: Soft, sad melody. Use "Grandfather's Clock."*
	DOOM: The age of the script has passed. The play is dead. The movie is moribund.
2 Cut to CU (closeup) of script of commercial held by Lovely Young Woman (LYW).	*LYW:* You are too gloomy, Doom. Commercials still need scripts. See—here's one for Genuine Gentians for Gents.
3 Repeat of scene 1.	*DOOM:* One ad's not an avalanche. Scripts are dead.
4 Cut to CU of LYW listening to radio.	*LYW:* Radio needs scripts, too—all kinds. For spot announcements, and news stories, and commentators, and documentaries. Even for short stories.
5 Return to scene 1 . . . increase lighting by 30%.	*DOOM:* Hmmm—I *am* feeling a little stronger. Still—*radio?* Does anyone listen these days?
6 Cut to CU of LYW watching a sound-slide show.	*LYW:* Have a little faith, Doom! Sure, people listen. They also watch millions of sound-slide shows—and everyone of those needs a script!
7 Cut to animated film of six scripts detaching themselves from mountain. They stretch and begin to move around.	*DOOM:* You know, my pulse is getting stronger.
8 Cut to CU of LYW watching a home 8 mm movie.	*LYW:* Home movies, too, Doom—more each year. And some people are writing really classy scripts to make those home films zip!

340

9	Cut to animated film of scripts doing calisthenics.	*DOOM:* Tell me more.
10	Cut to CU of LYW watching a puppet show. Five small children are also watching.	*LYW:* And the schools are buzzing with students studying scripts—there are puppet shows, and mini-plays in classes, and assembly programs! There's a revival of the operetta and musical—they need scripts, too—and some schools have their own TV studios. *They* write scripts every day!
11	Cut to animated film of six more scripts leaving mountain. They join the others. Some are running; some doing slow jigs.	*DOOM:* I'm getting interested now! I'm really not that old. Maybe I'll take a refresher course . . .
12	Cut to CU of a dozen television sets, each with a different picture.	*LYW:* Talking about television—how can anyone say the script is dead when television uses hundreds of them daily?
13	Cut to animated film of more scripts leaving mountain. Much activity—some are talking, some gesturing, some walking around excitedly.	*DOOM:* Faith I've got now! But how about a little more hope? Don't you have some tucked away in that gorgeous brilliant brain?
14	Cut to wide-angle picture of Cinemas 1, 2, and 3.	*Raise volume of music:* TICK TOCK, TICK TOCK.
15	Picture of drive-in movie.	TICK TOCK. TICK TOCK.
16	Picture of long lines waiting to get into theater.	*LYW:* Movies are IN—finding a whole new audience! Just reach out and grab yourself a piece of the action. And Doom . . .
17	Return to scene 1—reduced now to a few scattered scripts. Show all the rest moving around.	*DOOM:* Yes, dear.
18	CU of marquees on Broadway.	*LYW:* Don't let Tennessee Williams hear you say the play is dead. Or Neil Simon. Or Peter Shaffer. Or, for that matter, Enid Bagnold or Elie Wiesel, or Jules Feiffer. Their plays are SRO all over the country! And each one uses a nice, fat juicy script!
19	Cut to animated film of scripts dancing gleefully in large circles.	*DOOM:* WOW! I'm changing my name. Just call me BOOM from now on. Tell me, Lovely Young Woman—would you be interested in a little romantic dialogue? With a plot, of course, and a bar or two of music?
20	Cut to CU of one candle, burning brightly.	*MUSIC: "Grandfather's Clock" jazzed up.*

1 *All About You.* Change your appearance for a few hours. Dress up for dinner. Wear a wig. Alter your hairstyle. Add jewelry. Subtract make-up. Wear something different. Describe your experiment.

_____

_____

Now answer these questions:

(a) Did the change in your appearance affect your actions or your speech? If so, how?

_____

_____

(b) How did other people react?

_____

_____

(c) Any conclusions?

_____

_____

2 *Coffee Break.* During the next 24 hours, watch five people drinking coffee or tea or cocoa. Notice *everything* about each drinker: method of holding cup, position of fingers, frequency of sips, lip movements. Keep notes below on all five drinkers.

_____

_____

_____

_____

_____

_____

_____

_____

3 *Instant Stardom.* You just won a contest. Your prize: for just one night you will be the STAR of your favorite TV program.

(a) Which character in which show will you choose to be?

_____

(b) What is there about this character that appeals to you?

_____

(*c*)   Would you change the portrayal in any way?

_____

4   *The Ten Oddest* . . . Every human being has at least one odd little habit. Clay may pinch his left earlobe; Gwen may wiggle her right eyebrow; Tod may punch out his left cheek with his tongue when he's bored. Look. Notice. Record. Make a list of the ten oddest "gesture" habits that you detect.

_____

_____

_____

_____

_____

_____

_____

_____

5   *Voice Venture.*   Select a singer or actor whose voice you find fascinating. From records or television, tape a few minutes of this person's speech. Listen; analyze; imitate. Keep working at it until you feel you do a really good imitation. Then tape it. Try it on your friends and note their reactions.

_____

_____

_____

_____

Notice *your* reaction. How does it feel to hear your own voice "in costume"?

_____

_____

6   *TV Spectacular.*   The three richest companies in the world have agreed that you and only you can dream up the greatest TV program ever. You have all the money you need; and all the actors you want. Sketch the kind of program you think would walk away with the #1 Nielson rating. (The program may be a daily, a weekly, or a one-time spectacular.)

_____

_____

_____

_____

_____

7 *Moving Day*. Take a short story you know well—perhaps Poe's "The Tell-Tale Heart" or Connell's "The Most Dangerous Game." "Move" the story three times, each time to a distinctly different setting. After each move, discuss briefly how the new setting would affect the story. (Example: move Poe's "The Pit and the Pendulum" from a dungeon in Spain to Matt's Butcher Shop on Typical Lane. The story would become a simple tale of murder or a farce; it would lose the suffocating dignity and stature it now has. Move it again—this time to Mars, 2025 A.D. You would expect a sci-fi yarn, complete with blinking lights, strange noises, and a monster or two.

_____

_____

_____

_____

_____

_____

_____

_____

_____

8 *Cause and Effect*.   Hit a ball and it will move—simple cause and effect. But if you hit it at a certain angle, it may pop up and then land on your own head! Stretch your imagination by thinking up far-out results of the following causes (far-out, but possible!). We've deliberately not specified age or setting, so your imagination is almost unrestricted.

(*a*)   Ted eats a bag of peanuts.

_____

_____

_____

(*b*)   May playfully throws a snowball at Roger.

_____

_____

_____

(*c*)   Lee chops a large limb off a white birch tree.

_____

_____

_____

9 *Grab Bag.*   A grab bag is, by custom, a collection of interesting odds and ends. A dialogue grab bag can be tremendously helpful for any writer. Start one now. Simply collect unusual bits of dialogue from people, movies, news broadcasts, or books. Watch especially for occupational or regional "tags"—you may need them someday. (Examples: Mark Twain once noted that when a seaman wants a gangplank moved, he'll roar: "Here, now, start that gang-plank for'ard! Lively, now! *What*'re you about! Snatch it! *snatch* it!" Two more intriguing bits: "golly marbles" in South Carolina is the name of a disease; and "wrangle-tangle" in Georgia means "to quarrel.") Start collecting. Begin with three samples right here; then enter these in a section of your journal and add new ones whenever possible.

_____

_____

_____

10 *A Plethora of Plots.*   You can create plots by the bushelful if you apply a little imagination to a phrase that may have many meanings. Consider the title, THE VELVET ARM. It might be

—about a robbery in which a mysterious VELVET-clad ARM snatched a million-dollar necklace; or

—about a treasure map concealed in the VELVET ARM of an old chair; or

—about a fashionable thief who carried a dainty VELVET-covered ARM (i.e., gun); or

—about a diplomatic police officer (a VELVET ARM of the law); or

—about a dashing airforce squadron (a VELVET ARM of the services).

Try it with A HOME RUN (check your dictionary to see the many possible meanings of *run*). Aim for at least five possible plots.

_____

_____

_____

_____

_____

_____

_____

48. DIALOGUE FOR TWO

Paul and Jennifer meet. They stop for a moment.

"Hi."

"Hi."

"How are you?"

"Fine. How are you?"

"Fine."

Pause.

"Nice weather, isn't it?"

"Very nice."

Pause.

"Well—goodbye."

"Bye."

The above dialogue is so realistic that you have probably heard it three times a day—except, of course, on rainy days.

Is it therefore *good* dialogue—good for a play? It might be—if Paul and Jennifer, after going steady for several years and then breaking up, are meeting again for the first time. Then their short, curt exchange would have a powerful impact. But in any other situation it would be dead—dull—like most "real" conversation. If real conversation won't do, how does one go about creating good stage conversation?

Keep It Natural

The first rule is—**keep it natural.** But conversation that is natural for a 17-year-old student is not necessarily natural for a 35-year-old bank teller or a five-year-old girl. So the writer's first problem in handling dialogue is—to match speech patterns with specific characters.

Sanders and Mulligan are soldiers. Their position is under attack. Sanders sticks his head up and a bullet whistles past his left ear. What does Mulligan shout?

(*a*) You had better come down here where it is safer.

or (*b*) Get down, you fool!

a or *b*? ____

You *know* what Mulligan would say. When you hear or read conversation, you know instinctively whether it is right—for the person, for the occasion, for the time period. Unfortunately, the same instinct isn't always on duty when you're writing.

Test your instinct on the following problems:

Jessica is a confident young businesswoman of 23. Her car has stalled on the thru-way and she is waiting for a patrol car. A truck pulls up and the truck driver invites her into his cab. "I'll take you to the next service area," he says. Jessica replies:

(a)   No, thanks. But I would appreciate it if you would ask them to send a tow truck.

or (b)   Gee, whiz—but no—I mean, well, man . . . But maybe they could send a truck, you think?

a or *b*? ____

Louis is a seven-year-old who is quite immature. He whines a lot and has temper tantrums. One day he asks his mother if he can visit Kevin. When his mother says it is too close to lunch time, Louis replies:

(a)   All right, Mother. But may I go after we have had lunch?

or (b)   Waaaa! I wanta go! Why can't I? You never let me go anywhere!

a or *b*? ____

For the next two problems, *you* supply a suitable reply.

Pam is fourteen—sullen and defiant. She has had failing grades in most subjects for the last three years. Today she didn't do her math homework, the fourth time this week. Her teacher, Ms. Harrison, says: "Pam, since you can't do your homework at home, please report at 3 o'clock. Perhaps you can concentrate better here."

Pam replies:

____

____

Michael Landers heads his own business—the BCX Plastics Company. He is person-able, well-liked by his employees, and intelligent. On his way home one night, he is thinking of a pending business deal and he steps harder than he should on the accelera-tor. A police officer waves him to the side of the road. "You were doing 45 in a 25-mile speed zone, Mister."

Landers replies:

____

____

Keep It Moving

Don't let your dialogue get bogged down. Know how a record sounds when the needle is trapped in a groove? Too often dialogue slips into this pattern.

Mary: I'd like to go to the dance, but. . . .Well, I don't know if I will.

Janet: The gym looks real nice.

Mary: Yeah. But it might be boring. You know, a lot of kids milling around . . .

Janet: But everyone's going, Mary. Don't you think you should?

Mary: Maybe. Or maybe not. I guess I'll have to think about it.

Janet: I think you should go. It may look odd if you don't.

Mary: I don't see why. I have a right to go or not to go. If it's going to be boring, why should I go?

This conversation may sound realistic, but on stage it would put the audience to sleep. The writer must ask: "*Why* is Mary reluctant to go to the dance?" Perhaps she has no date; perhaps her parents won't let her go; perhaps she can't dance. The writer must know the reason, and the dialogue must reflect this knowledge and move the story forward.

Let's say that Mary is reluctant to go because she can't dance. The conversation might go like this:

Mary: I'd like to go to the dance, but. . . . Well, I don't know if I will.

Janet: The gym looks real nice.

Mary: Yeah. But dancing's awfully silly—just a lot of feet making stupid designs on a waxed floor.

Janet: That's not true!

Mary: It is *so* true! People wriggling and jumping around like monkeys! *I*'d rather do something intelligent—like reading a book.

Janet: You read a book? You hate to read! What's come over you anyway?

Mary: Maybe I'm growing up! I'm going to read a lot from now on. You've never heard of a dancer becoming president, have you? Or head of a law firm. Or anything. I hate dances! I hate them—I hate them!

The main difference between the two bits of dialogue is that the second is progressive: it moves the action forward. It suggests *why* Mary doesn't want to go to the dance. It shows her hurt and her fear—and her envy. It forces Mary's emotions to the surface and it forces Janet to begin to suspect the cause of her friend's reluctance.

Try your own snatch of dialogue. Here's the situation: Ron and Wade, both seniors, are talking in the hall. In two minutes they will be taking their science final. Ron, a lazy student, has not studied and wants Wade to slip him the answers. Wade has already been accepted into a pre-law course. If he is caught helping Ron, his acceptance will probably be withdrawn and he will definitely lose the scholarship he needs. Provide the dialogue between the two boys. End with Wade's making a decision.

_____

_____

_____

_____

_____

_____

_____

_____

_____

_____

_____

_____

_____

_____

_____

_____

_____

_____

Keep It Lively

Even if your dialogue is natural *and* progressive, it won't work unless it is also lively. So let's try a lively conversation. This time it's between two girls. Arlene and Kitty are juniors, both are fine secretarial students, and both are applying for the same job—filing clerk for Dr. Kidneystone. The doctor has already agreed to hire one of them, but he wishes to interview both of them once more. We'll be Arlene, you be Kitty. Arlene is sneaky and mean. Make Kitty sweet or sarcastic or arrogant, or anything you like.

Arlene: Well, Kitty—I guess it will be one of us.

Kitty: _____

_____

Arlene: I can't imagine *you* working in a doctor's office! All that blood pouring out on the floor, and the patients screaming . . .

Kitty: _____

_____

_____

Arlene: There's probably a skeleton in one of his closets, too. Just think of opening a door and being hugged by a bunch of bones!

Kitty: _____

_____

_____

_____

Arlene: And there's something else—infections. You can really pick them up when you're around sick people a lot. Of course, *I* am as healthy as a horse!

Kitty: _____

_____

_____

_____

Arlene: Oh, well. I'm feeling pretty confident. I'm sure Dr. Kidneystone will select the healthiest and brightest applicant!

Kitty: _____

_____

_____

_____

(The nurse opens the door. "The doctor will see you now," she says, nodding to one of the girls.)

❋   ❋   ❋   ❋

"Experimental Theater"

Here are two experiments that will help you close up this chapter and get ready for the next.

First—borrow a tape recorder. Ask a good friend to work with you. Switch on the recorder and get into a conversation. You will both be self-conscious at first, but try to forget the recorder. Later study the tape carefully. How long are the sentences? Were there many interrupted sentences? Was there much repetition? Make a few notes below about speech patterns of you and your friend.

_____

_____

_____

_____

_____

_____

Second—again borrow a tape recorder. This time ask a group of friends (perhaps at lunch) if they would mind if the conversation is recorded. (*Don't* record conversations unless you have permission from everyone involved. It's a violation of privacy.) If you get permission, insert a 30-minute tape and turn on the recorder.

Later, when you are alone, transcribe at least part of it . . . that is, write it out in longhand. Try to find at least one identifying characteristic in each person's speech pattern. One might say—"you know?"—all the time. Another might end all sentences with a question. A third might overuse the word "fabulous" or "nice." Record your observations below.

_____

_____

_____

_____

_____

_____

_____

_____

_____

You are ready—hopefully—for group dialogue, a far more complex technique. Tune in your ears and proceed to Chapter 49—your Encounter Session.

49. GROUP DIALOGUE

If you have ever been to an Encounter Session, you know that one of its purposes is to sensitize people so that each will better understand how others feel, think, and react. In a way, that's exactly what a writer does when handling group dialogue: he or she tries to understand each of the characters well enough to be able to anticipate how each will feel, think, and react to others. It's quite a challenge!

Acquiring Some Characters

Your first task is to acquire three characters. Aim for variety. You might choose, for example, a 45-year-old farmer (male), a 55-year-old nurse (female), and a 20-year-old head of a shoe department in a large store (female). It helps if you have a real person in mind for each of these characters. Now set up your own cast of characters.

1 _____

2 _____

3 _____

Give each one a name and a brief physical description. For example, Ned Forbes—the 45-year-old farmer—about 5′9″, 170 pounds, brown thinning hair, brown eyes, wrinkled skin, wearing overalls (denims) and plaid shirt, boots. (See Chapter 17 for suggestions.)

YOUR TURN:

1 _____

_____

_____

2 _____

_____

_____

3 _____

_____

_____

Next step—give each of your three characters a salient characteristic and two lesser characteristics. (See Chapter 34 if you need some ideas.)

Example: Ned Forbes
          salient characteristic—miserliness
          two lesser traits—honesty; doesn't talk much

1 _____
_____
_____

2 _____
_____
_____

3 _____
_____
_____

Last step in developing your cast: give each one a speech characteristic. Maybe Ned Forbes uses double negatives a lot; or maybe he frequently repeats: "Honesty is the best policy"; or maybe he uses only very short sentences. Be sure that the speech characteristic you choose for each character is one that will be obvious in dialogue (not a nasal twang, for example).

YOUR TURN

1 _____
2 _____
3 _____

Setting up a Situation

Set up a situation in which your characters will almost be forced to converse.

Our situation: The three people, all strangers, are in a dirty bus depot in a small town. It is close to midnight. The next bus will be along in about forty minutes. It's a cold, rainy night—too miserable to be outdoors; the stationmaster has gone off duty and the three are alone in the room. Suddenly the outside door opens and a bag of gold coins is thrown on the floor. For a minute the three are silent, staring at the closed door and at the gold. Then they begin to speak.

Your situation: _____

_____
_____
_____
_____
_____
_____
_____
_____

Creating Group Dialogue

One restriction here: you may *not* use any narration; you must tell the full story of the incident *through* dialogue. You know your characters fairly well, and you should know how they will respond to the situation.

Ned Forbes, the miserly but honest farmer, might start the conversation, mumbling: "Honesty is the best policy . . . I guess." The 20-year-old might respond by humming "Hawaii's just around the corner!" And the nurse, a practical woman but also a timid one, might add: "Shouldn't we count it first? To see how much there is? Before we do *anything*, I mean."

Fine—your dialogue has started. Each of the characters has made a commitment based on his or her values.

At this point you may want to pause for a few minutes to decide how the situation will be resolved. Will the thief return, bleeding, looking for his loot? Will the police rush in to confiscate it? Will the three divide it equally? Or award it by a lottery? Will the gold coins turn out to be play money? Or chocolate wafers wrapped in gold foil? Decide the resolution of *your* situation.

Ready? Now you must create dialogue that will move your characters from their opening speeches to the resolution.

As you proceed, remember two things:

Let each piece of dialogue be *appropriate* to the character speaking. (e.g., The nurse might say, "Don't you think we should. . . ?" Ned Forbes never would.)

Have the characters relate to each other in various ways. (e.g., The nurse and the young woman might take sides against the farmer; or each might stand alone, viewing the other two with suspicion.)

Here is how the dialogue should look on the page:

Forbes.	Honesty is the best policy . . . I guess.
Girl.	Hawaii's just around the corner.
Nurse.	Shouldn't we count it first? To see how much there is? Before we do *anything*, I mean.

Begin.

_____

_____

_____

_____

_____

_____

_____

_____

_____

_____

_____

_____

_____

_____

_____

_____

_____

_____

_____

_____

_____

_____

_____

_____

_____

_____

_____

_____

_____

_____

What you have just written is a playlet—brief, but a playlet all the same. Test it out by having three other students read the script. As the playwright, sit back and listen carefully. Is your dialogue *natural?* Is it *progressive?* Is it *lively?* Does it *flow smoothly?* If all your answers are "yeses," you can feel rather good. If some of them are "nos," take back your script and do some revising.

Dialogue is *the* key element in playwriting and—as you will see in Unit IX—it is a key element in short story writing. Get into the habit of jotting down bits of dialogue you overhear in the halls or on a bus. In your spare time, create dialogue for unusual "dream" situations. See yourself having lunch with Robert Redford and Liza Minnelli . . . what do they say? what do you say? See yourself being falsely arrested in a strange town . . . what do the police say? what do you say? See yourself as a passenger on a hijacked plane . . . what does the hijacker say? the flight attendant? the pilot? the other passengers? you?

Daydreaming (Chapter 4) can help you find ideas; it can also help you to develop skill in writing dialogue. Don't make all your characters speak as *you* do. Get inside their skin— be them—then let them speak as *themselves*.

50. TIME FOR A STORY

If dialogue is the key to a good play, then the *storyline* is the lock. Neither can exist alone; partnership is essential.

What is a storyline? A storyline is the plot—and the plot is made up of two elements: cause-and-effect relationships, and conflict.

Cause-and-Effect Relationships

The British author, E. M. Forster, summed it up well when he said:

> "The king died and then the queen died" is merely a recounting of two events.

> "The king died and then the queen died of grief" is a plot.

Notice the difference between the two statements: in the latter, the second action is *caused* by the first action.

Read the following problem:

> Ken and Steve work in a factory. Steve invents a gadget that will save the company thousands of dollars. Ken steals it and, using it as a lever, within a few months wheedles his way into an administrative position. The workers hate Ken—they know he's a cheat. The boss has heard rumors of the theft, but he believes Ken.

Keeping the cause-and-effect relationship in mind, which of the following two solutions would be more effective?

> Ken leaves the office after an especially unpleasant day. He has just fired Steve and two other workers. It's raining hard, and as Ken goes to get his car, he's hit by lightning and is killed.

> or

> The gadget is patented and put into operation. For a few days it works well. Then one day all the major machinery begins to overheat. Ken is helpless—he has never understood the technology that produced the gadget. As the machinery grinds and smokes, Steve goes forward and makes a few adjustments. The owner of the factory has seen the whole thing and beckons the two men to his office.

Of course the second resolution (or solution) is better. What is wrong with the first?

_____

_____

_____

Now concoct a resolution of your own. Using the cause-and-effect relationship as a guide, resolve the following problem:

> Jake knows a lot about racing cars, but he is lazy and often takes short cuts. On the day of the big race he mends a broken wire instead of replacing it. At the three-quarter mark in the race, Jake's car is well in the lead. What happens?

_____

_____

_____

_____

_____

Now try it the other way around. Start with an effect, and create a suitable and logical cause.

_____

_____

_____

_____

_____

> Ellen watched as her house burned down. She had lost everything—her husband Jim, her three children, her home. After ten years, she was right back where she had started—at zero.

Conflicts

Closely related to the cause-and-effect is the *conflict*. You cannot write even a playlet without one, so you may as well learn the five basic types.

> FIRST—**is the conflict between human and God.** (This is the hardest type to handle today.)

> *Example:* Tom believes that God wants him to enter a monastery, but he fears the hardships of monastic life. Tom creates reason after reason why he shouldn't enter.

The other four types of conflict are more common. After each example we give, *you* give an example.

> SECOND—**is the conflict between human and nature.**

> *Our example:* Karen and Fred, driving along a deserted highway, are trapped in a blizzard. The snow is 15 inches deep, and the temperature is below zero. If they stay in the car, they will probably freeze. If they leave the car, they will probably freeze.

Your example: _____

_____

_____

_____

_____

THIRD—**is the conflict between human and society.**

Our example: Dr. Simon starts a campaign to eliminate pollution from the river that flows through the town of Hasset Falls. But eliminating it means eliminating the HRL Plant which employs 60% of the town's residents. The people come to hate Dr. Simon for forcing them to decide between pure water in the tap or food on the table.

Your example: _____

_____

_____

_____

_____

FOURTH—**is the conflict between human and self.**

Our example: Vera works for the mayor of her town. She discovers he is accepting bribes from several sources. If she reports this to a newspaper, the town will benefit; but the mayor, a good friend, will lose his position and may go to jail. If she doesn't report it, she becomes an accessory—helping to cheat her friends and neighbors and risking a jail sentence herself.

Your example: _____

_____

_____

_____

_____

FIFTH—**is the conflict between human and human.** (This is the most common of all and the easiest to handle.)

Our example: (a continuation and development of #4) Vera decides to talk with the mayor, urging him to confess. If he is guilty, this confrontation will throw them into direct conflict.

Your example: _____

_____

_____

_____

Before you take the next step, select a conflict that interests you, one you would like to develop. It may be one of the four you devised above, or it may be a brand-new one. If the latter, summarize it below.

_____

_____

_____

_____

_____

Now comes the tricky part—to take the basic conflict and to develop it in accordance with the cause-and-effect rule.

Our example (based on conflict #5 above): As you read, notice that each step is the cause of the one that follows it, and the effect of the one that precedes it.

Vera, a shy quiet woman, learns the mayor is taking bribes.

She wonders whether to report him and decides not to. To avoid thinking about it, she invites some friends to dinner.

That night the friends talk about a state official accused of accepting bribes. They insist he cheated the taxpayers and damaged public morale.

Vera thinks some more; this time she decides to talk with the mayor.

She tells Mayor Trim she knows about the bribery and urges him to confess.

He agrees. She feels wonderful. As she leaves his office, she hears him pick up the phone and dial a number.

Vera goes out to lunch. A car jumps the curb and hits her, then speeds away. She is knocked down, but is not hurt. It didn't seem like an accident.

After lunch she goes back to the office. She checks the files and books and discovers the mayor has already accepted over $100,000 in bribes. The crime is too large, and he agreed to confess too quickly. She realizes she may be in danger and remembers the "accident."

She goes across the hall to the office of the mayor's assistant and tells him her suspicions. David is shocked. He offers to take her home and does.

She invites him into her apartment for coffee and some more talk. But his conversation soon makes her suspicious. When she is alone for a moment, in the kitchen, she calls the police.

A few minutes later as she is pouring the coffee, she feels David's fingers around her neck. She screams. The police arrive (thanks to her call), and he confesses. The mayor is also arrested.

Left alone, Vera shrugs and opens the newspaper. She reads the "Help Wanted" ads.

The script, as it stands, wouldn't make a very good play. It needs further complications, possibly one or two more characters, and a couple of unusual "twists." But it is coherent. It moves inevitably once the conflict has been established—and that is the first important thing for the scriptwriter to learn.

Take a deep breath now and tackle your first script outline. Do it in items (or scenes) and be sure there is a cause-and-effect relationship linking scene to scene.

_____

_____

_____

_____

_____

_____

_____

_____

_____

_____

_____

_____

_____

_____

_____

_____

_____

_____

_____

_____

_____

_____

51. STAGE DIRECTIONS

As a stage writer, you must also be a stage director. Let's consider the case of Ned Forbes, the 45-year-old farmer you met in Chapter 49. As Ned's creator, we must know where he's supposed to stand or sit, how he walks, how he uses his hands, what mood he's in—and somehow we must convey all this information to the actor.

In this chapter, use the playlet you wrote on pages 354–355 to experiment on, as you explore the world of stage directions.

Setting

Begin by indicating at the top of your play the fully described setting. You will find this stage diagram helpful in indicating placement of characters. Below the diagram is an example appropriate for *our* playlet; you provide one appropriate for *yours*.

	Upstage Center	
Upstage Right		Upstage Left
Right	Center	Left
Downstage Right	Downstage Center	Downstage Left

AUDIENCE

OURS

Scene: Midnight in a small railroad station in Craig Hollow. The waiting room is small and dirty. On three sides are worn benches. On the fourth side is a cage for the ticketseller, now barred and locked for the night. The only light comes from a single bulb hanging from the ceiling. Ned Forbes is slouched on a bench at the right. Across from him, on the left, is Christine Madden, R.N., still wearing her nursing uniform and cap. Miss Madden, sitting very erect, is crocheting. Between them, upper center, is 20-year-old Susie Alban, wearing a halter top, jeans, and earth boots.

The three, obviously strangers, are carefully maintaining privacy. They neither speak nor exchange glances. The station door opens and a paper bag is thrown in, landing in the center of the room. As it hits the floor, the bag breaks, spilling gold coins in every direction. For a minute, the three look silently from the closed door to the coins, then back again. At last they begin to sneak furtive glances at each other.

YOURS _____

_____

_____

_____

_____

_____

_____

_____

_____

_____

_____

_____

_____

Action

Characters *do* things . . . constantly. And each action should move the story forward or broaden our knowledge of the character. You, the author, must provide your characters with the *right* things to do.

For example, in the first scene of our play, the nurse, Christine Madden, is sitting upright and crocheting steadily. As she makes her first speech, we want to show that she is shocked out of her usual routine. We give appropriate instructions:

> Madden (*dropping her crocheting and leaning forward*). Shouldn't we count it first? To see how much there is? Before we do *anything*, I mean.

(As you can see, on the printed page the directions are italicized. Underline yours to indicate italics.)

Another example: later in the scene, Ned Forbes says: "I'll count it." Now Forbes has been shown to be slow and deliberate in his movements. To emphasize his love of money, we give him a contrasting action.

> Forbes (*leaping forward and landing on all fours over the money*). I'll count it!

Do you see what you can accomplish by providing the right stage directions? Go through your own play now (pages 354–355), inserting directions wherever they seem necessary.

Voices

You will want to follow a somewhat similar procedure to indicate voice use. It is possible to take a short, empty sentence like "I went to the store" and make it mean a dozen different things. For example, if the playwright indicated that the words were to be spoken *arrogantly*, the actor would probably emphasize the "I" and—through tone of voice—suggest that no one else was capable of going to the store. If the playwright indicated that the words were to be spoken *mischievously*, the actor would try to suggest—again through tone of voice—that the character was teasing or involved in a prank.

Other possible voice directions:

(fearfully). I—I w-went to the st-store.
(singing smugly). I went to the store.
(shaking her fist). I went to the store!
(shaking his head violently). I went to the store!

If you read each of these aloud, in accordance with the direction given, you will discover how voice direction can aid both writer and actor. Try it, using the short sentence—"Ah, what a day!" In each case, precede the sentence with a direction that indicates *how* it should be read. Do *not* use any of the above directions.

(_____). Ah, what a day!
(_____). Ah, what a day!
(_____). Ah, what a day!
(_____). Ah, what a day!
(_____). Ah, what a day!
(_____). Ah, what a day!

Go through your own play again, this time inserting voice directions wherever they will be helpful.

Stage "Business"

There is one other kind of stage direction with which even the beginning playwright should be familiar: the handling of stage "business." This may vary from a word or two, to several lines—and it is powerful enough to change a serious drama into a comedy.

In our "gold coin" play, we showed Ned Forbes leaping forward and landing on all fours over the money. Suppose we want a comic touch there. We add a stage direction.

Forbes (*leaping forward and landing on all fours over the money*). I'll count it!

(*At almost the same time Susie and Madden also leap forward. As the three heads collide, there is a loud crack.*)

Suppose instead of giving it a comic touch, we want to sustain and increase tension. We would add this stage direction instead:

> Forbes (*leaping forward and landing on all fours over the money*). I'll count it!
>
> > (*Madden and Susie immediately rise and move forward, Madden to Forbes' right, Susie to his left. They say nothing but watch intently as his hands scoop together the gold coins. As he goes to pick them up, each grasps one of his shoulders.*)
>
> Susie (*lightly, but meaningfully*). Not yet, farmer boy!
>
> Madden (*fearfully, yet obviously meaning it*). And not that way!

Stage business is not just decorative. It is vital if the actors are to interpret the play as you want them to. You can't afford to neglect this aspect of playwriting.

Another kind of stage business might be called the "motif" approach. Suppose you intend to end your play by having the villain lose his car keys just as the police turn into the street. All during the play you might have him playing with the keys: tossing them up in the air, dropping them on a table, twitching them at the other characters. Near the end, when he throws them into the air, his attention is diverted and he doesn't notice them land among the foliage of a huge philodendron.

The motif must be used skillfully and subtly, or it will take over the play and distract the audience from the main business. Used well, it provides unity and additional suspense.

Turn now to your own play. Decide where stage business is needed and add it.

❃ ❃ ❃ ❃ ❃

When you have finished, copy the complete script including the four types of stage directions. Make it a clean, easily readable copy. Then ask several friends to read it. If you have done your work well, you should be pleasantly surprised at how effectively it reads. (Of course, if instead of being pleasantly surprised, you're horribly disappointed, there's only one remedy: revise!)

52. CAST OF CHARACTERS

Imagine a play in which the following four people are the only characters.

Imagine, further, that all four wear identical clothing and use identical speech patterns. It would be deadly boring, wouldn't it?

Yet this is the sin of many inexperienced playwrights. Their characters may be described as individuals but they don't *act* as individuals. If the nurse slouches like the farmer, and the 20-year-old is timid like the nurse, and all three speak in short, curt sentences, the audience will quickly realize they aren't "real" and therefore not worth caring about.

So the question is—how do you make your characters individual? You've already experimented with these techniques:

.. detailed physical description
.. voice and speech patterns
.. physical movements and gestures

These will do for a rapidly written playlet. But for the longer play—the play intended to grip and persuade and arouse emotion—something more is needed.

Become Someone Else

As your first exercise, *become* someone else. Choose a celebrity, or a friend or relative. Get *inside* the other's body, talk with the other's lips, see with the other's eyes. If you can, imitate the other person's facial expressions and speech patterns. Ready?

Answer each of the following questions twice: first as yourself; and second as this other person.

1 You are walking down the street and a rowdy twelve-year-old hurtles into you, knocking you down.

How would *you* react? _____

_____

How would the *other* person react? _____

_____

2 You and this "character" are sitting in the living room, watching TV. A bulletin interrupts the program. "The President has just announced that, as of two hours ago, all mass transportation in this country has ceased to move. The reason is not known. We repeat: all mass transportation has ceased to move. Trains, planes, and buses—none are working. An investigation is now underway, and all citizens are requested to stay tuned in for further information."

What would *you* say? _____

_____

_____

What would the *other* person say? _____

_____

_____

Join a Group

The second exercise demands that five of you get together and develop a cast of characters. Create five different characters and describe each briefly: occupation, age, sex. (If three, four, or six people wish to work together, they should create three, four or six characters. The number of characters must equal the number of people in the group.) Match the characters by sex only; that is, if two of you are male, create two male characters. Write the descriptions below.

1 _____

_____

2 _____

_____

_____

3 _____

_____

_____

4 _____

_____

_____

5 _____

_____

_____

Now agree on who will become which character. Then separate. Indicate below the character *you* are to become:

_____

For the next thirty minutes, concentrate on becoming this person. Filling in the following outline should be helpful:

1 Write a brief physical description.

_____
_____
_____
_____

2 List a salient characteristic and two minor characteristics.

_____
_____
_____

3 Identify noticeable voice and speech patterns.

_____
_____

4 Identify habitual gestures (e.g., flicking hair from brow, playing with keys).

_____
_____

As you write *about* this person, take on his or her attributes. Does he play with a pencil? Play with yours. Does she sit with a stiff, erect back? Sit with a stiff, erect back. Begin a slow metamorphosis of yourself into this other person.

Now, *as this other person,* answer these questions:

5 How would you evaluate the present federal government?

_____
_____

6 What is your favorite dessert?

_____

7 How do you feel about members of the opposite sex? Do you like them? Or find them beyond comprehension? Or what?

_____
_____
_____
_____

8 If you had an extra $10 bill in your pocket, what would you do with it?

_____

_____

_____

_____

STOP. Check your answers. Would you have given the same answers if you had been answering for yourself? If you would have, then you are *not* getting inside your character. You have to try harder. Continue. Remember—the answers should reflect the created character's personality, not your own.

9 If you had a totally "free" day, how would you spend it?

_____

_____

_____

10 Which historical personage do you most admire? _____

Why? _____

_____

_____

11 How often do you wash your hair? _____

12 At what time do you get up in the morning? _____

At what time do you go to bed at night? _____

Add below anything else that will make your knowledge of this character deeper and more realistic.

_____

_____

_____

(If you are wondering what frequency of hair-washing has to do with knowing a character, here's the answer: our habits and our handling of small details are part of our general behavior pattern. If you know how often character "A" washes his hair, you will be better able to predict what he will logically do in a certain situation. If you doubt us, perhaps you'll believe Ibsen. Talking about Nora in *A Doll's House*, Ibsen said: "The things I know about that young woman that aren't in the play would surprise you.")

When all five of you have completed this task and have become five other people, meet again.

Here's your situation. The five of you were on a plane flying across the Sahara Desert. The motor failed, the plane crashed—and only you five survived. The temperature is 120°. It is 11:10 a.m. As far as you can see, there is only sand—no roads, no houses, no people, no camels, nothing—just sand, the wrecked plane (the radio is broken), and you five.

Isolate yourselves in a corner of the room and improvise. You should be asking yourselves—*As the character I have become*, what would I do? what would I say? how would I think? This is difficult. *You* may be honest and wouldn't think of stealing the little food that is in the plane; but if the character you have become is sneaky and selfish and cruel, he *will* steal it.

It may take you a minute to get "into character," but once you have managed to do so, you will be (mutually) creating a small play. Keep it going for at least five minutes, preferably ten. Again, separate.

Continue in character. As this character, write a first-person point of view description of the event. (Example: at first I was the only one conscious. The other four were either dazed or in a coma. I figured this was a good time to. . . .)

_____

_____

_____

_____

_____

_____

_____

_____

_____

_____

_____

Now evaluate yourself. Did you stay in character throughout the "play"? Were your actions and words logical for the character? Was it difficult to do?

_____

_____

_____

_____

_____

_____

_____

Become a Group

When you actually write a play, you will go one step further—you will become *each* character so that you may be three or even five different people simultaneously. You must become a juggler, juggling different voice and speech patterns, different behavior patterns, and different idea patterns.

Last exercise: create three new characters—any type you like. Describe each fully, including appearance, habits, personalities, etc.

First character: _____

_____

_____

_____

_____

_____

Second character: _____

_____

_____

_____

_____

_____

Third character: _____

_____

_____

_____

_____

_____

Create a situation in which the three are alone, and are facing a specific problem.

_____

_____

_____

_____

_____

_____

Finally—write a playlet. Include all necessary stage directions. Follow the format you have been using.

FORMAT

Fred. You can go. I'm not.

Jane (tearfully). But you promised! You absolutely promised! You said . . .

_____

_____

_____

Finished? Then read all the lines of character "A." Are they consistent? Do they sound like "A"? Follow the same procedure with "B"—then with "C." Don't try to take a short-cut and read all three together. You can test consistency of character only by concentrating on one role at a time. Make any revisions necessary.

Have some friends take the three parts and "put on" the play. Listen and watch. Are they capturing what you wrote? Did *you* capture what you hoped to?

Playwriting is not easy. If you are now able to get inside characters, to speak as they would, to act as they would, and if you have learned to put together a good storyline, you should be able to write a play that at least resembles a play.

Write *useful* playlets as often as possible. Each time one of your playlets is produced, you will learn a good deal about writing and about audiences.

How do you *use* playlets? Here are a half dozen suggestions. With a little brainstorming (see Chapter 1) you can probably come up with another half dozen.

Is your class sponsoring a dance? Instead of a regular announcement, write a playlet that will persuade students to purchase tickets.

Write playlets, dealing with various aspects of school life, that can be used in the orientation of new students.

Try a playlet about some successful new venture in your school. Present it to the PTA. The parents will love it!

Create playlets based on subject-matter: in history class, a dramatization of the signing of the Declaration of Independence; in science class, a dramatization of the discovery of penicillin.

Learn a little about puppets. Write a script, then have the puppets act it. Present it for your younger brothers and sisters. If it works, offer to the small fry of the neighborhood. They'll love you for it, and if your script is any good at all, their enthusiastic applause will encourage you!

Write a script, enlist some actors and someone with an 8 mm movie camera, and produce your own short film. If you write a murder story, you can show it in a few classes. If you are a bit more modest and write a tour of historical places in town, you may find yourself being booked for presentations to many of the social and business groups. And what a boost *that* is to the young playwright!

Go to it!

53. THE SOUND-SLIDE SHOW

Interested in breaking into show biz right now? You can—with the modest (but demanding) sound-slide show. No exercises this time—but a total production from script to presentation!

First—Check Out Your Resources

Your choice of subject may be limited by what is available. Here are some possible resources:

1 *Home Slides.* If you or your parents are 35 mm fanatics, you probably have a good supply of slides of various family members, summer trips, birthday parties, etc.

2 *School Slide Collection.* Check with your AV department and the school library. If there is a slide collection, check it out to determine the number and types of slides available. Also check to see if you can borrow the slides for two or three weeks.

3 *Film and Processing.* Here you start from scratch: take your own slides. But it's expensive. If you have plenty of money, you may prefer to work alone. A 30–40 slide production will cost you about $12. If money is limited, work in a group of four and split the cost; or check to see if your school provides film and processing for school projects.

4 *A Combination Deal.* It is also possible to combine two or all of the above: for example, to put together a show based on home slides but supplemented by a few newly taken specials.

Check out your resources and decide which approach you will adopt:

Second—Choose Your Subject

You now know what is available, and you can move to your second decision: what will the presentation be about?

For a home show: You might put together something about your 24-year-old brother Richard, to show to his fiancée.

For a school show: You might present your school as it appears to a freshman on his or her first day.

For independent filming and processing: You might dramatize an athletic event, produce a short school or community drama, capture on film an anniversary, jubilee, or auction.

Think and decide. Your choice:

_____

_____

_____

_____

_____

Third—Produce a Working Script

A working script is similar to a storyline. You know the story you are going to work with. Find your angle.

Our angle (for a home-slide production script): It will be based on 24-year-old Richard's habit of referring to his "poverty-stricken" childhood. We will mock Richard's claim to poverty by showing toys, parties, etc., from his birth to the present time.

YOUR ANGLE _____

_____

_____

_____

_____

_____

Our storyline (excerpt only, to serve as an example):

Slide 1–Richard at one week old; fancy bassinet; boxing glove rattles; football; etc.

2–Richard at two years, in Davy Crockett outfit.

3–Richard at third birthday party; cake, decorations, presents.

4–Richard at third birthday party; new fire truck; with two cousins.

. . .

11–Richard on stagecoach (part of summer trip).

12–Richard chopping wood (same summer trip).

. . .

18–Richard dressed for senior prom; tux.

. . .

36–Richard in shiny new car (taken a week ago).

YOUR STORYLINE: (If you are working with slides already made, you may find it easier to select the slides, organize them, and then write your storyline. If you are taking new slides, you may prefer to develop your storyline first.)

Slide 1–_____
2–_____
3–_____
4–_____
5–_____
6–_____
7–_____
8–_____
9–_____
10–_____
11–_____
12–_____
13–_____
14–_____
15–_____
16–_____
17–_____
18–_____
19–_____
20–_____
21–_____
22–_____
23–_____
24–_____
25–_____
26–_____
27–_____
28–_____
29–_____
30–_____
31–_____
32–_____
33–_____
34–_____
35–_____

36-_____
37-_____
38-_____
39-_____
40-_____

Fourth—Study Your Visuals

Now study your visuals until you know them thoroughly. If you have not already done so, organize them in accordance with your storyline. Study them again.

Fifth—Write the Script

The narration you will now write is called "voice-over"—literally, voice "over" pictures. The term is used in television, but it is equally correct here. When a voice accompanies pictures, you will want to use a special writing technique. NEVER EXPLAIN WHAT YOUR AUDIENCE CAN SEE; GIVE ADDITIONAL INFORMATION OR SUPPLY EDITORIAL COMMENTS. And be sure that whatever you say relates directly to the picture on the screen.

Don't say: This is 12-year-old Richard chopping wood in Cooperstown.

Do say: Even at 12, poor Richard spent hours chopping cords of wood to keep his family warm.

Notice the difference between the two bits of narration. The first is informative; but the viewer can *see* it and doesn't have to be told. The second ties the picture into the storyline—turns a summer adventure into a jest at Richard's self-styled "poverty." It also uses hyperbole to add a touch of humor.

Set up your script in two columns. The left-hand column will contain brief descriptions of the slides; the right-hand column will contain the narration.

OUR SCRIPT (sample only):

Slide	*Narration*
3–Closeup of Richard at third birthday party.	Poor Richard. Even on this third birthday, he was forced to work—cutting a cake and unwrapping large heavy packages.
4–Richard with new fire truck and two cousins.	While the grownups ate cake and drank soda, the poor little tyke had to brave the weather to fight fire and smoke, assisted only by two inexperienced helpers.

Got it? Don't be afraid to use hyperbole, irony, and sarcasm if you're writing a humorous script. But serious or comic, make sure your narration *supplements* the picture, rather than repeats it.

YOUR SCRIPT: (Mark your first picture #2; do not write on the first two lines or the
last two lines.)

Slide	Narration
1- _____	_____
_____	_____
2- _____	_____
_____	_____
3- _____	_____
_____	_____
4- _____	_____
_____	_____
5- _____	_____
_____	_____
6- _____	_____
_____	_____
7- _____	_____
_____	_____
8- _____	_____
_____	_____
9- _____	_____
_____	_____
10- _____	_____
_____	_____
11- _____	_____
_____	_____
12- _____	_____
_____	_____
13- _____	_____
_____	_____
14- _____	_____
_____	_____
15- _____	_____
_____	_____
16- _____	_____
_____	_____

17-_____   _____
_____   _____
18-_____   _____
_____   _____
19-_____   _____
_____   _____
20-_____   _____
_____   _____
21-_____   _____
_____   _____
22-_____   _____
_____   _____
23-_____   _____
_____   _____
24-_____   _____
_____   _____
25-_____   _____
_____   _____
26-_____   _____
_____   _____
27-_____   _____
_____   _____
28-_____   _____
_____   _____
29-_____   _____
_____   _____
30-_____   _____
_____   _____
31-_____   _____
_____   _____
32-_____   _____
_____   _____
33-_____   _____
_____   _____

34-_____ _____

_____ _____

35-_____ _____

_____ _____

36-_____ _____

_____ _____

37-_____ _____

_____ _____

38-_____ _____

_____ _____

39-_____ _____

_____ _____

40-_____ _____

_____ _____

Sixth—Write an Introduction

Now is the time to choose an opening slide that will support your storyline. We have selected a slide of Richard as a squalling infant, dramatic with tears and clenched fists. We then add a bit of appropriate narration as an introduction.

1–Richard as crying infant. From the very beginning, life for poor Richard was hard and painful. He learned as a tiny infant to face it with resignation and a brave smile.

The narration is the key. The first statement at once indicates that this is about Richard's hard life; but the second statement, contradicting what the viewer *sees*, signals the viewer that this is a jest, designed to evoke mocking laughter, not sympathy.

Choose your own "first" slide now. Write a brief introductory note that suggests the content and tone of the show.

YOUR INTRODUCTION

1-_____ _____

_____ _____

When you are satisfied with it, copy it on the first two lines of your script (page 378).

Seventh—Write a Conclusion

Next—the conclusion. The last slide need not be in chronological order, but it should emphasize the theme, either seriously or humorously. We have chosen a slide of Richard, age 16, lying on his back in a hammock, his eyes closed but a grin on his face.

40–Richard in hammock.

A hard life—a painful life—that knocked him flat while he was still a boy. Poor Richard—scarred for life by the toils and tribulations of his childhood!

YOUR CONCLUSION:

40–_____   _____

_____   _____

Add your concluding narration to the script (page 380), last two lines.

Eighth—Add Music

This—the final step—is not essential, but it adds a professional touch to any production. Think about the music you have heard and enjoyed. Then select one or more pieces that parallel the mood of the narration. Play a little of it (just a few seconds) at the very beginning. For the most part, turn the volume down while you are narrating, but occasionally (at key points) turn it up for a few bars. At the end, turn it up high and close with a crashing crescendo!

Using music this way means you will have to put in a couple of hours with a tape recorder. Time your show—it will probably run about seven minutes. Select music that will also run about seven minutes (or a little longer) and tape. Then experiment at combining the narration and the music until you can do it easily, without fumbling.

OUR MUSIC   Liszt's "Hungarian Rhapsody No. 2"

YOUR MUSIC   _____

Production!

Give your show a title—

OURS   Poor Richard's Almanac (a natural!)

YOURS   _____

Summon your audience, darken the room, turn on the slide projector and tape recorder, keep your notes in hand—and presto! You have a production. Your audience will love it, and you will find it far more satisfying than simply showing a batch of slides.

Hint for the Future: If you work with your own slides, number them, save the narration, and you can give the presentation again at any time with only ten minutes notice. A collection of such presentations will serve as ice-breakers for large gatherings and will provide hours of pleasure for you and your family.

54. RADIO ROUNDUP

Who writes for the radio? The chances are you've never even considered the question, much less thought about the answer. Yet millions of radios are "on" every hour of the day, and (except for straight music stations) someone somewhere is writing the material. A local station is the best bet, of course, for the beginner.

There are many kinds of radio-writing. Here are a few to stimulate your own wireless system.

Spot Announcements

Most local radio stations are eager to provide time for spot announcements—if the cause is good and the topic is of interest to listeners. Look around you. Is the sophomore class sponsoring a campaign for food and clothing for the needy? Get the details. Write it up . . . but keep it short. Most spot announcements run for only 20 to 30 seconds.

> Have you ever wondered what it's like to be hungry and cold? If you have, help the unlucky—those who don't have to wonder, because they *know*. Tomorrow the sophomore class of the Average High School is opening a campaign to collect food and clothing for the needy. When *your* doorbell rings, have a can of food ready—or an old coat—or a warm blanket. Help someone *now* and you'll feel a lot better when you sit down to your own dinner!

Make up your own spot announcement—any topic.

_____

_____

_____

_____

_____

_____

_____

_____

_____

_____

After you have written several good spot announcements, check with your local radio station. If they are willing to run one or two, and if they like your writing style, you'll have an "in"—a chance to write other, longer bulletins and even programs.

Commercials

Interested in writing commercials that have zip? Whether the commercials used by your local radio station are staff-written or written by the individual advertisers, they're another possible market.

Suppose you hear the following commercial:

> The XYZ Department Store is having a big sale today. All ski jackets, boots, ski pants, etc., are for sale at 50% off.

That commercial has two things in its favor: it includes all the necessary information, and it uses short sentences and simple words to convey that information. But it also lacks two essential qualities: zip and repetition. Compare it with the revised version below.

> Good news travels fast! That's why you'd better hurry down to the XYZ Department Store! For today only, XYZ is selling all winter outfits at a smashing 50% discount! That means ski pants, ski jackets, boots—*everything*—all with 50% off XYZ's already low prices. Remember: today only, at XYZ. Winterize now—and you'll enjoy winter more!

Notice that the second commercial includes all the information that the first did; the sentences are short, the words are simple. But everything is said at least *twice*—and said with *vigor*.

Here's another "blah" commercial for you to "zip"perize:

> A new medication, Maximum Relief, is now on the market. It sells for 79¢. Rub it on your chest, arms, or legs, and all your pains will disappear. It relieves congestion, too. The big economy size tube costs only $1.33. Available in Ma's Drug Store.

YOUR VERSION _____

_____

_____

_____

_____

_____

_____

_____

_____

News Stories

Local stations favor local news. Most have their own reporters to cover fires, arrests, etc., but few have enough reporters to cover less startling news. Probe your brain. Is something interesting scheduled in the next week or two at school? A school play, maybe? Or a parents' night? Or a visit by a representative of the state education department?

While you're thinking, practice by writing about Parents' Night at Average School. To be sure you have all the necessary information, follow the "5 W" pattern:

What: Parents' Night at Average School
When: Monday, Nov. 19th, from 8 to 10:30 p.m.
Where: In Average School on Typical Lane
Who: All parents of students who attend Average School are invited
Why: To help parents to become acquainted with the teachers and schedules of their daughters and sons

If you were writing a newspaper story, you would simply include all of the above material in the lead paragraph, writing as crisply and concisely as possible. There's one important difference when you're writing for radio: IT TAKES TEN TIMES LONGER FOR THE EAR TO HEAR THAN FOR THE EYE TO SEE. With this in mind, as you write, remember to repeat the major points for anyone who may not have grasped them the first time around.

YOUR NEWS STORY _____
_____
_____
_____
_____
_____
_____
_____
_____
_____

News Analysis

The news analysis on radio is similar to the feature in the newspaper. It goes *beyond* the facts; it permits some editorializing. Try a short news analysis story based on the Parents' Night story that you've already written. Point out the importance of parents knowing something about the school in which their children "live" for six or seven hours a day. Suggest that education and schools have changed since the parents went to school—and that it might help them to find out how and why. Use the two points above and/or any others you consider important, and write a brief news analysis. Keep your sentences short and crisp. Repeat anything you want them to remember. Spice with brief quotations, anecdotes, and statistics.

YOUR NEWS ANALYSIS STORY _____
_____
_____
_____

_____

_____

_____

_____

_____

_____

_____

Before we go on, think of two events scheduled in the next couple of weeks that would make a good news story or news analysis story. Consider sending one or both to your local radio station.

Interviews

A good interview is a sure-fire way of attracting the attention of your local radio station. You don't have to interview a coast-to-coast celebrity (although that's fine if you can manage it); just use your nose for news and think. There are always the mayor and the president of the Board of Education; but they may have been interviewed already, many times. Try someone different. How about Rolfe Quade who owns the ice cream store on Typical Lane? The last time you were in he had some interesting ideas about the cause of inflation and what inflation was doing to the small storeowner. That might make an interesting interview. If it's February and Washington's Birthday is coming up, consider interviewing that new social studies teacher—the one who lived near Mount Vernon and worked there one summer. Maybe there's a student in your school from another country. Has he or she been interviewed? Another strong possibility.

Now for your procedure.

- First—check to find out if the person you're interested in is willing to be interviewed.
- Second—draw up some provocative questions related to the topic.
- Third—ask the interviewee one or two of the questions; write down the answers. (Be sure both questions and answers are especially good.)
- Fourth—ask for an appointment with someone at the radio station. Explain your interview idea; exhibit the sample questions and answers.
- Fifth—if you get a go-ahead from the station, have a chat with your interviewee, revise and sharpen your questions, and set up the interview.

For practice only, experiment with steps one and two.

Step One: Choose a possible interviewee and an angle.

INTERVIEWEE _____

YOUR ANGLE _____

_____

Step Two: List at least ten questions that you can use in the interview. *Restrict your questions to the relevant:* don't ask that social studies teacher where she was born *unless* the answer is related to Mount Vernon.

_____

_____

_____

_____

_____

_____

_____

_____

_____

_____

If you like the idea of conducting a radio interview, you should be able to go ahead now with a real one.

One-Speaker Shows

If you have a specialty—something you know really well—you may be interested in developing a five- or ten-minute program.
Some ideas:

- You have a secret for catching trout and you live in an area where trout-fishing is big.

- You have a recipe from your great-grandmother for cookies exactly right for St. Patrick's Day.

- You read some poetry by Kipling, fell in love with it, and would like to start a Kipling revival. You've already read some of his poems to several classes and have had an excellent reception.

Any one of these ideas *could* make a fine radio program *if* you write well (before the program) and speak well (during the program).

Set up your own one-speaker show.

Select an idea: _____

_____

_____

_____

Write the script: (keep it under ten minutes)

_____
_____
_____
_____
_____
_____
_____
_____
_____
_____
_____
_____
_____
_____
_____
_____
_____
_____
_____
_____
_____

If you like the result, offer it to your school or local radio station. If they're not interested, you have a fine, already-made oral report the next time some teacher decides to assign one!

Project Time

There are several other types of radio shows, all more lengthy than the ones you have already mastered. Study the possibilities carefully, think, then choose *one* type for your own wrap-up project.

- *Educational Shows:* These can be on any topic of interest to local listeners. Is there a litter problem in your town? Are the potholes gargantuan? Are hurricanes more damaging than they have to be because people don't know how to prepare for them? If you decide to work with this type of show, choose your topic carefully, collect expert information and some good quotations, find an anecdote or two—then write.

- *Documentaries:* The local documentary is often overlooked. When is the last time your local radio station presented a history of your town? How about a story about some famous person who was born in your town? Is there an old lake with a legend—a bridge that has had to be rebuilt five times—a fascinating cave? Any one of these could make a fine documentary. You will want to do a great deal of research to get information that is fresh and unusual. When you write your script, include as many names, street names, school names, etc., as possible. Local listeners *love* to hear familiar names.

- *Story Telling:* The story-telling hour (or quarter of an hour) can be aimed at children or adults. Simply take a story you yourself like very much. You can handle it in two ways:

    1 retell the story in an informal, chatty style, with some "hamming" at crucial points; or

    2 dramatize the story for no more than two or three actors.

*   *   *   *

Whichever project you choose, follow this procedure:

    collect all information necessary;

    plan your script;

    write your script;

    record your program on tape.

> **When the project is complete (and don't forget how helpful a musical background can be), play it for the class or for your family. If they enjoy it, ask permission to play it in several other classes. If the reception is still good, take your script and your tape to your local radio station. Maybe—just maybe—you'll hear your own words coming out of Marconi's miracle!**

Unit IX
The Short Story

INTRODUCTION

Here's a riddle that's making the rounds:

> *Question:* What's the tallest building in town?
> *Answer:* The public library. It has the most stories.

Maybe. Maybe not.

Let's take a stroll down Main Street and see if it's true.

Here's 24 Main: the Medical Center. In Doctor A's office is a skier; he just broke his leg and the Olympic competition starts in three days. Doctor B is examining a battered child. In Doctor C's office a young woman is in tears; she's allergic to her fiance. And Doctor D, his head in his hands, is trying to decide whether five cases of psittacosis indicate an epidemic.

25 Main, just across the street: a Mom and Pop grocery store. They've been burglarized three times in the last two months. After 35 years, Mom is tired of groceries and guns and wants to go to Europe. Pop doesn't. The entire shipment of milk they received this morning is sour, and they've already sold thirteen quarts.

26 Main: a department store. Jennie and Bob, at the jewelry counter, are intent on engagement rings ... for less than $20. The store detective just spotted an old woman hiding a child's bathing suit under her coat. The back door was found open this morning ... left open by accident? or ...?

27 Main: insurance offices. A house burned down ... three children died ... the parents "stepped out" for a moment. A car pile-up on Route 101, involving 136 cars. A woman lost her ring at the zoo; she thinks the giraffe swallowed it. A strange rash of burglaries in the northeast section of town: only study lamps stolen.

28 Main: a pretzel shop. The young woman attendant is studying while making pretzels. In three hours she will take a final exam. An old man asks for two pretzels but discovers he's three cents short of the purchase price. A jogger comes in; he *needs* salt—buys a bag of pretzels, scrapes off the salt, and gulps it down.

The public library has the most stories? No—it just has the most *printed* stories. Wherever there are people, there are stories....

> .. a million years ago, in the caves;
> .. 4000 years ago, along the Nile;
> .. 3000 years ago, in Homer's Troy;
> .. 2000 years ago with the gladiators;
> .. 1000 years ago at the Round Table;
> .. 500 years ago in the Mermaid Tavern;
> .. 150 years ago, in Poe's anguish;
> .. 50 years ago, in F. Scott Fitzgerald's antics;
> .. today, in you.

1 *All About You*. It's good to be aware of the key episodes in your life: things or people or events that changed you or your thinking. Brood a bit, then describe three key episodes and explain briefly how each influenced you. (Examples: a serious illness; a victory or a defeat; a special birthday; falling in love; reading a particular book.)

_____
_____
_____
_____
_____
_____
_____
_____

2 *Filling in the Middle*. Write a mini-story (about 100 words) that begins and ends with the following two sentences:

Rudi hated to go home with his left ear bleeding and his right eye almost

closed. _____
_____
_____
_____
_____
_____
_____
_____ It was a good day for a yellow crocus.

3 *Town Tales*. Browse awhile through an atlas or gazetteer. Find ten unusual town names. (Examples: Skull Valley in Arizona and Truth or Consequences in New Mexico.)

_____   _____
_____   _____
_____   _____
_____   _____
_____   _____

Choose the one you find most intriguing; then create a myth that explains how the town got its name.

_____

_____

_____

_____

_____

_____

_____

4 *Dead End.* Unintentionally you drove down a dead-end street. Pursuing you is a car full of criminals. In front of you is a ten-foot stone wall. To the left is open water (at least three miles wide), and to the right is a swamp known to be dangerous. What do you do?

_____

_____

_____

_____

_____

_____

5 *Story Magazine.* A new magazine is being started—one that will publish stories for teen-agers. You have been asked to act as Story Consultant, and your first assignment is to list the five kinds of stories (mystery, sports, etc.) that should be in each issue. After thinking about your own likes and dislikes and those of your friends and acquaintances, which five types would you list?

_____

_____

_____

_____

6 *Instant Story.* This game can be played in class, at a party, or even by yourself. Player A gives a phrase: something like "tuna fish on rye." Player B must respond, within sixty seconds, with a possible story plot based on the phrase. If successful, Player B then gives the next phrase. The result should be brains working overtime and a good deal of hilarity. Get started by listing below three phrases that would strongly challenge another player.

_____

_____

_____

7 *Cause-and-Effect Chain*.   Construct a cause-and-effect chain of at least 10 incidents. Begin with something simple:

> The dog was chewing on a bone.
> The bone got caught in his throat.
> The dog's owner took him to the vet.
> The vet, while extracting the bone, got
>   bitten on the finger.
> The finger became infected. (etc.)

If possible, make the last incident the same as the first, thus completing the cause-and-effect chain. (This is harder than it sounds!)

_____
_____
_____
_____
_____
_____
_____
_____
_____
_____
_____
_____

8 *Improvisation*.   Here is a wire coathanger. List ten ways it can be used other than to support an article of clothing.

_____   _____
_____   _____
_____   _____
_____   _____
_____   _____

9 *Newspaper Dissection.* Take your writer's journal and the daily newspaper. Ready?

Study the obituaries and society pages. Any interesting names? Note them.

Read page 1. Any ideas for stories? Read between the lines. Was the head of a country exiled? Think about his family. Has a corporation been accused of bribery. Think how this would affect the executives that are innocent, the board of directors, the stockholders. Make notes.

Examine rapidly the inside pages—especially the one- and two-inch stories often at the bottom of columns. Any ideas there? Make notes.

Scan the editorials and the Letters to the Editor. They often contain values and/or ideas that can become the themes of short stories. Note them.

Study the pictures. Sometimes they show an unusual hair style, a scar, some physical trait that can be useful in identifying a character. Note any.

Examine the comic strips; analyze the gag lines (usually in the final frame). How many depend on word play? On slapstick? On incongruity? Make notes.

Look through the Help Wanted ads . . . the Lost and Found ads . . . the Personals. Any interesting ideas? Note them.

Study the store ads. Ah, that fur coat—how magnificently it is described . . . what loving details! Exactly what you may need someday when you're writing. Copy the description—in quotes—so you remember not to plagiarize.

Got the idea? Continue on your own. Many professional writers follow this procedure *every* day. Their journals and files are rich in materials of all kinds. Follow suit.

10 *Literary Party Puzzles.* Make up your own literary party puzzles. For example, can you identify the animal or insect that would complete each of the following titles?

"The _____'s Paw" by W. W. Jacobs

"The Celebrated Jumping _____ of Calaveras County" by Mark Twain

"The Gold _____" by Edgar Allan Poe

"The Lady or the _____?" by Frank Stockton

"Under the _____'s Paw" by Frank Norris

Make up at least one literary party puzzle, using short story titles with jewelry, colors, shapes, or whatever. Try them on each other.

55. THOSE FABULOUS FABLES

QUIZ:

    Who won the race: the tortoise or the hare?
    How did the fox describe the grapes he couldn't reach?
    What happened to the grasshopper that sang all summer?

If you know—

    that the tortoise won because the speedy hare was overconfident;
    that the fox called the grapes sour, belittling what he could not attain;
    and that the grasshopper that sang all summer starved all winter;

then you know your *Aesop's fables.*

Aesop was a Greek (possibly a slave) who lived in the 6th century B.C. He wrote dozens of little stories, most of them about animals and each teaching a moral or lesson. Twenty-five hundred years later Aesop's fables are still being read and loved by children and adults. Why? What is their secret?

The answer seems to be that they provide an index to human behavior. What is more fascinating than our own behavior and that of our friends? Aesop explains it all, more interestingly and more succinctly than the psychiatrists.

Some brief case histories:

    We consider running for office, can't get nominated, then declare loudly and at length that everyone in office is a crook and we wouldn't stain *our* hands with politics. ("The Fox and the Grapes")

    We are brilliant and beautiful, sure to win the coveted scholarship. We bask in the admiration of others, rest, and wait. And are stunned when someone less brilliant and beautiful, plodding away hour after hour, walks away with the prize. ("The Tortoise and the Hare")

    Our friends get part-time jobs; we loll all summer. Summer's the time for relaxation, right? Come fall, they take off for a week-long camping trip, with new tents, an almost new canoe, and sacks of provisions. We suggest they might like another camper. They look at our empty hands, shake their heads, and grin. ("The Ant and the Grasshopper")

You see? Aesop knew psychology before psychology was born. That's secret #1 when you're writing a short story: work with an aspect of human behavior that is universal, that everyone has experienced.

Since Aesop was so successful, we'll begin the writing of the short story by imitating and adapting one of his fables. Here's one that is not too well-known: "The Lion and the Mouse."

One day while a lion was sleeping, a mouse scampered across his body. The lion awoke, grabbed the mouse, and threatened to eat it. The mouse begged for mercy, promising to repay the lion's favor. Amused, the lion let the mouse go, sure the mouse could never do a favor for *him*. A few days later some hunters captured the lion and imprisoned him in a net. The mouse came along, saw the lion's sad condition, and nibbled through the ropes to set free his benefactor.

MORAL: **Both the great and the little need each other.**

The *fact* that we all need each other is common knowledge. But in reality we often forget it. It is easy for the "great" to believe that they do not need help from the "little"; yet most of us have been both the lion and the mouse.

Now it is time for you (a sophisticated 20th century swinger) to get help from Aesop (an ancient Greek slave). Read the fable four times, slowly and carefully, until you understand it well. Then proceed to Step #1.

Step I—Add a Setting

Start rewriting Aesop by providing a setting. Choose one you know quite well: your own town, the side of a mountain, the sandy coast of the Pacific. After you have made your choice, describe the setting in two or three sentences.

_____

_____

_____

Step II—Change Animals to People

Next—for each animal substitute a person. For the lion, you might substitute a 6' senior who's a bit of a bully; for the mouse, a 5' freshman who's terrified of the senior. Other possible substitutions: the dreaded head of a crime racket and a peaceful "ordinary" citizen; a parent and a child; the President of the United States and a poor immigrant. Use your imagination. Then describe below the two characters you will be working with. In each case include some physical description and some character traits.

_____

_____

_____

_____

_____

_____

_____

_____

_____

Step III—Add Conflict

In reworking this fable, you will need two conflicts: one at the beginning of the story (when the lion does the favor), and one at the ending of the story (when the mouse does the favor). Example: (for the senior-freshman version)

CONFLICT #1   the freshman accidentally brushes against the senior in the hall. The senior threatens to twist the freshman's arm but spares him.

CONFLICT #2   the senior is accused of stealing money from a locker. The freshman (who witnessed the theft by someone else) tells the truth, thus saving the senior's reputation.

As you develop your two conflicts, keep your setting and characters in mind.

CONFLICT #1 _____

_____

_____

_____

_____

CONFLICT #2 _____

_____

_____

_____

_____

Step IV—Add Details

By now *your* story should be taking on a form of its own. Go back, check your notes, and add details. The setting: is it winter? is there ice on the side of the mountain? what time of day is it? Add relevant details to your notes on setting, characters, and conflicts. List below.

_____

_____

_____

_____

_____

_____

_____

_____

_____

_____

Step V—Retell the Story

Finally—retell the story of "The Lion and the Mouse." Tell it in your own words, using your own setting, characters, and conflicts. Keep *one* thing from Aesop: the moral. (It will provide unity and a basic structure.)

With the modern reader in mind,

    add *dialogue*

    and *suspense* (don't let the second conflict be resolved too quickly).

Begin.

_____

_____

_____

_____

_____

_____

_____

_____

_____

_____

_____

_____

_____

_____

_____

_____

_____

_____

_____

_____

_____

_____

_____

_____

After you have completed your story, revise it carefully and make a clean copy. Then swap fables with other students. Read as many as possible and discuss them.

Most of the fables should be fairly effective—after all, Aesop provided the framework! Notice that all the stories are different, although all are built on the same foundation. That's the second secret of short story writing: know that your experiences, your insights, your wisdom and your ignorance are all peculiar to you. No one else has exactly the same combination. That's why *you* can write a story no one else can write. And that's an awesome thought.

> **Tolstoy with all his greatness, Cather with all her sensitivity, Steinbeck with all his social concern—not one of them could write the stories you can ... because not one of them *is* you. If you write a story truly—from your own strengths and weaknesses—it *has* to say something special. Isn't that comforting? (Now all you have to do is learn how to express what you feel and think and are!)**

56. IT ALL DEPENDS ON YOUR POINT OF VIEW

Rain falls, steadily, for 24 hours. It falls on everyone alike.

To the farmer, it's a joy: his crops are saved.

To the carnival operator, it's disaster: empty rides and empty sideshows.

To the mother, it's an annoyance: children underfoot, interruptions, and noise.

To the child planning to attend a picnic, it's heartbreak.

The same water—the same amount—the same rate of downpour; yet for each person the rain is different, because each sees it from a different *point of view*.

Until now, you have been looking at life from one viewpoint: your own. As a writer, you must look at life from many different viewpoints.

Here's another example from the comic strip, "Figments," by Dale Hale.*

FIGMENTS   **BY DALE HALE**

The little girl cutting out paper dolls sees her act as a proud accomplishment and sees herself showing them off in triumph. The father sees his reading of the newspaper disturbed by her "act of vandalism." The mother sees the litter that will be left and sees herself having to pull out the vacuum cleaner. Again, each point of view is different, because the three people involved have different interests and duties.

One of the first concerns of any short story writer is to determine the viewpoint from which to tell a particular story. It is not an academic exercise; it makes a world of difference. The only way you can prove this to yourself is to experiment: write the same incident from six different points of view.

The Basic Story

To begin, set up the data for a brief incident. Here's ours:

---

*Copyright © 1976, Los Angeles Times. Reprinted with permission.

Tom and Jerry, car salesmen, are planning to cut down a large elm tree in Tom's backyard. It was Tom's idea that the tree should come down; but it was Jerry's idea that the two of them, without expert help, could chop it down. It's Saturday morning and the two are ready to start.

The data for *your* incident (use only two characters):

_____

_____

_____

_____

_____

_____

_____

_____

Viewpoint #1: The Omniscient Author

One point of view is the omniscient (all-knowing) author's. In this version, the omniscient author knows both characters and knows what they think and feel.

Tom breathed heavily, staring at the old elm. "It's bigger than I thought," he said doubtfully. But Tom was often doubtful. "Hope we can take it down without smashing everything else."

Jerry dropped his ax and shrugged off his jacket. "Ah, it's easy . . . if you know how." He picked up the ax, swinging it as if he were John Wayne, and approached the tree confidently. "Here—let an old pro show you how!"

Write up your incident from the omniscient author's point of view.

_____

_____

_____

_____

_____

_____

_____

_____

_____

_____

_____

Viewpoint #2: First Person, Main Character
(Told by Tom)

Another variation has one of the main characters tell the story, using the first person point of view. Here's the same incident told as Tom sees it.

I stared at the old elm and began to feel doubts. I was right about wanting the tree down, but wrong, maybe, in thinking that Jerry and I could do it alone.

"It's bigger than I thought," I told him. "Hope we can take it down without smashing everything else." If Jerry agreed, we could do what I'd wanted to do in the first place—hire an expert.

But Jerry's not like me. He's always sure of himself. "Ah, it's easy," he bragged, as he took off his jacket, "if you know how." He walked over to the elm, swinging the ax. "Here—let an old pro show you how!"

As you probably realize, with the first person approach, it is easier to win the reader's sympathy for Tom. One disadvantage is that *only* Tom's feelings can be explored. Tom can react to what Jerry does or says, but he cannot know what Jerry is thinking or feeling.

Your chance now: tell your story, in first person, from one character's point of view.

_____

_____

_____

_____

_____

_____

_____

_____

_____

_____

_____

_____

_____

_____

_____

_____

_____

_____

_____

Viewpoint #3: First Person, Main Character
(Told by Jerry)

You will understand better how point of view operates if you now try telling the story from the other character's position. Here's the incident as Jerry sees it.

> Tom's a nice guy, but a bit of a conservative. Know what I mean? He's afraid to do anything he hasn't done a dozen times already. I looked at the old elm he wanted down. "That it?"
>
> Tom nodded. "It's bigger than I thought," he said. "Hope we can take it down without smashing everything else."
>
> I grinned, trying to put some starch into him. "Ah, it's easy if you know how!" I tossed my jacket over a small azalea and picked up the ax. The wooden handle felt good in my hand. I had never chopped down a tree before, but I'd seen it done, lots of times, on TV. I let the ax swing idly the way John Wayne does sometimes, and walked over to the elm. "Here— let an old pro show you how!" I quipped.

Do you see the difference? In #2, the emphasis is on Tom: his caution, his awareness that he should have followed his own common sense, his realization that Jerry is a bit of a braggart. In #3, the emphasis is on Jerry: his confidence and his superiority to "poor" Tom.

Tell your incident again, this time from the second character's point of view.

_____

_____

_____

_____

_____

_____

_____

_____

_____

_____

_____

_____

_____

_____

_____

_____

_____

Viewpoint #4: Third Person, Main Character
(Told Through Tom)

In this variation, the author, somewhat detached, tells the story *as if* from one character's viewpoint. For most young writers, this is an easier technique than either first person or omniscient author. Here is a version told by the author, *through* Tom.

> Tom stared at the old elm doubtfully. He was right about wanting the tree down—he was sure of that—but wrong in letting Jerry talk him into doing it by themselves.
>
> "It's bigger than I thought," he said hesitantly. "Hope we can take it down without smashing everything else."
>
> He looked at Jerry. Both he and Jerry were car salesmen. What did a car salesman know about chopping down trees? Jerry looked sure of himself, though, shrugging off his jacket and picking up the ax, running his thumb along the blade.
>
> "Ah, it's easy," Jerry was saying confidently, "if you know how." He walked over to the elm, the ax swinging lightly at his side. "Here—let an old pro show you how!"

Notice that the author can show more sympathy for Tom, more doubt about Jerry's competence than in the first-person narration. But our knowledge is still limited to what Tom can see or hear. Try another version of your incident as told *through* one of the two main characters.

_____
_____
_____
_____
_____
_____
_____
_____
_____
_____
_____
_____
_____
_____
_____
_____
_____
_____

Viewpoint #5: Third Person, Main Character
(Told Through Jerry)

This is similar to #4—only this time the author tells the story through the other main character. In the version below, told *through* Jerry, notice that Jerry's cockiness becomes confidence, while Tom's caution becomes timidity.

> Jerry stared at the old elm confidently. Poor old Tom—always the conservative, always timid about trying something new! Why, the two of them could get this old tree down in no time! "Come on, feller. Let's get started."
>
> But Tom was shaking his head. "It's bigger than I thought," he said cautiously. "Think we can take it down without smashing everything else?"
>
> Jerry grinned. "Sure we can, neighbor. It's easy, if you know how!" He tossed off his jacket and picked up the ax, feeling the wooden handle solid and alive in his hand. He had never chopped down a tree before, but he wasn't about to admit that to cautious Tom. Besides, he'd seen it done, lots of times, on TV. He let the ax swing idly at his side, the way John Wayne does, and sauntered over to the tree. "Here—," he said almost exultantly, "let an old pro show you how!"

Write a new version of your incident, this time told *through* the second main character.

_____

_____

_____

_____

_____

_____

_____

_____

_____

_____

_____

_____

_____

_____

_____

_____

_____

_____

_____

Viewpoint #6: First Person, Minor Character

This approach is a bit different from the first five. Here another character is added—an unimportant character who does not play an active role in the story. We will add Tom's fifteen-year-old son and let him tell the story. The advantage of this approach is that the writer, through the narrator, can channel the reader's sympathy. Notice that the fifteen-year-old is clearly on his father's side and is ruthless in his view of Jerry.

> Frankly, I'd rather be in school than here. When Dad said this morning that he and Jerry Monahan were going to chop down the old elm, I said I had to clean out the basement, but Dad said it would be good for me to learn how to chop down a tree and I should watch him and Jerry do it and I could pick up the twigs and stuff afterwards. Fat lot I'll learn! That Monahan guy doesn't know *anything*.
>
> Dad was walking around the tree, staring at it doubtfully. "It's bigger than I thought," he said. "Hope we can take it down without smashing everything else."
>
> Monahan was standing with his feet apart, making like a lumberjack. "It's easy if you know how," he said, trying to talk out of the side of his mouth like Jimmy Cagney. Then he picked up the ax and—good grief!—ran his thumb along the edge, like he knew what he was doing.
>
> "But Jerry—" That was Dad, having second thoughts.
>
> Monahan didn't have any, though. He strode over to the tree, raised the ax as if he were John Wayne, and shouted: "Here—let an old pro show you how!"

Write a new version of your incident, adding a third, minor character and telling the story first person, through his or her eyes.

_____

_____

_____

_____

_____

_____

_____

_____

_____

_____

_____

_____

_____

_____

_____

_____

_____

_____

_____

_____

_____

＊　　＊　　＊　　＊

Many stories almost demand to be told from a particular point of view. Others are more difficult: you may have to try several points of view before you find exactly the right one. It depends on the story *and* on what you want to say. If you want to show that Jerry Monahan is a "talker" rather than a "doer," you may prefer the first person, minor character (#6) point of view. If you want to emphasize Tom's timidity, you may prefer the third person, main character (#5—Told Through Jerry) point of view.

It also depends on you—on the style that is easiest for you, that you are most comfortable with. Some authors master all the styles. Most choose one or two and use them almost exclusively. Edgar Allan Poe used the first person, main character, viewpoint most of the time. "The Tell-Tale Heart" is told from the murderer's point of view; "The Pit and the Pendulum" is told from the victim's point of view—and both are fine stories. Nathaniel Hawthorne told "The Ambitious Guest" from the omniscient author's point of view—and that's a fine story, too. And Arthur Conan Doyle wrote the Sherlock Holmes mysteries from a first person, minor character point of view: Dr. Watson tells the stories, while raving non-stop about Holmes' brilliance.

> *So—as the carnival barker says—"You pays your money and you takes your choice." Only you, and the particular story you want to tell, should determine the point of view you finally use. But learn to use all six. Why settle for less?*

57. THE CHILDREN'S HOUR

Here's a project. When you have finished, you will understand a child's point of view (maybe) and a child's interests (peculiar). *Then* you can begin to write for children.

First tackle younger brothers and sisters, nieces and nephews, and the neighborhood small fry. Work only with children under ten. Ask each one: what is your favorite food and how do you cook it? Have the child write out or dictate the recipe for you. *Do not edit*.

Here is a sample of what you will get, if you are lucky. It's one of many "kid" recipes collected and published a few years ago.*

SKABBETTI

41 sausages as big as your ear
41 meatballs not as big
41 orange potatoes or tomatoes
41 skabbetti
41 clean oil

First you decide what will it be tonight—sausage or meatballs?
When your father tells you which one, then you cook.
Mix the sauce in the blender so your elbows don't hurt.
When the skabbetti is done from the cooking in the broiler (two degrees or maybe three), get it in the silver pan with holes in it by your spoon with holes in it.
Then spread out the sauce.
It serves your whole family and all your father's friends.

When you and your friends have collected several dozen recipes, *then* edit. Choose the best: the ones that delight or amuse or enchant. Type on ditto masters; illustrate casually (with a light, humorous touch); run off and staple.

You now have a very special recipe book: one you can give as gifts or sell for a small fee to the proud parents of the miniature chefs! But you can also use this recipe book in another way: as a beginning textbook for writing for children.

Here's how.

Gather in a small group, with each person equipped with a copy of the recipes. Now read them closely and analyze them. What techniques do children instinctively use? How do they look at life? What do they notice?

---

*"Skabbetti" from SMASHED POTATOES: A KID'S EYE VIEW OF THE KITCHEN by Jane G. Martel. Copyright © 1974 by Jane G. Martel. Reprinted by permission of Houghton Mifflin Company.

Using the SKABBETTI recipe as an example, let's make a first run. The youngster who developed this recipe used

> repetition (notice the five 41's)
> hyperbole (41 potatoes *is* hyperbole, isn't it?) (Review pages 193–194.)
> simile (sausages as big as your ear)
> details (the silver pan with holes; the spoon with holes)
> litotes (the 2 or 3 degree temperature in the broiler)
> alliteration (<u>s</u>pread out the <u>s</u>auce) (Review pages 71–73.)
> internal rhyme (potatoes or tomatoes)

The same youngster can also teach you a great deal about children.

> They have total faith in their parents: it's time to cook when your father tells you to.
> They personalize everything: you use the blender "so your elbows don't hurt."
> They don't know the names for even common household utensils, but they do notice details (the pan and the spoon).
> They have sublime confidence in themselves: by simplifying a process verbally, they turn a difficult task into an apparently easy one.

Analyze at least three of your recipes, noting the technical devices used by the children and what their writing can tell you about a child's point of view.

_____

_____

_____

_____

_____

_____

_____

_____

_____

_____

_____

_____

_____

_____

_____

_____

_____

_____

The Bible says—"A little child shall lead you." Now that a little child has you by the hand, you are ready to write for children.

✵   ✵   ✵   ✵

Create a child's picture book. It's fun to do and not very difficult. And the story is short—usually between 300 and 900 words. The age group you are writing for is the 4 to 8. They're an enthusiastic audience, but a demanding one, too.

BEFORE YOU WRITE—

Start With Their Interests

From their "recipes," you already know that children are interested in food and family. They also love animals. Add below seven more topics that would interest children. (If you don't live with a small child, then talk with some, or remember your own childhood, or watch children's TV shows.)

food	
family	
animals	

Choose a Couple of Characters

Children like two kinds of characters above all others: children and animals. Decide which you want to work with. Then dream up two specific characters and describe them briefly. Examples: Sally, a five-year-old who makes magnificent somersaults; or Tibby Tailor, the darning needle (dragonfly) that can sew a straight seam.

1 _____

_____

_____

2 _____

_____

_____

Settle on a Setting

When you're writing for children, make your setting an ordinary one or a far-out one—nothing in between. The back garden is fine, or the playroom, or the kitchen. The moon is also fine, or the bottom of the ocean. But avoid Las Vegas, or Venice, or 19th century London.

YOUR SETTING _____

_____

Pattern a Plot

For small children, a plot should be simple and repetitious. Remember Rudolph with the red nose? Rudolph had one goal: to be one of the reindeer to pull Santa's sleigh on Christmas Eve. To achieve his goal, Rudolph had to overcome a number of problems, all fairly similar. Goldilocks (in "The Three Bears") tasted porridge three times, sat on three chairs, and tried out three beds. When the bears came home, they followed the same rigmarole verbally . . . and how children love this repetition!

Create a plot for your picture book story. Remember: simple and repetitious.

_____

_____

_____

_____

_____

Manage a Moral

Just about every children's story teaches a moral. What's more, children want them to. Kids have a strong sense of "what's fair." But they don't want the moral tacked on to the end. That went out with Aesop. So before you begin to write, decide what your moral will be; then tell the story so the moral filters through the action.

YOUR MORAL _____

_____

AS YOU WRITE—

Watch Your Language

Remember that you're writing for children. Keep your sentences short and direct, your words simple and colorful. Appeal to their senses: use words that will make their noses twitch, their eyes widen, and their ears flap. Use alliteration: they love it; and bits of rhyme (not as a poem, just tossed in for fun). Use crazy, unusual imagery—but make sure the images are relevant for children. Almost any youngster is fascinated by a lemonade lake or a lollipop tree!

Just for practice, write a sentence or two describing your setting (page 410). When you have finished, check it against the suggestions listed above. Find out your strong points so that you can use them; find your weak points so that you can eliminate them.

_____

_____

_____

_____

_____

Delight With Dialogue

This is tricky. *You* are a long way from your childhood. Don't trust your memory. Listen to children talk. You may think that "goody!" is out of date, but watch a five-year-old who has just been told he's going to the circus. He'll clap his hands, cry "Goody!" and jump up and down. It's not out of date for *him*; therefore it's not out of date for *you*, as a writer.

One other thing about dialogue for children. Remember onomatopoeia, and make your meaning come through the sounds of words. (Remember too that most picture book stories are read aloud.) Let the bee buzz, buzz; let the wolf howl; let the small girl who has fallen cry "boo hoo." Children enjoy the sounds and are amused by them. Every onomatopoeic word will bring a chuckle from a fascinated four-year-old.

Try a few lines of dialogue for the story you are getting ready to write.

_____

_____

_____

_____

Delete the Description

Description is *not* a favorite with small children. Keep it to a minimum. When you must use it, make it brief and exciting. It's all right to describe a lion if you do it ferociously, or a pig if you do it laughingly; but don't get bogged down in a lot of dull details. Children can be ruthless in saying: "Skip that page!"

Describe one of your characters "ferociously" or "laughingly."

_____

_____

_____

_____

Inject With Imagination

You are getting old and may be embarrassed by wild flights of the imagination. Not so the small child who revels in it. Animals talk, and dreams come true; mirrors are to walk through, and trees dance; a day is a million hours long, and bunnies harvest carrots made of orange marshmallow. Have yourself a ball: enter a child's dreamworld and let your imagination leap and soar!

Dream up one or two bits of magic that will brighten your story.

_____

_____

_____

_____

NOW WRITE—

You have everything you need. Get worked up about it; get excited. Write it the way you would tell it if you had a couple of real four-year-olds to amuse. Remember: 300 to 900 words.

_____

_____

_____

_____

_____

_____

_____

_____

_____

_____

_____

_____

_____

_____

_____

_____

_____

_____

_____

_____

_____

_____

_____

_____

_____

_____

_____

_____

_____

_____

_____

_____

_____

Story finished—and revised? Then you still have three more steps.

1   Read it (or tell it) to a real child. Find out where it works and where it doesn't. Revise again, if necessary (and it will be!).

2   Next, type or print on a sheet of paper the words you think should appear on a single page (a description of one brief action, for example), perhaps fifty to eighty words. On the facing page illustrate appropriately. If you can draw (or if you have a friend who can), that's fine. If you can't draw, cut pictures from magazines or catalogs—they work, too. Continue alternating text and illustrations until the story is finished.

3   Provide a title page (title of story and _your_ name), a cover, and staple.

You now have completed one picture story book. Give it as a gift to some small friend; offer it to the kindergarten of your school district; submit it (if it's _very_ good) to a publisher. (But if you do the latter, check Chapter 63 to see manuscript specifications.)

Gift Suggestion:

The very nicest gift you can give to a small child is a personalized picture book. Just take the one you have written—or write a new one. Give the nicest character in the story the name of your small friend. Add a few special features: the name of the street the child lives on, the name of a friend or parent. _That_ gift, be certain, will be the child's favorite and will receive the supreme award: it will be worn out by constant and affectionate use.

---

58. FLASHBACKS AND TRANSITIONS

What makes some stories drag, like a tired, overweight ex-fighter, while others prance briskly, tossing left hooks and right crosses, until the reader dissolves in delight? The Golden Gloves champ won't become a World Champ until he has learned the *invisible* techniques of his profession: not the showy ones, but the ones that make the showy ones work.

As a writer, you can have an ingenious plot, crisp dialogue, and a setting that has never been used before and is totally captivating—and your story still won't come alive. Why? Usually it's the result of a sin of omission: you have not mastered a particular technique or you have forgotten to use it. Yet a few techniques spell the difference between a story that thousands will enjoy and the story that only you, the proud unseeing parent, can read from beginning to end.

The Essential Flashback

Think about the word "flashback"—something that flashes one back to the past. It's a verbal time-machine that permits a writer to speed backwards and forwards. With it, you can gain instant access to the memory banks of your characters; you can construct small bridges that link the past and the present in an illuminating pattern. It's as important to you as footwork is to the boxer. So begin with......

The Minor Flashback

This may be just one sentence. Suppose your main character, Sarah, is old and poor. She decides to plant tomatoes and a few vegetables to supplement her inadequate income. You want to emphasize Sarah's courage but also her naïveté. So—as she is studying seed catalogs and dreaming big dreams of huge harvests, you insert a quick flashback. "Once, years ago, she had tried her hand at gardening . . . a few daisies and some lovely roses, she remembered proudly." In one sentence you have proved her inexperience by citing her *only* experience. Most readers, more knowledgeable than Sarah, know there is a vast difference between playing with a few daisies and the backbreaking labor necessary to grow sufficient vegetables to sustain life. Most will feel sympathy, anticipate her failure, and admire her gallantry. All this, thanks to one short sentence.

Try it. Here's your situation. Joe Ferguson is standing at the edge of his fields. The wheat is coming up strong and beautiful. It should be a fine harvest. In his mind he is already spending the proceeds: a new tractor, the roof of the barn repaired, maybe a new floor for the kitchen. Construct a one-sentence flashback in Joe's memory that will send a shadow across his happiness and across the printed page.

_____

_____

_____

Major Flashback #1: Drawing a Parallel

The major flashback is longer: perhaps a brief paragraph, even two. It can be handled in a number of ways, for a number of reasons.

Jim Wade has just heard a rumor. Someone saw Jim's wife, Emily, carrying a suitcase and going into the bus depot. She was heard to say: "Enough is enough. A woman can't take more." Jim and Emily have been married for sixteen years; he trusts her completely, but he jumps into the car and heads for the depot—just to check. As he drives, he is tormented by a fear that the rumor may be true. She wouldn't leave him . . . would she? No, there's a mistake.

To heighten Jim's anguish, the author throws in a flashback that *parallels* the current situation.

> It was raining—just as it had been raining twenty years ago. He'd been engaged to Cora . . . Cora with the red hair and green eyes and swirling skirts. Involuntarily he grinned, then quickly sobered. Cora had worn his ring, had whispered with him on the porch swing, had promised. . . . Then, just twenty years ago—that was in May, too—she had disappeared, run off with a farm equipment salesman. Sweat formed on his forehead as he clenched the steering wheel.
>
> But—Emily wasn't Cora. She wouldn't. . . . He saw the depot, double-parked, and jumped out of the car.

The former betrayal strengthens the possible current betrayal. Our sympathy for Jim grows. We too had been sure that Emily *wouldn't*. Now we're not so sure!

Your turn: Elaine Wells has just been fired from her job. She has worked for this company for eight years, but times are bad and she and a lot of others have been laid off. She is waiting for a bus to go home. She's scared—near panic. How will she tell the children—Jeff who, at 17, is full of dreams about going to college, and 12-year-old Marilaura who expects a new bike at her next birthday? More important, how will she buy food, pay the rent?

Write a flashback covering a memory of a *parallel* incident . . . one that increases Elaine's fear or alleviates it.

_____

_____

_____

_____

_____

_____

_____

_____

_____

_____

_____

Major Flashback #2: Drawing a Contrast

The exact opposite of the parallel flashback is the contrasting flashback. Ted Belasco, a coal miner for 23 years, is preparing to go down into the mine to try to rescue some workers who were down there just before the explosion. There's still danger, and Ted is grim and justly fearful. This time, to heighten the mood, the author uses a contrasting flashback.

> He remembered the first day he'd gone into the mine. It was June—school was just out—and as he waited, with a lunch box just like his father's, he felt like—like a *man*. In the hot sunshine, near the mine entrance, he made plans, big plans—he would work for a few years, then go off to college to study engineering. He felt fearful, but proud, too, as his mother embraced him, and his little brother stared enviously at the lunch box.
>
> Now, 23 years later, he was waiting again at the entrance to the mine. But this time he just felt fearful. The pride was gone . . .

The early hope of escape emphasizes Ted's present imprisonment; the early dreams of success emphasize the fact that Ted isn't going anywhere—except back into the mine.

Your turn: Penny (or Philip—as you will) is in a train on her way to her aunt's house 300 miles away. Not for a visit this time, but to stay. Her parents were killed in an automobile accident, and Penny, at fifteen, has been made a ward of her aunt. She's rebellious, unhappy, and fearful.

Write a *contrasting* flashback that will emphasize Penny's present sad situation.

_____

_____

_____

_____

_____

_____

_____

_____

_____

_____

The Necessary Transition

Another technique that is "invisible" to the average reader although it has an effect is the *transition*. You've already learned something about transitions (see pp. 146–149); but transitions in a short story should be more subtle and require more careful handling than transitions in essays or articles. You must slide from scene to scene easily and clearly, and you must do it in as few words as possible.

Transition #1: The Chronological

This is the easiest transition approach. Let's say that Jason Schmitt is leaving the house to go to the office. You could follow Jason out of the door, into the car, down the driveway, over Route 28 to Route 149 to Route 3, to the parking field of the plant, to the gate, to his workbench. But if none of that is important, it's sheer waste. So you do this instead.

> Jason grabbed his jacket and cap, kissed his wife, and dashed out of the door. As he turned the key in the ignition, he shouted: "So long, hon. Have a good day!"
> Fifteen minutes later he tossed his jacket into his locker and headed for his workbench.

The three words—"fifteen minutes later"—form a transition, taking the place of the dull detailed happenings of those fifteen minutes.

Try your own *chronological transition*, using any characters and situation that you wish.

_____

_____

_____

_____

_____

_____

_____

_____

_____

_____

_____

_____

Transition #2: The Echo Effect

The "echo" effect is a touch more difficult, but it's extremely useful. You can't fill your story with "fifteen minutes later"—but the echo effect can be used frequently without staling. This transitional approach requires that a word in one scene "echo" a word from the preceding scene, thus making a kind of bridge. Like this—

> Amanda slammed her desk drawer shut. She would *not* retype that letter for the fifth time—not if old Masterson stood on his head and whistled "Dixie." It was time for lunch, and if Masterson didn't appreciate her abilities, Ken would.
> Ken did. As they wolfed down cornbeef sandwiches, Amanda . . .

Here are two echo effects: from "Ken would" to "Ken did" (direct); and "time for lunch" to "cornbeef sandwiches" (indirect). Together, they get Amanda out of the office and into a restaurant, from Masterson's grouchiness to Ken's solicitude.

This time try an *echo effect transition*, again using any characters and situation you like.

_____

_____

_____

_____

_____

_____

_____

_____

_____

_____

_____

Transition #3: The Long-Range Echo Effect

If you want to skip several days and not just twenty minutes, you may prefer the long-range echo transition. It is similar to the simple echo transition, but is a bit more complicated.

> In two days—if nothing went wrong—Dominic would be in the country. He winced from the heat as the hot sun bounced off the concrete, from the angry shouts, from the noise and the dirt, and from the taste of dust. It would be different in the country . . . he hoped.
>
> In the country the sun is just as hot, but it warms rather than burns. As Dominic dug his bare toes into the grass, he listened to the cows mooing and the chickens cackling, and to the monotonous drone of the tractor as his uncle turned over a new field. He spied a late strawberry, plucked it, and popped it into his mouth. As a little of the juice trickled down his chin, he grinned.

Notice the pattern of echoes: the feel of the sun, the noises, the tastes. The pattern carries the reader two or even three days forward in time; and the recurring echoes prevent a time gap and the confusion a time gap can cause. Notice also that the passage of time is marked by an extra space between the two paragraphs.

You can use this type of transition to cover several days or several months. Just construct it with careful attention to details. If you move from August to November, for example, remember that the November sunlight is weaker, the air colder, the trees starker. Ready? Try your own *long-range echo transition*, with the characters and situation of your choice.

_____
_____
_____
_____
_____
_____
_____
_____
_____
_____
_____
_____
_____

> *There are other techniques that can be helpful to a short story writer, but these two (flashback and transition) are essential. Master them well and they will serve you well—allowing you to move easily and fluidly through time and space.*

59. SAINTS AND SINNERS

This is the story of Model L—better known as Mo Dell. Mo is 77 years old and a retired plumber. In this story he is going to join a senior citizens' softball team as a last-minute sub.

Your job is to clothe Mo from the outside in . . . as a fiction writer would. In order to do this, you will actually write a mini-story about Mo Dell, developing him in various ways so that he will become a model for your future efforts at characterization.

Section One

Begin by making some notes about Mo.

PHYSICAL FEATURES   (grey hair, scar on left cheek, etc.). You decide.

_____

_____

_____

_____

CLOTHING   (old grey fedora, shapeless brown tweed overcoat, etc.)

_____

_____

_____

_____

HABITUAL GESTURES   (scratches his head; plays with his hat; chews on his fingernails)

_____

_____

_____

_____

We suggest (but do not insist) that you use the omniscient author point of view (page 401). As the story starts, Mo is alone. Take that one fact, add a couple of notes from the lists above, and write an opening paragraph.

Example:

He played with the brim of his hat and pinched the crown. It was the worst looking crown you've ever seen. It had a right to be. It was pinched all day long. It was all Mo had to do, pinching that hat. Sometimes he thought that's what 77 years of living added up to: sitting on a park bench with only a pinched hat for company.

Your first paragraph:

_____

_____

_____

_____

_____

_____

_____

Section Two

In this section, add a second character, Phil Loftus. Phil is a senior citizen who plays softball. You can make him a member of the town team or the rival team; and you can make him any kind of person you like. We suggest you consider making him a *foil*—a character whose qualities emphasize the main character's qualities, usually through contrast ... but you need not follow this recommendation.

About Phil Loftus:

PHYSICAL APPEARANCE _____

_____

A GESTURE OR MANNERISM _____

_____

A COUPLE OF OUTSTANDING TRAITS _____

_____

A SPEECH IDIOSYNCRASY _____

_____

More About Mo Dell:

A SPEECH IDIOSYNCRASY _____

_____

A COUPLE OF OUTSTANDING TRAITS _____

_____

Using the information above and *through* dialogue, introduce Phil Loftus and get the two men into a discussion of softball and age. You might begin with something like this:

> "Mind if I sit down?" Phil Loftus was only three or four years younger than Mo, but he walked like he had springs in his shoes and mischief in mind.
>
> Mo shrugged, his eyes still intent on the pinched crown of his hat. "Sit," he said.

Your turn: Your section should be two or three times longer than the above. Remember: work primarily through dialogue.

_____
_____
_____
_____
_____
_____
_____
_____
_____
_____
_____
_____
_____

Section Three

Special abilities make characters real and understandable. Perhaps when he was young, Mo held the record for the 100-meter sprint. Or perhaps Phil prides himself on his ability to persuade people to try new things. These two facts would help us to understand the characters better and could also be used to show motivation or to influence outcome. Before you continue with your story, provide each man with one or two relevant special abilities (relevant in that they can be related to the storyline).

MO DELL _____
_____

PHIL LOFTUS _____
_____

Now proceed to the writing of section three of your mini-story. Use at least one brief flashback (pages 415–417) to reveal a special ability of either Mo or Phil. Make sure this flashback furthers the action of the story.

_____
_____
_____
_____
_____

_____

_____

_____

_____

_____

_____

_____

Section Four

Make this section a confrontation between Mo and Phil. Perhaps Phil persuades Mo to play softball; perhaps he challenges Mo; or perhaps Mo decides to play because Phil claims he can't. *You* decide. Then set up the conflict, probably in dialogue form, between the two men. It *must* end with Mo's making a decision: to play softball at least once, as a sub, for the town team.

_____

_____

_____

_____

_____

_____

_____

_____

_____

_____

_____

_____

_____

_____

_____

Section Five

This last section should include both a climax and a conclusion. The only requirement is that Mo must go in as a sub and play softball. What happens—why it happens—how it happens—these are for you to decide. But everything that happens here must be the result or effect of what has gone before. What Mo *is* has to determine the result. If you can, create a surprise ending; they are especially effective in very short stories. But even a surprise ending must be consistent with what you have already let the reader know about Mo and Phil.

_____

_____

_____

_____

_____

_____

_____

_____

_____

_____

_____

_____

_____

_____

_____

_____

_____

_____

_____

You now have a short short story, that is, a mini-story. It may or may not be good—there are too many variables for guarantees to be given. But you do have a *real* short story and one in which the two characters are *real*, acting in accordance with their personalities and abilities. And that's a long step toward your goal.

> **In the future as you start to write a story, remember to explore first the exterior and interior of your characters: their physical appearance, their traits, their gestures, their speech idiosyncrasies, and their abilities. Whether they are saints or sinners—or somewhere in between—their *completeness* will add texture to your stories and increase interest.**

Post-Mortem

Before you go on to the next chapter, compare the stories about Mo and Phil as written by at least a dozen writers. Notice how different Mo and Phil are in the various stories. Notice how the storylines diverge, and how multiple conclusions are possible. This will simply emphasize something you already know: that each story, if truly written, is distinctive: the results of *your* personality, *your* style, *your* imagination.

60. FROM THE VILLAGE PARK TO ZANZIBAR

You do not live in a vacuum. You live in a house, on a ball field, in a classroom, on a mountain slope. And so does Mo Dell and just about every other fictitious character that has ever been created. The setting is part of you, as you are part of the setting. The character without a setting is like a cartoon figure: interesting, but not quite real . . . not quite worthy of our tears or concern.

We have seen that a character is more than a description; Mo needed a habitual gesture, a way of speaking, a flash of memory, a special ability to make him breathe. A setting is more than a description, too; it needs a point of view and a particular mood before it comes alive.

Consider a park, any park. Our basic notes might read as follows:

> Trees (maples, elms, a few oaks, and a couple of weeping willows) on all four sides. Northwestern quadrant: well-kept paths, azalea bushes, flower gardens, green benches every ten feet. Southwestern quadrant: playground, swings, slides, immense sand box. Northeastern quadrant: pagoda-like bandstand for concerts, much lawn, rhododendrons and hydrangeas. Southeastern quadrant: tennis court, pool, softball field.

An architect's blueprint might include all these details; so might a brochure advertising the town. But no writer would. It is too objective, too comprehensive, too *inhuman*.

Point of View

Study your setting from a particular point of view. You will find that this makes a world of difference.

Begin by making quick but complete notes for your own room. Be objective. Mention everything and give equal weight to all objects and features. Use the notes for the park description as a guide.

_____

_____

_____

_____

_____

_____

_____

_____

_____

Now think about your room for a moment. How does it look to *you*? What is the focal point of the room for you? Perhaps the poster of a rock star presiding over your phonograph; perhaps (because you're working as well as going to school and are often tired) your bed; perhaps a series of ship models that you started when you were ten years old and that still inspire pride. Start with the focal point and describe the room as it looks to you . . . not notes this time, but a paragraph that will show the room through you, and you through the room.

_____

_____

_____

_____

_____

_____

_____

_____

_____

_____

_____

_____

That's *one* of your rooms—for you have more rooms than you think.

Now become your mother (or your father). Walk to the door of your room and look in. Select the details she would see and mention, as well as the order in which she would notice them. (For example, she very well might first notice your pajamas lying on the floor, or the balls of fluff in every corner!) Describe your room from her point of view.

_____

_____

_____

_____

_____

_____

_____

_____

_____

This next one is really tough—role-play a two-year-old. A two-year-old is about two feet tall, so begin by getting down to her level. A two-year-old is curious, thirsting for mischief, delighting in touching and handling and breaking. Squat at the door of your room and see it as a two-year-old. Describe it from her point of view.

_____

_____

_____

_____

_____

_____

_____

_____

One more—a young dog, a puppy. On all fours, his tail wagging, he pauses at the open door, his bright eyes examining all that is to be seen. What do his eyes study most intently? The slippers under the bed? The tennis ball in your sneaker? *Become* the puppy (yes, this is extremely hard!) and describe the room from his point of view.

_____

_____

_____

_____

_____

_____

_____

_____

You see? **You already have *four* rooms, not one—it all depends on the point of view.** And you can multiply your room still more by seeing it as—your grandmother, a visitor from Mars, a college admissions person, a prospective employer, your younger brother or sister, etcetera, etcetera.

Mood

The other factor that makes settings "come alive" is mood. (Review Chapter 24.) Work with yourself, since you know yourself (hopefully) better than you know anyone else. Let's explore the relationship between mood and setting.

You come home from school. It's been a vile day: everything went wrong. As you enter the house, your mother begins screaming at you because you forgot to put out the garbage. You go into your room, slamming the door behind you. Describe your room as a haven, a refuge, where you can get away from people for a little while.

_____

_____

_____

_____

_____

_____

_____

_____

This time you're angry, but in a different way. At the dinner table you announced excitedly you were going to spend the summer hitchhiking your way across the continent. It took your parents about four seconds to turn thumbs down on *that*! They wouldn't even discuss it. You go to your room and you feel like a caged animal. Describe your room *as* a cage, as a prison.

_____

_____

_____

_____

_____

_____

_____

_____

_____

Once more—this time you're happy. You had an unusually good day in school, the boss gave you a raise, and—since this is your birthday—you received the transistor radio and the camera you have been wanting. That night you go to your room, and you're warm with love and gratitude. Now what objects do you see most clearly? Describe your room as a good place to be, offering protection and concern.

_____

_____

_____

_____

_____

_____

_____

_____

There is another way in which mood and setting are interrelated. Unless you are most unusual, you have windows in your room—windows that open up on the world outside. Imagine your room (and you in your room) under the following circumstances:

.. warm sunny day in late June, windows open, warm pleasant breeze

.. hot close day in August, raining hard, windows closed, no air

.. freezing winter night, blizzard raging, snow battering shingles and gale-force winds rattling windows

.. crisp autumn afternoon, pale sunlight, somehow both warm and chilly, clouds racing across sky

There are no right answers for the following questions, but thinking through to *an* answer will help you to see the closeness of story and setting.

Which room would you choose as a setting for a mystery story that would be frightening to a reader?

_____

Which room would you choose as a setting for a short story about a future camping trip?

_____

Which room would you choose as a setting for a scene of emotional turmoil?

_____

Here's a story situation. You have been chosen as one of a dozen young people to found a colony on the moon. You will be there at least ten years, and you will face many unknown dangers. You are leaving tomorrow, and you are alone for a couple of hours in what you are already thinking of as "your old room." Your mood is half nostalgic for the safe and sure world you are leaving, and half impatient for the new and exciting world to which you are going. Describe your room, making your description a reflection of your own mood. (And don't forget that the view from your windows is part of your room.)

_____
_____
_____
_____
_____
_____
_____
_____
_____
_____

It is only fair to point out that some authors use the setting as a *foil*: for contrast. Alfred Hitchcock is adept at this. Imagine a really beautiful morning—a loving family—a suburban home—the sun shining and the stillness of the air broken only by the laughter of children. Introduce suddenly a desperate escaped convict. Bang! The fear, the horror are intensified by the contrast with the setting. It's a fine technique, but a difficult one.

Experiment with this story situation. You are at a school dance. The gym has been decorated so skillfully it is hardly recognizable. Everyone looks beautiful and is happy. The music is fantastic. The night is perfect. But your date just disappeared onto the dance floor with a most desirable partner. You are alone and feeling sorry for yourself. Write a paragraph or two reproducing this scene; start with the "perfect" setting and work up to the "impossible" mood.

_____

_____

_____

_____

_____

_____

_____

_____

_____

_____

_____

It's good to know the setting *can* be used as a foil, but in most stories the inexperienced writer is wise to aim for unity—keeping the storyline, the mood of the characters, and the mood of the setting consistent.

One Word More

A natural tendency of young writers is to seek the exotic setting. It's more fun to write about Zanzibar or the canals of Venice or the top of Mount Everest—or even about the craters of the moon. But beware! It's also more difficult and demands hours of research. If you want to set your story in Zanzibar, learn all you can about Zanzibar (see Chapter 15). Then dream yourself into Zanzibar until you experience the heat and the markets and everything you learned in books. After that, you may try using Zanzibar as a setting . . . but there will still be pitfalls. The speech patterns must be right, and the human relationships; the geography and the history; the work-pattern and the life-pattern including simple obvious things like the usual dinner hour; the customs and the beliefs.

It is much easier (and safer) to use a familiar town or section of the country as a setting. But if you must use an exotic setting, know that it can be done, has been done, is being done—and that you can do it too *if* you are willing to spend the enormous time and effort necessary.

As a final experiment in setting, select an exotic place—research it—dream it; and use what you learn in composing the opening paragraphs of a possible story. The experience is good for you, and it will probably send you scampering back to the old hometown!

YOUR CHOICE OF SETTING: _____

_____

YOUR OPENING PARAGRAPHS:

_____
_____
_____
_____
_____
_____
_____
_____
_____
_____
_____
_____
_____
_____
_____
_____
_____
_____
_____
_____
_____
_____
_____

61. "A PIECE OF THE ACTION"

Years ago, when television was very young, there was a serial named "Boston Blackie." It was an adventure story, and in each episode the superhero jumped across chasms, ran faster than trains, and performed dozens of feats of "derring-do." At first, people watched breathlessly, but as it became obvious that Boston Blackie had not nine lives but 9000, the suspense lost its edge and dissolved into farce. When enough people were laughing instead of gasping, the show died.

And that is the best lesson you can learn about plotting: **you need action and suspense, but if you overdo it, if you pile them up heedlessly, you will have comedy not adventure.**

Creating the Basic Plot

Begin with a conflict. You may have one in mind, or in your journal. If you don't, simply select a Virtue and a Vice. (Henceforth, we'll refer to these as the two V's.)

Love is usually a virtue; *pride* is usually a vice. Place both in the same human heart and conflict almost has to occur. Here's how it works in the concrete. John loves Mary; he truly loves her—that's his virtue. But Mary comes from a wealthy family, and John's family is poor. He is too proud to show his love—and that's his vice. Already there are two conflicts, the one within John between his pride and his love; and the potential one between John and Mary (which Mary may or may not know about).

Here are two lists: one of virtues, one of vices. Select one virtue and one vice.

VIRTUES	VICES
generosity	miserliness
kindness	cruelty
loyalty	vindictiveness
courage	cowardice
honesty	dishonesty
dependability	jealousy
prudence	rashness
justice	greed
diligence	laziness
modesty	pride
love	hate
self-confidence	self-doubt

_____ (others) _____

_____ _____

Your choice: (They need not be a related pair, such as generosity and miserliness. Generosity can be opposed by jealousy, or miserliness by diligence.)

VIRTUE _____

VICE _____

Now set these two V's into conflict, either within one person or between two persons. From that conflict, develop your basic plot, as we did with love and pride and John and Mary.

_____

_____

_____

_____

_____

_____

Developing the Plot

You have your initial conflict, but it doesn't truly become a plot until it moves. Ask yourself: "What happens?" At this point the plot can develop in any one of hundreds of directions. This first step is crucial: it will (through cause and effect) determine the rest of the plot.

In the John-Mary-love-pride plot, this might be the first incident:

> John finally decides to ask Mary to go to the movies, but his pride makes him so clumsy, so ungracious, that Mary is bewildered and almost automatically refuses. Feeling really rejected now, John is furious. He quits school, giving up his dream of being an architect, and gets a job as a used-car salesman. He will show Mary; he'll soon have as much money as her father.

Notice that John's actions are the direct result of his character. Go ahead and set up your first incident, using your initial conflict.

_____

_____

_____

_____

_____

_____

_____

_____

_____

_____

The second incident should be the result of the first. In our plot—

John does very well financially. A few months later he appears in front of the school in a long shiny car. His pride has outdistanced his love, and he's primarily concerned with his own image. When Mary comes out of school, he honks the horn to catch her attention and beckons her over to the car. He insists that she let him drive her home. On the way he talks only of himself in an arrogant fashion. Mary grows more and more quiet. At her house he tries again—this time demanding a date. But this time Mary is not confused: she doesn't especially like the new John, and she refuses. Doubly furious, he steps hard on the accelerator and zooms away. His pride lets him draw only one conclusion: he still doesn't have enough money to win "her majesty's" approval. He decides to leave town and go to the city where Big Money can be made.

Dream up your second incident. Make sure it is a logical development from the first, and that it shows some growth (good or bad) in the characters.

_____

_____

_____

_____

_____

_____

_____

_____

_____

Most stories employ three incidents to move from the beginning to the end. Here is our third incident, deliberately incomplete.

Twenty years later John returns to his hometown. He is wealthy, thanks to a career of ruthlessness. But he is not happy. He dated many women but found for none the love he had felt for Mary. He meets Mary and they talk. She has never married and is working as a children's librarian. She seems happy and at peace. John, more confident now, admits that he loved her when they were young. She smiles and says she had loved him, too— him and his ideals and dreams.

Your third incident:

_____

_____

_____

_____

_____

_____

_____

_____

_____

_____

_____

_____

_____

Resolving the Conflict

The resolution (or ending) of the story must follow all that went before, must resolve the conflict, and must reveal the pattern underlying the plot.

This is the end of our third incident, and our resolution.

> John, excited, insists that all his ideals and dreams have come true; he has money, a big house, servants, everything she could possibly want. Will she marry him? Mary shakes her head. The ideals and dreams he discarded long ago; and the young man who once possessed them no longer exists. Quietly she stands up, kisses him on the cheek, and walks away. Momentarily John is shattered by this third refusal. He goes out to his new Rolls Royce, studies it, then jumps in and roars away. Mary has never understood *anything*. His eyes burning, he tells himself over and over that he doesn't need her, doesn't want her. He speeds back to the city.

As the story ends, John still possesses his two V's: pride and love. But pride has been growing faster than love, and we know now that it will always be the stronger. The conflict is over, precisely because John doesn't realize it is over.

Your resolution:

_____

_____

_____

_____

_____

_____

_____

_____

_____

_____

_____

_____

Your plot is complete. Through three carefully selected incidents, you have revealed a pattern of life. Our lives are composed of hundreds, perhaps thousands, of these criss-crossing patterns. You chose one plot and, by following it, illuminated one aspect of human nature—and that is what a short story is supposed to do.

With your plot in mind, make the following decisions:

1 *From what viewpoint should this story be told?* (We would tell our John-and-Mary story either from John's point of view (third person) or from the omniscient author's.)

_____

_____

_____

2 *Would you use a flashback? If so, where?* (We would turn the entire story into a flashback, starting with John racing back to the city for the last time.)

_____

_____

_____

_____

_____

You now have all you need. Think some more about your characters so that you will know how they speak and think and feel; then write your story. Good luck!

_____

_____

_____

_____

_____

_____

_____

_____

_____

_____

_____

_____

_____

_____

62. THE MAGIC INGREDIENTS

There is a world of difference between a short story in a pulp confession magazine and one by James Joyce. Or between an adventure yarn by Kipling and a gentle bit of introspection by Katherine Mansfield. Yet all share one characteristic, one magic ingredient: *emotion*.

We humans experience many emotions: love and hate and fear; terror and doubt; envy and faith and joy. We know that our memories are made up not of incidents, but of the emotions connected with the incidents. It isn't the automobile accident we remember, but our terror just before the impact.

We are also creatures of *curiosity*: curious about strange places and people, about coincidences, about the inexplicable operation of justice and injustice.

Curiosity and *emotion*: these are the two magic ingredients you must capture—and convey—when you write a short story, and you must do it from the first sentence to the last.

Consider Beginnings

Your first sentence is all-important. With it, you will either hook or lose your reader. Examine the following "first" sentences. After each one, explain its appeal—why most people would want to continue reading.

Example:

"Jeff Peters has been engaged in as many schemes for making money as there are recipes for cooking rice in Charleston, S.C."

(from "Jeff Peters as a Personal Magnet" by O. Henry)

This sentence appeals to our curiosity: how can one make money fast? and to our greed: how can *I* make money fast?

1 "All contact lost," said the bulkhead loudspeaker in the Firing Control Center, its tone detached. "Over and out."

(from "The Displaced Missile" by Jacob Hay)

_____

_____

_____

2 "I am told that sin has somewhat declined since Satan met Sam Shay."

(from "Satan and Sam Shay" by Robert Arthur)

_____

_____

3 "At five o'clock on a September afternoon Ronald Frederick Torbay was making preparations for his third murder."

(from "Bubble Bath No. 3" by Margery Allingham)

_____

_____

_____

4 "A child of three sat up in his crib and screamed at the top of his voice, his fists clinched and his eyes full of terror."

(from "The Brushwood Boy" by Rudyard Kipling)

_____

_____

_____

5 "They say there never was such a funeral in the history of New York's theatrical life."

(from "Mother Knows Best" by Edna Ferber)

_____

_____

Now that you have closely examined a few "first" sentences, try writing some of your own.

6 *Situation:* Ellen Knotts has just had a baby. She feels she can't support it and has decided to put it up for adoption.

YOUR FIRST SENTENCE _____

_____

_____

7 *Situation:* Tod Backaluck and his three friends are planning to stow away on a spaceship destined for Mars. The story will be about the planning and the execution of their project.

YOUR FIRST SENTENCE _____

_____

_____

8 *Situation:* Jessie is desperate. She has no job and she is a stranger in a strange city. She wonders if life has any meaning at all. This will be a quiet story, with most of the action taking place inside Jessie's mind.

YOUR FIRST SENTENCE _____

_____

_____

This time write two more "first" sentences, even though you have no idea what stories they might lead into. Remember: curiosity + some emotion.

9 _____

_____

_____

_____

10 _____

_____

_____

_____

_____

Before we continue, check the story you wrote at the end of Chapter 61 (starting page 437). Is the first sentence good enough? If it isn't, rewrite it.

*　　*　　*

Consider Endings

The ending of a story is second in importance only to the beginning. (Review Chapter 33.) It must pack an emotional wallop, and it must satisfy the reader's curiosity.

But it must also do something else (and this is the hard part): it must satisfy the reader's sense of justice, of fair play. If, for example, you write a mystery story, and at the end a salesman who has never even been mentioned is found to be the culprit, the reader will reciprocate by hurling your story in a wastebasket and swearing never again to read one printed under your name. In brief, the ending must be *right*.

Most people divide endings into happy endings and unhappy endings. Happy endings are considered all right for magazine stories, but unhappy endings are necessary for "good" stories. This is nonsense. Whether the ending is happy or unhappy should depend on the storyline and the characters. Life is full of both happy and unhappy endings—depending on *what* is happening and *who* is involved. Consider John F. Kennedy. If a story ended after his inauguration in 1960, it would have a happy ending. If a story ended after his assassination in 1963, it would have an unhappy ending. But both endings would be *right*—for their particular stories. What is true of life is true of fiction.

Do you remember the John-Mary-love-pride plot developed in Chapter 61? The ending we used was to have John return, financially successful, and ask Mary to marry him. She refused because he was no longer the idealistic young man she had once loved. Given John's growing pride, his impulsiveness, his unwillingness to see himself truly, it seemed to us the inevitable ending . . . even though it is unhappy.

But the ending could be different. If the twenty years had taught John that financial success is not everything, that love is *more* important than pride, then the ending could have been happy.

Here are some other possible endings for the same story.

John returns after twenty years jubilant. He seeks out Mary and finds she has died. He is too late—and shocked into self-awareness.

John returns after twenty years filled with anger and wanting revenge. He finds Mary happily married and kills her. As he flees, he realizes that his pride (which was so important to him) will be leveled during the trial that is sure to come.

(or) . . . as he flees, he feels only self-pity—another bad break. It was all Mary's fault, or the police's, or anybody's but his.

John, happily married, returns after twenty years with his wife. He finds Mary happily married also. At first they are embarrassed, but then they realize that *they* have changed and that "first love" is not "only love."

One could go on and on. There are dozens of possible endings for almost any story, but—given the development of the plot and the characterization—only one *right* ending.

Stretch your imagination. Here is a story outline. Read it; then see if you can create three possible endings.

It is Christmas Eve. A tramp, cold and hungry, wants only one thing: to be arrested. In prison he will be provided with bed and food. He tries everything he can think of, even breaking a store window; but the police either feel merciful or refuse to believe he is guilty. Never did anyone try so hard to be arrested, and never did anyone so often fail.

How would you end this story?

ENDING #1 _____

_____

_____

_____

_____

ENDING #2 _____

_____

_____

_____

ENDING #3 _____

_____

_____

_____

_____

If you would like to compare your possible endings with O. Henry's actual ending, read "The Cop and the Anthem." Of course, O. Henry was a master of the surprise ending, so don't be discouraged if your endings fall short of his!

The surprise ending, by the way, is still effective and works best in very short stories. But it is not easy. The ending must follow the cause-and-effect sequence of the plot, yet be unexpected to the reader. Unless you have a special knack for the surprise ending, you probably should use it only when it seems natural.

Go back now to the story you wrote in the previous chapter, page 437. Reread your last paragraph. Is it effective? Is it *right*? If it isn't, think about it and revise. Then copy the revised story in your journal.

❄   ❄   ❄

The gift of storytelling is a precious one. If you have it, cherish it, nurture it, use it. Entertain your friends around a campfire on an October evening, or during a storm when the electric lines are down. Amuse the small children that you know—by telling them stories or by writing the stories down in brief personalized books. Amuse yourself by turning your own joys and concealed sorrows into stories about someone else. And then—when you really know how to tell a story—try to market it.

> **In an age of anxiety, of fear, of doubt, people turn to short stories for diversion and for understanding. We are now in such an age. We need storytellers who can make us lose ourselves in excitement and then find ourselves in new self-knowledge. You see, *it all started a very long time ago in the strange city of Merriment where the good King Sage had a beautiful daughter* . . .**

Part Three
PUBLISHERS' ROW

. . . wherein you will explore the marketplace, learning
    how to find markets and
    how to create them;
    how to prepare your manuscript and
    how to mail it;
    how to endure a rejection and
    how to glory in an acceptance.

Unit X
Marketing

63. PREPARING A MANUSCRIPT

You wrote a story or some poems or an article. You revised it several times. You put it away for a few weeks or a month, and when you read it again, you still found it good. Now what?

If you're like most writers, you're wondering if you can sell it—if there's a market for it. Don't be shy about admitting this to yourself. Even Emily Dickinson, the least public of all writers, *wanted* to be published. It's natural: a writer writes in order to communicate; and you can't communicate unless there's someone at the receiving end. Adela Rogers St. John, a veteran writer, once said: "Writing is not writing until it is read any more than an airplane is an airplane until it takes off and flies."

The first step in marketing your writing is to prepare the manuscript. There are a few basic rules:

1 *Type*. Editors and readers examine an enormous amount of material every day; they can't be bothered with handwritten submissions. So type. And use a typewriter that gives clean copy—no filled in *e*'s or broken *y*'s.

2 *Be accurate*. Before you type, check your manuscript for spelling, punctuation, and grammar. After you type, proofread carefully. If there are one or two errors on a page, you may correct them with pen. If there are more than that, retype the page.

3 *Margins*. Leave a 1¼ inch margin on all four sides. This not only contributes to a neat appearance; it also insures that there will be approximately the same number of lines on each page.

4 *Identification*. Type your full name and address in the upper lefthand corner of the first page. On each following page, type your last name only in the upper left.

5 *Numbering Pages*. Starting with page 2, number each page in the upper right-hand corner.

6 *Length*. Indicate the length of your story or article in the upper righthand corner of the first page. Round off to the nearest hundred (e.g., 500 words, or 1400 words, etc.).

7 *Title*. On page 1, drop 1/3 down the page and type title, accurately centered. Below the title, type your name, or your pen name if you choose to use one.

8 *Text*. After the title, skip about three lines, then proceed with text. *Double-space* all text. Even between paragraphs, only double-spacing should be used. And, of course, type on only one side of the paper.

9 *Quotes*. Quotations of more than three lines should be further indented (about 10 spaces) and single-spaced. Such quotations should not start or end with quotation marks. Shorter quotations should be placed in quotation marks and handled as regular text. Quotations within such quotations should be indicated by single quotation marks.

10 *Paper*.   Use only *white* paper, preferably a good bond of 14, 16, or 20 lb. weight. Make at least one good carbon; manuscripts are occasionally lost and the carbon is your insurance.

11 *Fasteners*.   Staples, pins, etc., should *never* be used on any manuscript. Use a paper clip only.

The rules above should be followed for all manuscripts. In addition, there are a few other rules for specific types of material.

For Poetry and Fillers: Type each poem or filler on a separate page. Type your name and address in the upper lefthand corner of each page. Double-space.

For Greeting Cards: In most cases ideas or verses for greeting cards should be typed on 3 x 5 cards, one to a card. Again, name and address should appear on each card.

For Play and Television Scripts: Since the rules for scripts are different and quite complex, they cannot be given here. Check any good, up-to-date reference on script-writing and follow the suggestions given.

✵   ✵   ✵   ✵

If you are serious about submitting work to publishers, you should be aware of several "truths." First, well-established publishers are honest . . . so don't waste time worrying that one of them will reject your manuscript but steal your idea. If they like your idea but not your writing, they will sometimes offer to buy it. Even if an article on a topic similar to yours appears a few months later, this doesn't mean your idea was stolen. Editors receive hundreds of manuscripts daily. Quite often several will deal with the same topic.

Second: don't try to "fool" an editor. Turning a page upside down or putting one page out of order will only annoy an editor. Most manuscripts *are* read; but they may not be read to the end. Often an experienced reader can tell after a page or two whether a manuscript is suitable for a particular market. So save game-playing for parties.

Your next step, after preparing a manuscript, is to select a market—a major problem for inexperienced writers.

64. SELECTING A MARKET

The easiest way to be certain that your manuscripts go to the right markets is to work through an agent. Unfortunately most agents will not accept work from unpublished writers. So give up that dream, get down to work, and *learn* the markets suitable for your type of writing.

Invest in a market handbook or borrow one from your local library. The best today are

> *Writer's Market* (published annually by Writer's Digest)
> *The Writer's Handbook* (published by The Writer, Inc.)

Each gives long lists of book publishers, general magazines, and specialized magazines. Each listing is annotated, giving address of magazine, names of editors, types of material desired, lengths, payment, etc. If you have written a story for children, you will find a list labeled "Juveniles." By studying the comments, you should be able to decide which magazine is most likely to be interested in your story.

Studying the list of markets is only a beginning, however. Do not send any manuscript to any publication until you have studied the publication itself. If you think your story would interest *Jack and Jill*, a magazine for children from five to eight, go to the library and read several issues. Notice the topics of the stories, and the themes; the length; the style; the vocabulary. If a magazine you are interested in is not available in the library, check the magazine stands; and if it is not available there either, send to the magazine and ask for a sample copy. Check the same two handbooks to discover which magazines are willing to do this.

Repeat: do not send anything to a publisher until you have studied the publication thoroughly. You are only wasting your time and money, and the publisher's.

State of the Market

The market for short stories is weak, but it is improving. The strongest demand is for non-fiction articles: interviews, how-to's, factual material of all types. The poetry market is stable with more demand for light verse than for serious poetry; but there are plenty of "little" magazines interested in the latter.

This may be the right time to point out that writing is a better avocation than vocation. Few poets can support themselves through writing; and even fiction writers have a hard time, unless they hit the bestseller lists. For most writers, the satisfaction lies in the act of writing rather than in checks received (although any writer will admit that the latter is also delightful!).

A Look at Types of Markets

Just looking at the various types of markets may stimulate your thinking . . . and writing. Here are a few. For more comprehensive lists, check the same two handbooks mentioned at the beginning of this chapter and *Literary Market Place*, "the directory of American book publishing."

> mystery magazines
> science-fiction magazines
> romance magazines
> art and music magazines
> western magazines
> education and medical journals
> comic books
> greeting card manufacturers
> hobby, home and garden magazines
> humor magazines
> trade and business magazines
> travel magazines
> television and radio networks
> summer, repertory and university theaters
> literary magazines
> religious magazines
> poetry magazines
> sports magazines
> children's magazines
> magazines for teen-agers

—as well as magazines or journals about jewelry, guns, skiing, military life, conservation, politics, groceries, law, mining, agriculture, photography, dairy products, and at least a hundred other topics.

If you really want to write and to publish your writing, there are plenty of markets. And if the markets that already exist don't satisfy you, turn to Chapter 66 and learn to develop your own.

65. MAILING A MANUSCRIPT

Now that you have a beautiful manuscript and a possible market, you are ready for the last step: sending it on its way. The rules are few and simple. And the most important is

ALWAYS ENCLOSE A STAMPED,
SELF-ADDRESSED ENVELOPE.

No publisher is willing to pay postage to return the many unsolicited manuscripts (and one of the sad facts of life is that most of your early submissions *will* be returned). If you hope to see your rejected "child" again, remember that stamped, self-addressed envelope.

Size of Manuscript

If your manuscript is fewer than five pages, fold twice, and mail in an ordinary long envelope (4″ × 9½″).

If your manuscript is more than five pages but fewer than twelve, fold once and mail in a small manila envelope (6″ × 9″).

If your manuscript is twelve pages or more but not book-length, place between cardboard and mail flat in a large manila envelope (9″ × 12″, or 10″ × 13″).

If your manuscript is book-length, place in a cardboard box (the kind typing paper comes in), and wrap securely in brown paper.

Postal Regulations

First class: Many writers prefer to send their manuscripts first class. First class postage insures faster and safer delivery. At the post office, after your manuscript is weighed, remember to purchase *two* sets of stamps, placing one set on the self-addressed return envelope.

For increased safety and assurance of delivery, send your manuscript by certified mail, with return receipt requested. This has an additional advantage: you will know the exact date your manuscript arrived at its destination.

Fourth class: If you wish, you may mail manuscripts fourth class; it is considerably less expensive. Write on the envelope, "Special Fourth Class Rate—Manuscript." (If your post office agent questions your use of this special rate, refer him or her to Postal Regulation 135.13.)

Accompanying Letter: An accompanying letter may, of course, be enclosed if you use first class mail. If you use fourth class mail, you may still enclose the letter but must write on the envelope, "First Class Letter Enclosed," and add additional postage.

The Accompanying Letter

You need *not* send an accompanying letter with your manuscript; the editor is aware that the poems, story, or article enclosed is being offered for publication. You *should* send an accompanying letter if there are special circumstances: for example, if you are submitting to a teen-age magazine, it might be wise to mention your age and grade level. They sometimes prefer to buy the work of young writers.

If you do write a letter, keep it short. Don't praise your work; the editor is quite capable of making an independent decision. Do not mention rate of payment; each publication has its own rate. Do not mention serial rights, reprint rights, etc.; that can wait until some editor expresses an interest in purchasing your material. As you can see, there isn't much you *can* say . . . so unless there are special circumstances that are relevant, just skip the letter. *After* you have made several sales, you may wish to include a list of your published works. *That* is relevant.

Rejections

Much of your early work will be rejected, usually with a cold, impersonal, printed rejection slip. What you must do, if you really hope to publish, is to shrug your shoulders when the manuscript is returned, reread it, and if you still think it is worthy of publication, send it immediately to another market.

When you are selecting a market for a particular piece of writing, select half a dozen. Write the six publications, with addresses, on the back of your carbon copy. When you mail it out the first time, note the date next to the first publication. When it returns, note that date also—then pack up the manuscript in a new envelope and send it to the second publication. A writer who is convinced that his or her article or story is good may send it to twenty or thirty publications; and occasionally it is purchased by the thirtieth.

Endurance is necessary, and faith. If you think it is difficult to accept the return of a test paper with a low grade, be assured it is far more painful to have your first (or any other) manuscript rejected. It takes guts to put the manuscript back in the mail, and to keep on writing. Authorship is not a profession for the weak.

66. DEVELOPING YOUR OWN MARKETS

If you really want to write, you probably have a good imagination, and that's fortunate: because if everything else fails, you can "dream up" your own markets.

Try the Local Approach

Often opportunities exist in your own backyard—if you are alert enough to recognize them. Consider the following possibilities:

..writing for your local newspaper (even fillers, for a start)

..writing ad copy for small storeowners

..ghostwriting speeches for candidates running for minor offices

..creating personalized story books and greeting cards for neighbors

..writing news releases for the school or for business clubs or charities

..writing a short play for an assembly program

..writing for your school newspaper or literary magazine or yearbook

..publishing a mimeographed booklet of current and future events in your school or community

..publishing a monthly news-letter (mimeographed) with each issue featuring a recreational or historical site in your area

..writing playlets for local religious organizations, especially for those working with children

Knowing your own community, you probably can add several more quickly. Add them.

_____

_____

_____

_____

_____

_____

Some of the above activities will yield little (or no) financial reward; but you are serving an apprenticeship. Everything you write will improve your writing; every reader who responds will be teaching you something valuable about your writing. There are more rewards than money. Reap them.

Use Your Expertise

Another way to create your own market is to become aware of your areas of expertise . . . and to use them.

From your family: if your mother is a dentist, you have probably heard dozens of anguished stories about small stubborn children who won't open their mouths. Select a few of the best anecdotes, include a couple of your mother's solutions, and write a short humorous feature. It might sell to a dental journal or women's magazine. (And this is one time to enclose an accompanying letter, indicating that you live with a dentist and know what you're talking about!)

From your friends: if your friend is a yo-yo expert, learn all you can about the techniques of yo-yoing. Go to the library and find out who invented the yo-yo and anything else about it that is available. Then write a story about yo-yos (you might even include some black-and-white glossies) for a children's magazine or a Sunday newspaper feature section.

From your own brain: think about *today*—what's important, what's interesting to most people. During the student protest movement in the 1960's, several ingenious writers developed fascinating articles paralleling student protest in the medieval period and current student protest. As a nation, we've become very faddish: we're always going crazy over hula hoops or pandas or crosscountry skiing. Become a mini-expert on the fad of the moment—then write about it. If you're fast and good, there's always a market for this type of writing. (And if you are interested in articles rather than in fiction or poetry, you might well consider taking up photography as a hobby. Often articles sell more quickly if they are accompanied by a couple of good pictures.)

✱   ✱   ✱   ✱

These suggestions should be sufficient to get you started. Whether you are writing articles or stories, light verse or sonnets, the basic formula for writing creatively remains the same:

See . . . with all your senses.

Observe . . . with your brain as well as your eyes.

Note.

Think. Dream. Muse and mull. Brainstorm. Then think again . . . until you come up with a brand-new angle.

Then see, observe, and note some more.

Think some more.

Write.

INDEX